Motivating Students to Learn

Motivating Students to Learn

Gurpreet Kaur

RANDOM PUBLICATIONS
NEW DELHI (INDIA)

Motivating Students to Learn

ISBN 978-93-5111-481-9

Published in 2015 in India by

RANDOM PUBLICATIONS

4376-A/4B, Gali Murari Lal, Ansari Road
New Delhi-110 002
Phone : +9111-43580356, 011-23289044, 011-43142548
e-mail: sales@randompublications.com,
info@randompublications.com, randomexports@gmail.com

Reprinted 2021

Type Setting by : Friends Media, Delhi-110089
Digitally Printed at : Replika Press Pvt. Ltd.

Preface

Teachers have a lot to do with their students' motivational level. A student may arrive in class with a certain degree of motivation. But the teacher's behavior and teaching style, the structure of the course, the nature of the assignments and informal interactions with students all have a large effect on student motivation. We may have heard the utterance, "my *students are so unmotivated!"* and the good news is that there's a lot that we can do to change that.

Educational psychology has identified two basic classifications of motivation - intrinsic and extrinsic. Intrinsic motivation arises from a desire to learn a topic due to its inherent interests, for self-fulfilment, enjoyment and to achieve a mastery of the subject. On the other hand, extrinsic motivation is motivation to perform and succeed for the sake of accomplishing a specific result or outcome. Students who are very grade-oriented are extrinsically motivated, whereas students who seem to truly embrace their work and take a genuine interest in it are intrinsically motivated.

This book is a great place to start for ideas and tips about increasing student motivation in your classes. It presents a handy distillation of research on motivation and uses examples that bring this material to life. In addition to general strategies, it addresses successful instructional behaviors, how to structure a course to motivate students, de-emphasizing grades and responding with other types of feedback to students, and tips to encourage students to complete assigned readings. The book is a comprehensive and practical guide for reconnecting with discouraged students and reawakening their excitement and enthusiasm for learning. With proven strategies from the classroom, this resource identifies effective processes the teacher can use to motivate students.

Author

Contents

1

Introduction

Human behavior is complex and people are naturally curious. Therefore, instructional designers should meet the challenges of designing instruction assisted by motivation; because it is of paramount importance to student success. Students work longer, harder and with more vigor and intensity when they are motivated than they are not. In other words, motivation helps individuals overcome inertia. This happens so because in the teaching-learning process, as in other various activities, there should be something that propels their mind or dangles in front to make them more active and vibrant, in classroom teaching, the major task is to nurture student curiosity as a motivation for learning. This is important because curiosity is motivation that is intrinsic to learning.

The source of motivation is complex. It can be categorized into external and internal. The latter sustains behavior. Intrinsic and extrinsic motivations are two types of motivation that affect achievement of students. However, the value of external motivation, for instance, reinforcement, is questioned from those who suggest that once it is withdrawn the behavior stops. Critics go on to say that students must have intrinsic motivation to accomplish the required activities. In intrinsic motivation the "doing" is the main reason for finishing an activity whereas in extrinsic motivation the "value" is placed at the end of an action. Infants and young Children appear to be propelled by curiosity, driven by an intense need to explore, interact with, and make sense of their environment.

Learning often becomes associated with drudgery instead of delight. A large number of students-more than one in four-leave schools before graduating. Many more are physically present in the classroom but largely mentally absent; they fail to invest themselves fully in the experience of learning. Awareness of how students' attitudes and beliefs about learning develop and what facilitates learning for its own sake can assist educators in reducing student apathy towards learning. Therefore, the role and importance of motivation is worth looking at in this regard.

Student motivation has to do with students' desire participate in the learning process. But it also concerns the reasons or goals that underlie their involvement in academic activities. Although students may be equally motivated to perform a task, the source of their motivation may differ. A student who is intrinsically motivated undertakes an activity "for its own sake, for the enjoyment it provides, the learning it permits, or the feelings of accomplishment it evokes". An extrinsically motivated student performs "in order to obtain some reward or avoid some punishment external to the activity itself" such as grades, stickers, or teacher approval. As stated above, the term motivation to learn has a slightly different meaning.

Others note that motivation to learn is characterized by long-term, quality involvement in learning and commitment to the process of learning. Factors that influence the development of students' motivation: According to educators, motivation to learn is a competence acquired "through general experience but stimulated most directly through modeling, communication of expectations, and direct instruction or socialization by parents and teachers. Children's home environment shapes the initial constellation of attitudes they develop toward learning. When parents nurture their children's natural curiosity about the world by welcoming their questions, encouraging exploration, and familiarizing them with resources that can enlarge their world, they are giving their children the message that learning is worthwhile and frequently fun and satisfying. When children are raised at home that nurtures a sense of self-worth, competence, autonomy, and self-efficiency, they will be more apt to accept the risks inherent in learning. Conversely, when children do not view themselves as basically competent and able, their freedom to enlarge in academically challenging pursuits and capacity to tolerate and cope with failure are greatly diminished.

Once children start school, they begin forming beliefs about their school-related successes and failures. The source to which children attribute their successes and failures have important implications on how they can approach and cope with learning situations. The beliefs teachers themselves have about teaching and learning and the nature of the expectations they hold for students also exert a powerful influence. As one notable educator remarked, "To a very large degree, students expect to learn if their teachers expect them to learn". School-wide goals, policies, and procedures also interact with classroom climate and practices affirm or alter students' increasingly complex learning-related attitudes and beliefs. Developmental changes comprise one more strand of the motivational web as well. For example, although young children tend to maintain high expectations for success even in the face of repeated failure, older students do not. Although younger children tend to see effort as uniformly positive, older children view it as a "double-edged sword". To them, failure following high effort appears to carry more negative implication-especially for their self-concept of ability-than failure that results from minimal or no effort.

What are advantages of intrinsic motivation? Does it really matter whether students are primarily intrinsically or extrinsically oriented towards learning? A growing body of evidence suggests that it does. When intrinsically motivated, students tend to employ strategies that demand more effort and that enable them to process information more deeply. Students with an intrinsic orientation also tend to prefer tasks that are moderately challenging whereas extrinsically oriented students gravitate toward tasks that are low in degree of difficulty. Extrinsically oriented students are inclined to put forth the minimal amount of effort necessary to get the maximal reward. Although every educational activity cannot, and perhaps should not, be intrinsically motivating, findings suggest that when teachers can capitalize on existing intrinsic motivation, there are several potential benefits. How can motivation to learn be fostered in the school setting? Although students' motivational histories accompany them into each new classroom setting, it is essential for teachers to view themselves as "active socializing agents capable of stimulating student motivation to learn".

Classroom climate is important. If students experience the classroom as a caring, supportive place where there is a sense of belonging and everyone is valued and respected they will tend to appreciate more fully in the process of learning. Various task dimensions can also foster motivation to learn. Ideally, tasks should be challenging but achievable. Relevance also promotes motivation, as does "contextualizing" learning, i.e., helping students to see how skills can be applied in the real world. Tasks that involve "moderate amount of discrepancy or incongruity are beneficial because they stimulate students' curiosity", and this is an intrinsic motivator. Extrinsic rewards, on the other hand, should be used with caution, for they have the potential for decreasing existing intrinsic motivation. What takes place in the classroom is critical; but "the classroom is not an island". Depending on their degree of congruence with classroom goals and practices, school wide goals either dilute or enhance classroom efforts. To support motivation to learn, school-level policies and practices should stress "learning, task mastery and effort" rather than relative performance and competition. What can be done to help unmotivated students? A first step is for educators to recognize that even when students use strategies that are ultimately self-defeating (such as withholding effort, cheating, procrastination, and so forth); their goal is actually to protect their sense of self-worth. A process called attribution retraining, which involves modeling, socialization, and practice exercise, is sometimes used with discouraged students. The goals of attribution retraining are to help students to: Concentrate on the tasks rather than becoming distracted by fear of failure; respond to frustration by retracting their steps to find mistake or figuring out alternative ways of approaching a problem instead of giving up; and attribute their failures to insufficient effort, lack of information or reliance on effective strategies rather than to lack of ability. Other potentiality useful strategies include: portray effort as investment rather than risk; portray skill development as incremental and domain specific and focus on mastery. Because the potential payoff-having students who value learning for its own sake-is priceless, it is crucial for parents, teachers, and school leaders to devote rekindling students' motivation to learn.

Definition of Motivation

Motivation is a theoretical construct used to explain the initiation, direction, intensity, persistence, and quality of behavior, especially goal-directed behavior. Motives are hypothetical constructs used to explain why people are doing what they are doing. Motives are distinguished from related constructs such as goals (the immediate objectives of particular sequences of behavior) and strategies (the methods used to achieve goals and thus to satisfy motives). For example, a person responds to hunger (motive) by going to a restaurant (strategy) to get food (goal).

Motives are usually construed as relatively general needs or desires that energize people to initiate purposeful action sequences. In contrast, goals (and related strategies) tend to be more specific and to be used to explain the direction and quality of action sequences in particular situations.

Motives, goals, and strategies can be difficult to distinguish in situations that call for intentional learning of cognitive content, because optimal forms of motivation to learn and optimal strategies for accomplishing the learning tend to occur together. In the classroom context, the concept of student motivation is used to explain the degree to which students invest attention and effort in various pursuits, which may or may not be the ones desired by their teachers.

Student motivation is rooted in students' subjective experiences, especially those connected to their willingness to engage in lessons and learning activities and their reasons for doing so.

Evolving Views of Motivation

Behavior Reinforcement Theories

Most contemporary views on student motivation emphasize its cognitive and goal-oriented features. These conceptions represent considerable evolution from earlier views, which were influenced heavily by behavioral theory and research (much of it done on animals rather than humans). Early behavioral views depicted humans as responsive to basic drives or needs, but otherwise relatively passive. As one observer put it, "The behaviorist view was that of a creature quietly metabolizing in the shade, occasionally goaded into action by the hot sun or the lure of a cold glass of beer".

Behaviorists later deemphasized drives or needs and instead focused on reinforcement as the primary mechanism for establishing and maintaining behavior. They define a reinforcer as anything that increases or maintains the frequency of a behavior when access to it is made contingent on performance of that behavior. For example, careful work on assignments leading to successful task completion might be reinforced by giving verbal or written praise, awarding high grades, affixing stars or other symbols of excellence, allowing access to some privilege, awarding points that can be exchanged for prizes or applied to a competition, or in some other way compensating students for their efforts or recognizing them for their accomplishments by providing rewards that they value.

In explaining how to establish and maintain desired behavior patterns, behaviorists usually talk about control rather than motivation. They speak of using reinforcement to bring behavior under stimulus control. The stimulus is a situational cue that (in effect) reminds learners that performing certain behaviors in this situation will gain them access to reinforcement. If the learners are not able to perform the desired behaviors immediately, gradual improvement toward the target performance level is shaped through successive approximations. Once the desired performance level is established, it is maintained by reinforcing it often enough to ensure its continuation. Any behaviors that are incompatible with the desired pattern are extinguished through nonreinforcement or (if necessary) suppressed through punishment.

Much of the culture of schooling reflects the behavioral view, especially grading and report card systems, conduct codes, and honor rolls and awards ceremonies. With respect to everyday motivation in the classroom, behavioral views lead to carrot-and-stick approaches: Teachers are advised to reinforce students when they display desired learning efforts and withhold reinforcement when they do not.

Behavioral models that emphasize manipulation of learners through reinforcement are still emphasized in applied behavior analysis treatments, especially in school psychology and special education. However, most behavioral models have evolved into more complicated forms that include at least some consideration of learners' thoughts and intentions. Meanwhile, cognitive models of motivation have developed that place more emphasis on learners' subjective experiences such as their needs, goals, or motivation-related thinking. These cognitive models of motivation include the concept of reinforcement but portray its effects as mediated through learners' cognitions. That is, the degree to which task engagement can be motivated by reinforcer availability depends on the degree to which learners value the reinforcer, expect its delivery upon completion of the task, believe that they are capable of completing the task successfully, and believe that doing so in order to gain access to the reinforcer will be worth the costs in time, effort, and foregone opportunities to pursue alternative courses of action.

Need Theories

Need theories were among the first motivational theories to emerge as alternatives to behavior reinforcement theories. These theories explain behaviors as responses to felt needs. The needs may be either inborn and universal (self-preservation, hunger, thirst) or learned through cultural experience and developed to different degrees in different cultures and individuals (achievement, affiliation, power).

Need theories have been criticized for relying on circular logic that fails to separate the hypothesized motive (need) from the behavior that it supposedly explains (e.g., students who work hard in school are said to do so because they are high in need for achievement, and the evidence that they are high in need for achievement is that they work hard in school). Such circular "explanations" identify and label clusters of behaviors without really explaining them. Scientific psychologists have rejected need theories because of circular logic problems with the concept of need and because of difficulties in generating convincing research support for the lists of supposed needs that have been compiled. Nevertheless, one motivation model based in need theory has remained popular and influential:

Abraham Maslow's Hierarchy of Human Needs

Maslow suggested that needs function within a hierarchy arranged in the following order of priority:

1. Physiological needs (sleep, thirst)
2. Safety needs (freedom from danger, anxiety, or psychological threat)
3. Love needs (acceptance from parents, teachers, peers)
4. Esteem needs (mastery experiences, confidence in one's ability)
5. Needs for self-actualization (creative self-expression, satisfaction of curiosity)

The hierarchy model implies that needs must be satisfied in the order given. Unless lower needs are satisfied, higher needs may not even be recognized, let alone motivate behavior. Physiological needs are basic to survival, but once they are met, attention can be directed to higher needs. If both physiological and safety needs are satisfied, people can appreciate warm, interpersonal relationships, and love needs may begin to motivate their behavior. If love needs are reasonably satisfied, people may begin to seek to satisfy their esteem needs and perhaps ultimately their self-actualization needs.

In the classroom, Maslow's hierarchy implies that students who come to school tired or hungry are unlikely to become engrossed in lessons.

Similarly, students who feel anxious or rejected are unlikely to take the intellectual risks involved in seeking to overcome confusion and construct clear understandings, and even less likely to try to be creative when working on assignments. This is especially the case when need frustration is chronic. Rational people want arrangements in place that will enable them to meet their basic needs routinely, not just for the moment.

Students do not always act in accord with Maslow's hierarchy. They may deprive themselves of sleep in order to study for a test, for example, or become so engrossed in an activity that they forget about their fatigue, hunger, or personal problems. Even so, Maslow's hierarchy is a useful reminder that, in order to motivate our students successfully, may need to address their lower needs along with their higher needs that are associated more closely with school learning.

Goal Theories

Behavior reinforcement theories and need theories both depicted motivated actions as reactive to pressures, either from extrinsic incentives or from internally felt needs. Gradually, motivation theories began to acknowledge that in addition to being pushed and pulled in this manner, are sometimes more proactive in deciding what want to do and why want to do it. As biological organisms, are naturally active (except when sleeping), so motivational concepts usually are not needed to explain the energization of behavior (e.g., Why is the person doing something instead of nothing?). They are needed, however, to explain the direction, intensity, persistence, and quality of behavior. That is, given all the possibilities that a situation affords, why does the person choose a subset of them, to the exclusion of the rest, and pursue those possibilities in the particular way that he or she does?

Reflecting this evolution, most motivational theorists have shifted from talking about our needs to talking about our goals: the objectives or intended outcomes of planned sequences of behavior. Most human activity is purposeful, although not necessarily from its inception (when free from pressing needs, may seek "down time," although even then usually make action decisions that imply goals, such as taking a nap or a bath to refresh ourselves or reading or watching television to inform ourselves or enjoy entertainment). Implied goals are built into activity settings, such as workplaces, gymnasiums, or classrooms. In classrooms, students are expected to engage in lessons and learning activities with the goal of achieving their intended learning outcomes, although students do not necessarily accept this goal and may pursue other goals in addition or instead.

Goals vary in scope, from primitive or concrete goals (grasping an object) through somewhat more abstract goals (continue to engage in activities that you enjoy) to still more abstract ones (try to be the kind of person you want to be). Whatever its scope, the existence of a goal indicates that the person has made a commitment to achieve some state or outcome, that progress in doing so can be monitored and assessed, and that the person can use the resulting feedback to make any needed adjustments in the strategies used to pursue the goal. Many goals subsume complex activities played out across extended periods of time. For example, the goal of climbing a mountain implies not just wanting to experience standing on top of the mountain, but experiencing all of the things involved in doing the climbing. In this case, the "going" is the main goal of the activity, not the "arriving".

Martin Ford has developed a theory of human motivation that includes a taxonomy of 24 goals arranged within six categories:

1. *Affective goals:* entertainment, tranquility, happiness, pleasurable bodily sensations, and physical well-being
2. *Cognitive goals:* exploration to satisfy one's curiosity, attaining understanding, engaging in intellectual creativity, and maintaining positive self-evaluations
3. *Subjective organization goals:* unity (experiencing a spiritual sense of harmony or oneness with people, nature, or a greater power) and transcendence (experiencing optimal or extraordinary states of functioning that go beyond ordinary experience)
4. *Self-assertive social relationship goals:* experiencing a sense of individuality, self-determination, superiority (in comparisons with others), and resource acquisition (obtaining material and social support from others)
5. *Integrative social relationship goals:* belongingness, social responsibility (meeting one's ethical and social obligations), equity (promoting fairness and justice), and resource provision (giving material and social support to others)
6. *Task goals:* mastery, task creativity, management (handling everyday tasks with organization and efficiency), material gain, and safety.

Ford's list is unusually lengthy. Goal theorists usually work with simpler taxonomies that contain just a few categories of goals but are more convenient and flexible to apply. However, longer lists such as Ford's are useful as reminders of the many competing agendas facing teachers who seek to motivate their students to focus on learning goals. Doing so successfully involves making it possible for students to coordinate their goals so that many different goals are being satisfied, and few if any are being frustrated, as they engage in classroom activities with motivation to learn.

When students adopt learning goals (also called mastery goals or task-involvement goals), they focus on trying to learn whatever the task is designed to teach them. In contrast, when students adopt performance goals (also called ego-involvement goals), they focus more on preserving their self-perceptions and public reputations as capable individuals than on learning what the task is designed to teach. Finally, when students adopt work-avoidant goals, they refuse to accept the achievement challenges inherent in the task and instead seek to minimize the time and effort they devote to it.

Goal theorists have developed a great deal of information about situational characteristics that predict people's tendencies to adopt these different goals in achievement situations. Other motivational researchers have explored related cognitive and affective experiences (success or failure expectations, self-efficacy perceptions, attributions of performance outcomes to causes), and the ways in which these motivational factors influence the quality of people's engagement in tasks and the ultimate levels of success they achieve. Classroom applications of goal theories emphasize (a) establishing supportive relationships and collaborative learning arrangements that encourage students to adopt learning goals and (b) avoiding creating the sorts of pressures that dispose students toward performance goals or work-avoidant goals. When conditions emphasized by goal theorists are established in classrooms, students are able to focus their energies on learning without becoming distracted by fear of embarrassment or failure or by resentment of tasks that they view as pointless or inappropriate.

Intrinsic Motivation Theories

The shift in emphasis from motivation as response to felt pressures to motivation as self-determination of goals and self-regulation of actions is most obvious in theories of intrinsic motivation. Even if they include need concepts, theories of intrinsic motivation depict people as pursuing their own agendas—doing what they do because they want to rather than because they need to.

Self-determination Theory. A prominent recent example is the self-determination theory of Edward Deci and Richard Ryan. When people are motivated, they intend to accomplish something and undertake goal-oriented action to do so. Motivated action may be either self-determined or controlled. To the extent that it is self-determined, it is experienced as freely chosen and emanating from one's self, not done under pressure from some internal need or external force.

The prototype of self-determined behavior is intrinsically motivated action that engage in because want to. Intrinsically motivated actions require no separate motivating consequences; the only necessary "reward" for them is the spontaneous interest and enjoyment that experience as do them. They often feature curiosity, exploration, spontaneity, and interest in our surroundings.

Self-determination theory specifies that social settings promote intrinsic motivation when they satisfy three innate psychological needs: autonomy (self-determination in deciding what to do and how to do it), competence (developing and exercising skills for manipulating and controlling the environment), and relatedness (affiliation with others through prosocial relationships). In other words, people are inherently motivated to feel connected to others within a social milieu, to function effectively in that milieu, and to feel a sense of personal initiative while doing so. Students are likely to experience intrinsic motivation in classrooms that support satisfaction of these autonomy, competence, and relatedness needs. Where such support is lacking, students will feel controlled rather than self-determined, so their motivation will be primarily extrinsic rather than intrinsic.

Flow. Mihaly Csikszentmihalyi has captured what peak experiences of intrinsic motivation feel like in his concept of flow. He interviewed people about their subjective experiences during times when they were absorbed in activities they enjoyed, expecting to find that most flow experiences occur during relaxing moments of leisure and entertainment. Instead, he found that they usually occur when are actively involved in challenging tasks that stretch our physical or mental abilities. He listed eight characteristic dimensions of the flow experience:

1. The activity has clear goals and provides immediate feedback about the effectiveness of our responses to it.
2. There are frequent opportunities for acting decisively, and these are matched by our perceived ability to act effectively. In other words, our personal skills are well suited to the activity's challenges.
3. Action and awareness merge; experience one-pointedness of mind.
4. Concentration on the task at hand; irrelevant stimuli disappear from consciousness; worries and concerns are temporarily suspended.
5. A sense of potential control.
6. Loss of self-consciousness, transcendence of ego boundaries, a sense of growth and of being part of some greater entity.
7. Altered sense of time, which usually seems to pass faster.
8. Experience becomes autotelic: The activity becomes worth doing for its own sake.

In summary, tend to experience flow when become absorbed in doing something challenging. We remain aware of the goals of the task and of the feedback generated by our responses to it, but we concentrate on the task itself without thinking about success or failure, reward or punishment, or other personal or social agendas. At least for awhile, we focus completely on meeting the challenges that the task offers, refining our response strategies, developing our skills, and enjoying a sense of control and accomplishment. We are most likely to experience flow when engaged in hobbies or recreational activities (e.g., artistic endeavors, sports, arcade or computer games), but we may also experience it on the job, in the classroom, or in any other activity setting.

Flow Potential Differs Across Both Persons And Situations. Some people develop a "flow personality." They seek out challenges and relish stretching their limits. When required to engage in a more routine activity, they tend to "complexify" it by trying to do it artistically, seeking to increase their efficiency, or in other ways setting goals that will make the activity more challenging and interesting for them. Other people rarely experience flow because they fear failure and therefore try to avoid challenging situations.

People report flow experiences most frequently during activities that offer high degrees of challenge in areas in which they perceive themselves as possessing high degrees of skill. Other situations produce different experiences. When skill is high but the task is not challenging, we experience boredom; when both challenge and skill levels are low, we experience apathy; and when we face a challenging task for which we think we possess low levels of skill, we experience anxiety.

In school, anxiety is the chief threat to flow potential. If students are routinely faced with overly challenging situations that are beyond their abilities to handle effectively, they may come to prefer the boredom of "safe" routines to the flow opportunities of challenging activities. Eventually, their potential for experiencing flow in the classroom will erode away.

Csikszentmihalyi, Rathunde, and Whalen suggested that teachers can encourage flow experiences in three ways:

1. by being knowledgeable about their subjects, teaching them enthusiastically, and acting as models pursuing the intrinsic rewards of learning;
2. by maintaining an optimal match between what is demanded and what students are prepared to accomplish (urging but also helping students to achieve challenging but reasonable goals); and
3. by providing a combination of instructional and emotional support that enables students to approach learning tasks confidently and without anxiety.

Subsequently, Csikszentmihalyi added modeling as a key to stimulating students' intrinsic motivation to learn. He depicted ideal teachers as intrinsically motivated to both learn and teach their subjects, and as displaying this enthusiasm in ways that encourage students to enjoy and look forward to learning about it themselves.

Motivation in the Classroom

The concepts of intrinsic motivation and flow are useful for interpreting a range of motivational situations. However, they are not feasible to serve as the primary concepts underlying models of motivation in education. These concepts apply best when people are freely engaging in self-chosen activities. Usually these are play or recreational activities rather than work or learning activities. Even when people are intrinsically motivated to learn, their learning usually features leisurely exploration to satisfy curiosity rather than sustained efforts to accomplish explicit knowledge- or skill-development goals. Finally, even when intrinsically motivated learning is more goal oriented, it tends to occur under autonomous and self-determined conditions. Unfortunately, these conditions are difficult to establish in classrooms, for several reasons.

First, school attendance is compulsory and curriculum content and learning activities are selected primarily on the basis of what society believes students need to learn, not on the basis of what students would choose if given the opportunity to do so. Schools are established for the benefit of students, but from the students' point of view, their time in the classroom is devoted to enforced attempts to meet externally imposed demands. Second, teachers usually must work with classes of 20 or more students and therefore cannot always meet each individual's needs. As a result, certain students sometimes are bored and certain others sometimes are confused or frustrated. Third, classrooms are social settings, so that failures often produce not only personal disappointment but public embarrassment. Finally, students' work on assignments and performance on tests are graded, and periodic reports are sent home to their parents. In combination, these factors tend to focus students' attention on concerns about meeting demands successfully rather than on any personal benefits that they might derive from learning experiences. It is hard to just enjoy an activity and "go with the flow" when the activity is compulsory and your performance will be evaluated, especially if you fear that your efforts will not be successful.

Even in classrooms where fear of failure is minimized, both teachers and students can easily settle into familiar routines as the school year progresses. To the extent that these routines become the "daily grind," classroom activities that were designed as means toward curricular ends tend to become ends in themselves. That is, attention becomes focused on what must be done to complete the activities rather than on the knowledge or skills that the activities were designed to develop.

You can make curricular and instructional adjustments that will increase the frequencies with which your students experience intrinsic motivation and flow in your classroom. Nor are you a private tutor who can individualize the curriculum to a single learner's needs and interests. Instead, you must work with classes of 20 or more students and concentrate on helping them to accomplish curricular goals.

These constraints make it unrealistic to adopt intrinsic motivation or flow as the model of student motivation that you will seek to maintain on an all-day, everyday basis. You can provide frequent opportunities for choice and autonomy and you can phrase instructions and feedback in ways that downplay your control over students, but it will remain true that students are required to come to your class to try to master a largely externally imposed curriculum, and that their efforts will be evaluated and graded. Under these conditions, intrinsic motivation will be the exception rather than the rule.

The same will be true of flow experiences, especially for students who are underchallenged and thus bored much of the time or overchallenged and thus anxious much of the time. Even students who enjoy a consistently good match between your demands on them and their current readiness to meet those demands will vary in their desire for flow experiences. Some will prefer the boredom of safety over the risk of challenge. Even those who are more disposed toward flow experiences cannot be in (or seeking) flow continuously because this would be exhausting.

It is worth noting that teachers are not the only people who experience constraints on their options as motivators. Most leadership roles are played out in contexts in which supervisees do not necessarily share their supervisors' goals, yet must be motivated to adopt those goals or at least commit to accomplishing the agenda that goes with them. Furthermore, they often must be willing to accept responsibility for accomplishing their portion of the agenda, even though they will not be rewarded as generously as their supervisors or even many of their peers. Thus, the aspects of motivational theory and research likely have the most relevance to potential appliers are those involved in motivating people to commit to goals that they ordinarily would not adopt on their own initiative, not those involved in providing people with opportunities to engage in preferred activities.

Student Motivation to Learn as Your Goal

If intrinsic motivation is ideal but unattainable as an all-day, everyday motivational state for teachers to seek to develop in their students, what might be a more feasible goal? It is realistic for you to seek to develop and sustain your students' motivation to learn from academic activities: their tendencies to find academic activities meaningful and worthwhile and to try to get the intended learning benefits from them.

Motivation to learn differs both from extrinsic, reinforcement-driven motivation and from intrinsic, enjoyment-driven motivation, although it may coexist with either of them. The difference between motivation to learn and extrinsic motivation is closely related to the difference between learning and performance. Learning refers to the information processing, sense-making, and advances in comprehension or mastery that occur when one is acquiring knowledge or skill; performance refers to the demonstration of that knowledge or skill after it has been acquired. Strategies for stimulating students' motivation to learn apply not only to performance (work on assignments or tests) but also to the information processing that is involved in learning content or skills in the first place (attending to lessons, reading for understanding, comprehending instructions, putting things into one's own words). Thus, stimulating students' motivation to learn includes encouraging them to use thoughtful information-processing and skill-building strategies when they are learning. This is quite different from merely offering them incentives for good performance later.

The difference between intrinsic motivation and motivation to learn is closely related to the difference between affective and cognitive task engagement experiences. Intrinsic motivation refers primarily to affective experience—enjoyment of the processes involved in engaging in an activity. In contrast, motivation to learn is primarily a cognitive response involving attempts to make sense of the information that an activity conveys, to relate this information to prior knowledge, and to master the skills that the activity develops. Students may be motivated to learn from a lesson or activity whether or not they find its content interesting or its processes enjoyable.

Student motivation to learn can be viewed either as a general disposition or as a situation-specific state. As a disposition, it is an enduring tendency to value learning—to approach the process of learning with effort and thought and to seek to acquire knowledge and skill. In specific situations, a state of motivation to learn exists when a student engages purposefully in an activity by adopting its goal and trying to learn the concepts or master the skills it develops. Students who are high in motivation to learn (as a disposition) tend to do these things routinely, as if they possess a motivated learning schema that is triggered whenever they enter a learning situation. Even students who do not have much motivation to learn as a general disposition may display such motivation in specific situations because the teacher has sparked their interest or made them see the importance of the content or skill. Students who are motivated to learn will not necessarily find classroom activities intensely pleasurable or exciting, but they will find them meaningful and worthwhile, and will take them seriously by trying to get the intended benefits from them.

Focus on the Nature and Quality of Motivation, Not its Quantity

Motivation to learn refers primarily to the quality of students' cognitive engagement in a learning activity, not the intensity of the physical effort they devote to it or the time they spend on it. For most tasks, there is a curvilinear relationship between motivational intensity and degree of success achieved. That is, performance is highest when motivation is at an optimal level rather than either below or above this optimal level. Furthermore, the optimal level varies with the nature of the task: High levels of arousal maximize performance on tasks that call for extraordinary effort, but lower levels maximize performance on tasks that call for controlled application of refined technique. Thus, it helps to be "psyched up" if your task is to break open a door or win a 50-meter dash, but such high arousal is counterproductive if your task is to sink a putt or make a free throw.

High arousal is likely to interfere with performance on activities that call for sustained mental concentration and thought, such as the learning tasks facing students in classrooms. Students are likely to handle these tasks most successfully when their motivation is positive (they are engaged in the task and free from distractions, anxieties, and fear of failure) but not overly high in an absolute sense. They are alert and oriented toward learning, but not "psyched up" or focused on winning a competition or obtaining a reward.

In other words, we always want to maximize students' motivation to learn, but not necessarily to maximize their total motivation. Similarly, we want to maximize successful achievement outcomes, but only insofar as this can be done by maximizing motivation to learn and supplying supportive incentives and rewards. Attempts to increase motivation still further are likely to be counterproductive, especially if they involve inappropriately pressuring students or making them unnecessarily anxious or dependent. We want to develop life-enhancing dispositions in students, not neurotic needs.

Stimulating and Socializing Motivation

Much of the motivational advice typically offered to teachers boils down to the following general principle: Find out what topics your students want to learn about and what activities they enjoy doing, then build these into your curriculum as much as possible. This is only part of what needs to be done, however. If you confine yourself to responding to the motivational orientations that your students bring with them, you will limit your options and fail to capitalize on opportunities to guide your students' motivational development in desirable directions.

People are born with the potential to develop a great range of motivational dispositions. A few such dispositions appear to be inborn as part of the human condition and can be observed in everyone. Most, however, especially higher level dispositions such as motivation to learn, are developed gradually through exposure to learning opportunities and socialization influences. The degree to which a particular motivational disposition develops, as well as the qualitative nuances it takes on in the individual person, are influenced by the modeling and socialization (communication of expectations, direct instruction, corrective feedback, reward and punishment) provided by "significant others" in the person's social environment. Along with family members and close friends, teachers are significant others in the lives of their students, and thus in a position to influence the students' motivational development.

In this regard, it is helpful to view motivation to learn as a schema—a network of connected insights, skills, values, and dispositions that enable students to understand what it means to engage in academic activities with the intention of accomplishing their learning goals and with awareness of the strategies they use in attempting to do so. The total schema cannot be taught directly, although some of its conceptual and skills components can. In addition, its value and dispositional components can be stimulated and supported through modeling, communication of expectations, and socialization of students into a cohesive learning community.

Children's development of motivation to learn and related self-actualization motives is especially dependent on modeling and socialization by adults. These motivational dispositions include key insights and cognitive strategies that are learned primarily as a result of sophisticated socialization at home and instruction at school. Students who have not had much exposure to these cognitive aspects of motivation may view school tasks as imposed demands rather than as learning opportunities, and thus engage in them (if at all) with work-avoidant goals and perhaps performance goals, but not learning goals. They will have to be helped to understand and appreciate what motivation to learn means before such motivation can begin to influence their decisions and actions.

Therefore, in addition to capitalizing on students' existing motivation, make the best of your opportunities to stimulate and socialize their motivation to learn. In each particular teaching situation, try to stimulate motivation to learn the knowledge or skills that the activity is designed to develop. Bring this motive to the forefront relative to any other motives that may be operating at the time. Over the long run, these everyday motivational efforts should have cumulative effects encouraging your students to develop motivation to learn as an enduring disposition.

Expectancy × Value Model of Motivation

Much of what researchers have learned about motivation, including implications for teachers, can be organized within an expectancy × value model. The expectancy × value model of motivation holds that the effort that people are willing to expend on a task is the product of (a) the degree to which they expect to be able to perform the task successfully if they apply themselves (and thus the degree to which they expect to get whatever rewards that successful task performance will bring), and (b) the degree to which they value those rewards as well as the opportunity to engage in the processes involved in performing the task itself. The word value, used here as a verb meaning to appreciate or see worth in, should not be confused with the noun values, meaning ethical principles or ideals.

Effort investment is viewed as the product rather than the sum of the expectancy and value factors because it is assumed that no effort at all will be invested in a task if one factor is missing entirely. People do not willingly invest effort in tasks that they do not enjoy and that do not lead to valued outcomes even if they know that they can perform the tasks successfully. Nor do they willingly invest effort in even highly valued tasks if they believe that they cannot succeed on those tasks no matter how hard they try. If required to engage in such tasks unwillingly, they are likely to experience negative affective and cognitive reactions. Thus, the expectancy × value model of motivation implies that teachers need to (a) help students appreciate the value of school activities and (b) make sure that students can achieve success in these activities if they apply reasonable effort.

Unique expectancy × value reasoning concerning potential task engagement occurs within each individual, but it is influenced by the social context in which the task is Classrooms are highly charged social contexts that complicate individual students' expectancy × value reasoning enormously, for good or ill.

Hansen suggested that students tend to adopt one of four general approaches to coping with classroom tasks, depending on their success expectations and task values. Engaging is likely when students see value in the task and are reasonably confident of their ability to meet its demands. When engaged, they seek to make sense of the task by discovering meanings, grasping new insights, and generating integrative interpretations. The outcomes even if they know that they can perform the tasks successfully. Nor do they willingly invest effort in even highly valued tasks if they believe that they cannot succeed on those tasks no matter how hard they try. If required to engage in such tasks unwillingly, they are likely to experience negative affective and cognitive reactions. Thus, the expectancy × value model of motivation implies that teachers need to (a) help students appreciate the value of school activities and (b) make sure that students can achieve success in these activities if they apply reasonable effort.

Unique expectancy × value reasoning concerning potential task engagement occurs within each individual, but it is influenced by the social context in which the task is embedded (where relevant). Classrooms are highly charged social contexts that complicate individual students' expectancy × value reasoning enormously, for good or ill.Hansen suggested that students tend to adopt one of four general approaches to coping with classroom tasks, depending on their success expectations and task values.

Engaging is likely when students see value in the task and are reasonably confident of their ability to meet its demands. When engaged, they seek to make sense of the task by discovering meanings, grasping new insights, and generating integrative interpretations. The task's unfamiliar aspects are viewed as challenging but are valued because they provide a basis for extending one's understandings.

Dissembling is likely when students recognize value in the task but do not feel capable of meeting its demands. They would like to complete the task successfully, but are uncertain of what to do, how to do it, or whether they can do it. These uncertainties threaten their identity and self-esteem, so they pretend to understand, make excuses, deny their difficulties, or engage in other behavior focused more on protecting their ego than on developing task-related knowledge and skill.

Evading is likely when success expectancies are high but task value perceptions are low. The students feel confident of their ability to meet task demands but don't see a reason to do so. In response to the grading system and other pressures, they may go through the motions by focusing sufficiently on the task to avoid teacher interventions and perhaps even to accomplish the task goal. However, their attention is scattered, frequently drifting to competing interests such as daydreaming, interacting with classmates, or thinking about their personal lives.

Finally, *rejecting* is likely when both success expectations and task value perceptions are low. Lacking both reasons to care about succeeding on the task and confidence that they could do so if they tried, students in this situation withdraw from the task. Some become passive and psychologically numbed. Others smolder with anger or alienation. Rejecting the task completely, they not only don't engage in it but don't even feel the need to dissemble by pretending to themselves or others that they are capable of meeting its demands.

References

Boekaerts, M. (2001). Motivation, learning, and instruction. In N. Smelser & P. Baltes (Eds.), *Inter-national encyclopedia of the social and behavioral sciences* (pp. 10112–10117). New York: Elsevier Science.

Deci, E., & Ryan, R. (1985). *Intrinsic motivation and self-determination in human behavior.* New York: Plenum.

Maehr, M., & Meyer, H. (1997). Understanding motivation and schooling: Where we've been, where we are, and where we need to go. *Educational Psychology Review*, 9, 371–409.

Stipek, D. (1996). Motivation and instruction. In D. Berliner & R. Calfee (Eds.), *Handbook of educa-tional psychology* (pp. 85–113). New York: Macmillan.

Thrash, T., & Elliot, A. (2001). Delimiting and integrating achievement motive and goal constructs. In A. Efklides, J. Kuhl, & R. Sorrentino (Eds.), *Trends and prospects in motivation research* (pp. 3–21). Boston: Kluwer.

2

Building a Learning Community

A learning community is a group of people who share common emotions, values or beliefs, are actively engaged in learning together from each other, and by habituation. Such communities have become the template for a cohort-based, interdisciplinary approach to higher education. This may be based on an advanced kind of educational or 'pedagogical' design.

Community psychologists such as McMillan and Chavis state that there are four key factors that defined a sense of community: "(1) membership, (2) influence, (3) fulfillment of individuals needs and (4) shared events and emotional connections. So, the participants of learning community must feel some sense of loyalty and belonging to the group (membership) that drive their desire to keep working and helping others, also the things that the participant do in must affect what happened in the community, that means, an active and not just a reactive performance (influence). Besides a learning community must give the chance to the participants to meet particular needs (fulfillment) by expressing personal opinions, asking for help or specific information and share stories of events with particular issue included (emotional connections) emotional experiences.

Learning communities are now fairly common to American colleges and universities, and are also found in the United Kingdom and Europe. The learning community approach fundamentally restructures the curriculum, and the time and space of students. Many different curricular restructuring models are being used, but all of the learning community models intentionally link together courses or coursework to provide greater curricular coherence, more opportunities for active teaming, and interaction between students and faculty.

Experts frequently describe five basic nonresidential learning community models:

1. *Linked courses*: Students take two connected courses, usually one disciplinary course such as history or biology and one skills course such as writing, speech, or information literacy.
2. *Learning clusters*: Students take three or more connected courses, usually with a common interdisciplinary theme uniting them.
3. *Freshman interest groups*: Similar to learning clusters, but the students share the same major, and they often receive academic advising as part of the learning community.
4. *Federated learning communities:* Similar to a learning cluster, but with an additional seminar course taught by a "Master Learner," a faculty member who enrolls in the other courses and takes them alongside the students. The Master Learner's course draws connections between the other courses.
5. *Coordinated studies:* This model blurs the lines between individual courses. The learning community functions as a single, giant course that the students and faculty members work on full-time for an entire semester or academic year.

Residential learning communities, or living-learning programs, range from theme-based halls on a college dormitory to degree-granting residential colleges. What these programs share is the integration of academic content with daily interactions among students, faculty, and staff living and working in these programs.

Establishing a Learning Community

It is commonly observed that certain preconditions must be in place before motivational strategies can be effective. Maslow's hierarchy of needs, for example, implies that lower level needs must be satisfied before higher level needs can become operative. Other examples have been developed by industrial and organizational psychologists studying factors that affect workers' satisfaction and productivity. Their studies indicate that workers' motivation is affected not only by the nature of their work and the rewards they expect to earn, but also by their job environment and other working conditions, their social relationships with co-workers, and especially, their feelings about their boss. Even workers who do not derive much intrinsic satisfaction from their work will put forth reasonable effort if they like their boss. However, they may develop apathy or resistance if they view their boss as oppressive.

Citing studies of management practices that have been used successfully in business and industry, William Glasser urged teachers to act as lead managers rather than boss managers. Lead managers motivate by reinforcing rather than punishing, showing rather than telling, empowering rather than overpowering, and emphasizing cooperative work toward shared goals rather than rule enforcement. Lead managers are more likely than boss managers to elicit students' cooperation and empower them to assume responsibility for controlling their lives at school.

Similar ideas about establishing caring and collaborative relationships with students and their families have been advanced by James Comer in *School Power*, by Nel Noddings in *The Challenge to Care in Schools*, by Robert Pianta in *Enhancing Relationships Between Children and Teachers*, by William Purkey and John Novak in *Inviting School Success*, and by Carl Rogers and H. Jerome Freiberg in *Freedom to Learn*. These books advocate creating a school environment in which students feel comfortable, valued, and secure. This encourages them to form positive emotional bonds with teachers and peers and a positive attitude toward school, which in turn facilitates their academic motivation and learning.

Many emerging ideas about optimal social contexts in classrooms center around the concept of learning community. we use the term with some hesitation because it has been given many meanings, some of which extend beyond what is intended here. For example, in some definitions, the term refers to collaborative learning planned and regulated primarily by the students themselves, with the teacher acting primarily as a resource person. Nevertheless, we have adopted the term because it points directly to two key features of optimal classroom environments. First, it emphasizes learning, which implies something more than merely completing academic tasks or even passing tests. It serves as a reminder that students come to school to acquire important knowledge, skills, values, and dispositions, and that their learning is supposed to be enriching and empowering.

Second, the term emphasizes that this learning will occur within a community—a group of people with social connections and responsibilities toward one another and the group as a whole. This implies that learning will be collaborative as community members encourage and support one an-other's efforts. A learning community features a social context in which students feel comfortable asking questions, seeking help, and responding to questions when unsure of the answer. Members share the belief that "We're all learning together," so confusion and mistakes are understood as natural parts of the learning process. The teacher has a special place in this learning community, but he or she is a learner too, and models this fact frequently.

Various lines of theory and research point to three important agendas for you to accomplish in establishing a learning community that will set the stage for effective motivation of students: (a) make yourself and your classroom attractive to students; (b) focus their attention on individual and collaborative learning goals and help them to achieve these goals; and (c) teach things that are worth learning, in ways that help students to appreciate their value. The first two of these agendas address the communal aspects of learning community; the third addresses the learning aspects.

Make Your Classroom Attractive

You—your own personality and everyday behavior in the classroom—can become your most powerful motivational tool. To do so, you will need to cultivate and display the attributes of individuals who are effective as models and socializers. These begin with characteristics that make people well liked: a cheerful disposition, friendliness, emotional maturity, sincerity, and other qualities that indicate good mental health and personal adjustment. Your attempts to socialize students will have positive effects to the extent that the students admire you, value your opinions, and believe that you are sincere in what you say and have their best interests in mind when saying it. Motivation to learn tends to be high when students perceive their teachers as involved with them (liking them, sympathetic and responsive to their needs), but students tend to become disaffected when they do not perceive such involvement.

Therefore, get to know and enjoy your students. Learn their preferred names quickly and use these names frequently as you interact with them. Greet them warmly each day and spend some time getting to know them as individuals. In the process, you will learn a lot about their backgrounds and interests that you can incorporate into your teaching in ways that are compatible with curricular goals. Also, help your students get to know and appreciate you as a person by sharing some of your background, life experiences, interests, and opinions. If you do this appropriately, it will help your students to become more open and genuine in their interactions with you, even while retaining their respect for your authority as the teacher. Finally, help them get to know one another by interviewing them publicly in ways that allow them to share information about their families, interests, hobbies, and noteworthy experiences.

Create an inviting physical environment in your classroom. To the extent possible, see that it is furnished comfortably and arranged in a way that is both aesthetically pleasing and compatible with your instructional methods. Include attractive displays and decorations that relate to the curriculum. As photos of your students and products from their completed assignments become available, incorporate these into your displays in ways that encourage the students to take pride in their accomplishments and appreciate those of their classmates.

Be an Authoritative Manager and Socializer of Students

In managing your classroom and socializing students, emphasize the strategies that have emerged repeatedly in studies of the most effective teachers: Teachers who approach management as a process of establishing a productive learning environment tend to be more successful than teachers who emphasize their roles as disciplinarians. That is, successful managers focus on helping their students learn what is expected and how to meet those expectations, not on threatening or punishing them for failing to do so. These teachers are clear and consistent in articulating their expectations. If necessary, they model and instruct students in desired procedures and remind students when these procedures are needed. They keep students engaged in worthwhile lessons and activities; they monitor their classrooms continually and respond to emerging problems before they become disruptive; and when possible they intervene in ways that do not disrupt lesson momentum or distract students who are working on assignments.

Unsurprisingly, students describe their favorite teachers as caring about them as individuals and seeking to help them succeed as learners, teaching interesting things, explaining content clearly, being pleasant and friendly, being fair, and as not playing favorites, humiliating them, appearing to look down on them when they make mistakes or ask for help, yelling at them, or overreacting to their minor misbehavior. However, students also say that they want teachers to articulate and enforce clear standards of behavior. They view this not just as part of the teacher's job but as evidence that the teacher cares about them.

A dependable classroom structure provides students with the information and assistance they need to enable them to learn successfully. You can provide structure by communicating your expectations clearly; by responding consistently, predictably, and contingently to students' behavior; by offering help and support to those who are struggling; and by adjusting your teaching strategies to individual differences. Students who experience optimal levels of this kind of structure are likely to be the most effortful, persistent, and highly engaged in classroom activities.

In managing your classroom and socializing your students, seek to maintain a classroom structure that is optimal not only in the degree of direction that you provide but also in the manner in which you exercise your leadership. Use authoritative strategies that help students to become active, self-regulated learners; avoid both authoritarian strategies that produce passive obedience rather than thoughtful self-regulation, and laissez-faire strategies that offer students autonomy but fail to provide them with needed guidance.

Parents who are the most successful in getting their children to adopt their ideals and internalize their standards for behavior are those who use authoritative rather than authoritarian strategies. Authoritarian parents make little attempt to explain their demands, which they expect to be obeyed without questioning or discussion. In contrast, authoritative parents explain the rationales for their demands and help their children to understand that the demands are made for the children's own good. The authoritative pattern that promotes optimal personal and social development in children includes the following socialization practices:

- Accepting the child as an individual
- Communicating this acceptance through warm, affectionate interactions
- Socializing by teaching the child prosocial values and behavioral guidelines, not just imposing "discipline"
- Clarifying rules and limits, but with input from the child and with flexibility in adapting to developmental advances (e.g., allowing more

opportunities for autonomy and choice as children develop greater ability tohandle these opportunities responsibly)

- Presenting expectations in ways that communicate respect for and concern about the child, as opposed to "laying down the law"
- Explaining the rationales underlying demands and expectations
- Justifying prohibitions by citing the effects of children's actions on themselves and others rather than by appealing to fear of punishment or essentially empty logic such as "good children don't do that"
- Modeling as well as teaching well-articulated value systems
- Continually projecting positive expectations and attitudes: treating chil dren as if they already are, or at least are in the process of becoming, prosocial and responsible people.

Authoritative socialization practices are optimal in the classroom as well as the home. Besides supporting your management system, they set the stage for successful motivation efforts by creating a positive classroom atmosphere and encouraging students to view you as a caring teacher whom they trust and want to please.

Use Appealing Communication Practices

The linkage between authoritative classroom management and successful student motivation was demonstrated in college classrooms in a series of studies done by communication theorists. Some of these studies focused on instructors' compliance-gaining strategies. They indicated that coercive, authoritarian approaches to gaining compliance had very negative effects on students' liking of instructors and on the degree to which they achieved the classes' learning goals. In contrast, the use of authoritative techniques helped pave the way for the instructors' motivational efforts by developing positive relationships between them and their students.

Other studies showed the importance of teacher immediacy, a term for actions that enhance physical and psychological closeness with students. Nonverbal immediacy includes eye contact, smiling, positive gestures, vocal variety, forward body lean, and a relaxed body position. Verbal immediacy includes use of humor, personal examples, "we" and "our" language, and students' first names. Immediacy behaviors increase students' liking for the instructor, their interest in the course, and their desire to study thoughtfully and do good work on assignments. Working together, the compliance-gaining and immediacy aspects of instructors' communication styles reinforce each other to produce positive effects on motivation and learning, especially in students who are not highly motivated at the beginning of the term. In contrast, students avoid interactions with instructors they perceive as uncaring or uninterested in them, and they stop coming to ask for help if repeated attempts do not elicit effective responses.

Individual and Collaborative Learning Goals

At any given time, you will want your students to focus on certain goals but may find that some of them pursue other goals in addition or instead. Many of these goals will be social rather than academic. Social goals sometimes complement academic goals (as when students seek to achieve at a high level in order to please you, their parents, or peers who value such achievement).

However, social goals also can undermine academic goals (as when students minimize their attention and work output in an attempt to please peers who have rejected the school's agenda, or more typically, when their attention is distracted from lessons and assignments to social interactions with classmates). You can increase the power of your motivational efforts by attending to your students' social goals as well as their academic goals. In particular, create a social environment in which everyone feels welcome and learning is accomplished through the collaborative efforts of yourself and your students.

During lessons and times when students are working on assignments individually, however, you will need to keep attention focused on learning goals rather than on social goals or other competing agendas.

You are likely to get the best results if you help students to frame their learning goals in terms of acquiring the knowledge or skills that you intend to teach, not just in terms of completing tasks or obtaining particular grades. This will encourage students to take more responsibility for managing their own learning by actively setting goals, seeking to construct understandings, persisting in their efforts to overcome confusions, and assessing and reflecting on what they have learned.

Teach Things that are Worth Learning

Even if you have set the stage by making yourself and your classroom attractive to students and by focusing their attention on individual and collaborative learning goals, you cannot expect them to sustain much motivation to learn unless they view the learning as meaningful and worthwhile. Students are not likely to be motivated to learn when engaged in pointless or meaningless activities such as the following: continued practice on skills that already have been mastered thoroughly; memorizing lists for no good reason; looking up and copying definitions of terms that are never used in activities or assignments; reading material that is written in such sketchy technical, or abstract language as to make it essentially meaningless; or working on tasks assigned merely to fill time rather than to accomplish worthwhile learning goals.

Plan With Major Goals in Mind

The key to making your students' learning experiences worthwhile is to focus your planning on major instructional goals, phrased in terms of desired student outcomes—the knowledge, skills, attitudes, values, and dispositions that you want to develop in your students. Goals, not content coverage or learning processes, provide the rationale for curriculum and instruction. All of the elements of your instructional program—content sources, discussion questions, activities, assignments, and assessment methods—should be included because you consider them useful as means to accomplish important instructional goals.

It may seem obvious to you that curriculum planning should be guided by major instructional goals, but research on instructional materials and on teachers' planning and teaching suggest that this principle is not often realized in classrooms. Teachers typically plan by concentrating on the content they will teach and the activities their students will do, without giving much thought to the goals that provide the rationale for the content and activities in the first place.

In effect, most teachers leave crucially important decisions about goals to the publishing companies who supply them with instructional materials. This would work out well if sustained focus on important goals guided the development of these materials. However, the textbook series typically treat content coverage as an end in itself. As a result, too many topics are covered in not enough depth; content exposition often lacks coherence and is cluttered with insertions and illustrations that have little to do with the key ideas that should be developed; skills are taught separately from knowledge content rather than integrated with it; and in general, neither the students' texts nor the questions and activities suggested in the teachers' manuals are structured around powerful ideas connected to important goals.

Adapt Instructional Materials to Your Goals

You will not be able to achieve a coherent program of curriculum and instruction simply by following the teaching suggestions that come with your textbooks. Instead, you will need to elaborate on or even substitute for much of the content in the texts and many of the activities suggested in the accompanying manuals.

To do so, examine your instructional materials and unit plans in light of your major instructional goals. Identify what content to ignore or downplay and what content to emphasize. You may need to augment the latter content if major ideas or themes are not well developed in the texts. Skip pointless questions and activities, and develop alternatives that will support progress toward major goals.

Develop Powerful Ideas in Depth

You won't have time to teach everything worth learning. Only so many topics can be included in the curriculum, and not all of these can be developed in sufficient depth to promote deep understanding of key ideas, appreciation of their significance, and exploration of their applications to life outside of school. This tension between breadth of coverage and depth of topic development is an enduring dilemma that teachers have to manage as best they can; it is not a problem that you can solve in any permanent or completely satisfactory manner.

In recent years, curricula have drifted into an overemphasis on breadth at the expense of depth. Critics routinely complain that textbooks offer "mile-wide but inch-deep" curricula featuring parades of disconnected facts instead of coherent networks of connected content structured around powerful ideas. Reports of teaching in classrooms suggest a similar picture. Although there are exceptions, most of these descriptions portray teachers as hurriedly attempting to cover too much content and students as frequently memorizing but not often reflecting and discussing. Students spend too much time reading, reciting, filling out worksheets, and taking memory tests, and not enough time engaging in sustained discourse about powerful ideas or applying these ideas in authentic activities. Still more recently, these unfortunate curricular trends have been exacerbated by increasing emphasis on high-stakes testing.

Disconnected factual information is not very meaningful or memorable. When students lack contexts within which to situate such information and richly connected networks of ideas to enhance its meaningfulness, they are forced to rely on rote memorizing instead of using more sophisticated learning and application strategies. They remember as much as they can until the test, but then forget most of it afterwards. Furthermore, most of what they do remember is inert knowledge that they are not able to use in relevant application situations.

There is general agreement about what needs to be done to enable students to construct meaningful knowledge that they can access and use in their lives outside of school. First, there needs to be a retreat from breadth of coverage in order to allow time to develop the most important content in greater depth. Second, this important content needs to be represented as networks of connected information structured around powerful ideas. Third, the content needs to be developed with a focus on explaining these important ideas and the connections among them.

Teaching with Emphasis on Powerful Ideas

As an example of the value of structuring content around powerful ideas, consider the topic of shelter. Elementary social studies textbook series typically emphasize that shelter is a basic human need and then go on to identify and illustrate a great variety of shelter forms (tipis, igloos, stilt homes, etc.). However, the texts typically say very little about the reasons why people live in these different kinds of homes and nothing at all about advances in construction materials and techniques that have made possible the features of modern housing that most children in the United States take for granted. Students often emerge from these units thinking that people from the past or from other societies have inexplicably chosen to live in strange or exotic forms of housing, without appreciating that local responses to shelter needs usually are quite inventive given the available construction knowledge, technology, and materials.

Units on shelter and other cultural universals (food, clothing, transportation, communication, occupations, government, etc.) will be much more powerful if taught with emphasis on how practices relating to the cultural universal have evolved over time, how and why they vary across societies today, and what all of this might mean for personal, social, and civic decision making. This will expand students' purviews on the human condition and help them to put the familiar into historical, geographical, and cultural perspective.

Rather than teach only that shelter is a basic human need and that different forms of shelter exist, instruction might help students to understand and appreciate the reasons for these different forms of shelter. Students could learn that shelter needs are determined in large part by local climate and geographical features, and that most housing is constructed using materials adapted from natural resources that are plentiful in the local area. They could learn that certain forms of housing reflect cultural, economic, or geographic conditions (tipis and tents as easily portable shelters used by nomadic societies, stilt homes as adaptation to periodic flooding, highrises as adaptation to land scarcity in urban areas). They also could acquire a better appreciation of the fact that inventions, discoveries, and improvements in construction knowledge and materials have enabled many modern people to live in housing that offers better durability, weatherproofing, insulation, and temperature control, with fewer requirements for maintenance and labor (e.g., cutting wood for a fireplace or shoveling coal for a furnace) than what was available to even the richest of their ancestors.

These and related ideas would be taught with appeal to students' sense of imagination and wonder. There might also be emphasis on values and dispositions (e.g., consciousness-raising through age-suitable activities relating to the energy efficiency of homes or the plight of the homeless). Development and application might include a tour of the neighborhood (in which different types of housing are identified and discussed) or an assignment calling for students to take home an energy-efficiency inventory to fill out and discuss with their parents. There might also be reading and discussion of children's literature selections on life in the past (e.g., in log cabins on the frontier) or in other societies or about the homeless in our society today, as well as activities calling for students to plan their ideal homes or simulate the thinking involved in making decisions about where to live given certain location and budgetary constrictions.

Similarly, units on history need not be seemingly random parades of facts. If planned with focus on instructional goals, they can be structured around powerful ideas that students can appreciate and apply. For example, units on the American Revolution might be planned to develop understanding and appreciation of the origins of American political values and policies. Treatment of the Revolution and its aftermath would emphasize the historical events and political philosophies that shaped the thinking of the writers of the Declaration of Independence and the Constitution.

Content coverage would focus on the issues that developed between England and the colonies and the ways that these impacted various types of people, as well as on the ideals, principles, and compromises that went into the construction of the Constitution (especially the Bill of Rights). Assignments calling for research, critical thinking, or decision making would focus on topics such as the various forms of oppression that different colonial groups had experienced (and the influence of this on their thinking about government), as well as the ideas of Jefferson and other key framers of the Constitution. There would be less emphasis on Paul Revere or other revolutionary figures who were not known primarily for their contributions to American political values and policies, and no emphasis at all on the details of particular battles.

Students might role play journalists or pamphleteers writing about the Boston Massacre or the Boston Tea Party, simulate a town meeting or Continental Congress session discussing possible responses to the Intolerable Acts, hold a debate on whether the Revolution was justified, or pretend to be citizens of Boston writing to friends elsewhere about their experiences.

These examples are not meant to imply that the suggested approaches are the only or even necessarily the best ones to take in addressing these two topics. Instead, they illustrate how clarity of primary goals encourages development of units and lessons likely to cohere and function as tools for accomplishing those goals, and in the process, to produce instruction that students find meaningful, relevant, and applicable to their lives outside of school.

The particular goals to emphasize will vary with one's educational philosophy, the ages and needs of the students, and the purposes of the course. Teachers of military history in a service academy, for example, would have very different goals and would approach the unit on the American Revolution with very different content emphases than those in the example.

Structure Activities and Assignments Around Powerful Ideas

The best learning activities and assignments are built around powerful ideas. Students will not necessarily learn anything important from merely carrying out the processes of an activity (i.e., spending "time on task"). The key to the effectiveness of good activities is their cognitive engagement potential—the degree to which they get students actively thinking about and applying key ideas, preferably with conscious awareness of their learning goals and control of their learning strategies. The most valuable activities are not merely hands-on, but minds-on.

The success of an activity in producing thoughtful student engagement with key ideas depends not only on the activity itself but on the teacher structuring and the teacher–student discourse that occur before, during, and after the activity. Activities are likely to have maximum impact when you introduce them in ways that clarify their purposes and engage students in seeking to accomplish those purposes; scaffold students' work, monitor their progress, and provide appropriate feedback; and lead the students through postactivity sharing of and reflection on the insights that have been developed.

In planning activities and assignments, begin with a focus on the unit's major goals and consider the kinds of activities that would promote progress toward those goals. This will help you to make good decisions about whether to use activities suggested in the manual that accompanies your textbook and about what other activities might need to be included. A synthesis of principles for designing and implementing learning activities concluded that all of the activities in a unit of instruction should meet four primary criteria:

1. *Goal relevance.* Each activity is essential, or at least directly relevant and useful, for enabling students to achieve the unit's learning goals.
2. *Difficulty level.* Each activity is pitched within the optimal range of difficulty—challenging enough to extend learning, but not so difficult as to leave many students confused or frustrated.
3. *Feasibility.* Each activity is feasible for implementation within the constraints under which you must work (space and equipment, time, types of students, etc.).
4. *Cost effectiveness.* The educational benefits expected to be derived from each activity justify its anticipated costs in time and trouble (both for you and for your students).

In selecting from among activities that meet all four of these primary criteria, you might consider applying several secondary criteria:

1. Students are likely to find the activity interesting or enjoyable.

2. The activity provides opportunities for interaction and reflective discourse, not just solitary seatwork
3. If the activity involves writing, students will compose prose, not just fill in blanks.
4. If the activity involves discourse, students will engage in critical or creative thinking, inquiry, problem solving, or decision making, not just regurgitate facts and definitions.
5. The activity focuses on application of important ideas, not incidental details or interesting but ultimately trivial information.
6. As a set, the activities offer variety and in other ways appeal to student motivation to the extent that this is consistent with curriculum goals.
7. As a set, the activities include many ties to current events or local and family examples or applications.

Emphasize Authentic Activities

Be conscious of potential applications of powerful ideas when selecting and implementing learning activities. As much as possible, allow your students to learn through engagement in authentic activities. Authentic activities require using what is being learned for accomplishing the very sorts of life applications that justify inclusion of this learning in the curriculum in the first place. If it is not possible to engage students in the actual life applications that the learning experiences are designed to prepare them for, then at least engage them in realistic simulations of these applications.

Where skills must be practiced until they become smooth and automatic, most of this practice should occur within whole-task application activities rather than be confined to isolated practice of subskills. Elementary students should have opportunities to read for information or pleasure in addition to practicing word attack skills, to solve problems and apply mathematics in addition to practicing number facts and computations, and to write prose or poetry compositions or actual correspondence in addition to practicing spelling and penmanship. All students should learn how and why knowledge was developed in addition to acquiring the knowledge itself and should have opportunities to apply what they are learning to their own lives or to current social, civic, or scientific issues.

Educators who do not distinguish between school subjects and the academic disciplines that inform them sometimes define authentic activities narrowly, as activities that engage students in doing things that disciplinary practitioners do (e.g., conduct inquiry using the forms of discourse and the investigatory tools that characterize the discipline). Most educators (myself included) view schooling more broadly—as development of students' full human potential and preparation for life in general, not just as induction into the disciplines. This broader view leads to definitions of authentic activities that emphasize life applications.

Newmann, for example, specified that authentic activities should afford students opportunities to construct knowledge through disciplined inquiry that has value beyond the classroom. Perkins suggested that mathematics curricula might place more emphasis on probability and statistics relative to quadratic equations, and that social studies curricula might place more emphasis on the roots of ethnic hatreds relative to the details of the French Revolution. The authenticity of literacy education has been augmented by establishing authentic audiences for students' reading and writing activities, such as by creating pen pal programs or student-run newspapers.

These examples illustrate that authentic activities involve both curricular elements (focusing on content that has potential applications in life outside of school) and instructional elements (developing this content through activities that afford students opportunities to use what they are learning for authentic purposes). Research on authentic activities indicates that they occur infrequently in classrooms, but when they do, they are associated with a variety of positive outcomes.

Teach for Understanding

In recent years, both the findings of research on effective teaching and the instructional guidelines issued by organizations serving subject-matter specialists have emphasized the importance of teaching school subjects for understanding. Students who learn content with understanding not only learn the content itself but appreciate the reasons for learning it and retain it in a form that makes it usable when needed. When the new learning is complex, the construction of meaning required to develop clear understanding of it takes time and is facilitated by the interactive discourse that occurs during lessons and activities. Clear explanations and modeling from the teacher are important, but so are opportunities to answer questions about the content, discuss or debate its meanings and implications, and apply it in problem-solving or decision-making contexts.

These activities allow students to process the content actively and make it their own by paraphrasing it into their own words, exploring its relationships to other knowledge and to past experience, appreciating the insights it provides, and identifying its implications for personal decision making or action. The teacher provides whatever structuring and scaffolding that students need in order to accomplish the goals, but gradually fades this assistance as students develop expertise. Ultimately, the students engage in independent and self-regulated learning.

Sociocultural Theories of Teaching

Other theoretical principles that have emerged recently and that fit well with ideas about teaching for understanding within a learning community are sociocultural views of teaching and learning. Sociocultural theorists view the learning that takes place in classrooms as part of the more general socialization that takes place as societies equip their new members with the knowledge and skills that they believe to be important. Based on the metaphor of on-the-job training, sociocultural theorists speak of learners as novices undergoing a cognitive apprenticeship under the supervision of one or more mentors. In addition to society in general, such enculturation occurs within smaller communities of practice when mentors impart to novices the knowledge and skills involved in functioning as a mathematician, historian, or chemist.

At first, novices learn through legitimate peripheral participation in communities of practice. They are legitimate members of the community, but their participation is peripheral because they mostly watch, listen, and carry out beginner-level aspects of the community's activities under the supervision of mentors. As they gain expertise, their social roles change and they move from peripheral toward more central forms of participation. They begin to function more fully as equals with the mentors who have been teaching them and to assume increasing responsibilities for regulating their own learning and for acting as mentors themselves in socializing new members into the community.

As novices acquire expertise, they learn to use the community's specialized discourse and tools. Communities of practice develop specialized vocabulary and forms of discourse that help them to carry out their activities (e.g., analyze a story with reference to concepts such as plot or characterization, or analyze a historical account with reference to concepts such as bias or primary vs. secondary sources). The tools used by communities of practice include not only physical tools but cognitive tools such as mathematical formulas, musical notation, or any of the processes and skills commonly taught as part of the academic disciplines. Novices ordinarily acquire the community's specialized discourse and learn to use its specialized tools in the context of carrying out the very kinds of activities that led the community to invent the specialized discourse and tools in the first place.

Sociocultural theorists emphasize that learning activities and situations are characterized by affordances and constraints. Affordances are exploitable opportunities—the potentials for thought and action that the activity offers. For example, a discussion affords opportunities to students to engage in verbal interaction about a topic, whereas an essay assignment affords opportunities to organize their thinking and communicate their ideas in writing. Constraints are limitations on the range of thinking and action that an activity imposes. A teacher might constrain a discussion by requiring that students' contributions be polite and on topic, and might constrain an essay assignment by limiting it to 300 words and requiring that each paragraph begin with a clear topic sentence. Some school activities and assignments are severely constrained, such as worksheets that limit students' responses to filling in a blank, circling an alternative, or supply the answer to a calculation problem.

References

Newmann, F., & Associates. (1996). *Authentic achievement: Restructuring schools for intellectual quality*. San Francisco: Jossey-Bass.

Purkey, W., & Novak, J. (1996). *Inviting school success: A self-concept approach to teaching, learning, and democratic practice* (3rd ed.). Belmont, CA: Wadsworth.

Rogoff, B., Turkanis, C., & Bartlett, L. (2001). *Learning together: Children and adults in a school community*. New York: Oxford University Press

Weinstein, C., & Mignano, A., Jr. (1993). *Elementary classroom management: Lessons from research and practice*. New York: McGraw-Hill.

3

Building Students' Self-Confidence

Teachers are some of the most powerful influences in a child's life. As a teacher, you can help children increase their self-confidence as you provide them with a chance to build on their achievements and be successful in and out of your classroom. Classroom activities provide children with infinite opportunities to affirm their abilities. As students strive to do more in and out of the classroom, they increase their self-confidence in performing specific activities and completing assignments. As a teacher, it is important for you to recognize your students' accomplishments and provide positive reinforcement. Positive reinforcement increases the likelihood that the student will repeat the desired behavior and encourages the student to try something more challenging.Furthermore, positive reinforcement enhances protective factors, which are crucial in helping children resist peer pressures to engage in risky behaviors, such as substance use, that can affect them later in life

Achievement Situations

Information about the expectancy aspects of motivation has been developed by studying people's reactions to achievement situations. Achievement situations require people to perform some goal-oriented task knowing that their performance will be evaluated. Some achievement situations pit people in direct competition with one another and produce winners and losers. Other achievement situations do not involve such personal competition but do involve characterizing performance with reference to standards of excellence.

If there is a single clear-cut goal, people either succeed or fail in their efforts to meet it. If the task allows for more graduated or varied assessment, the quality of performance may be characterized more precisely or comprehensively.

Performance can be evaluated with reference either to absolute standards of excellence or to norms that allow comparisons relative to some reference group (e.g., one's classmates). Subjective experiences of relative success or failure flow from these evaluations, viewed in the light of one's performance expectations (e.g., among students who earn a grade of B, any who expected a lower grade will feel successful but any who expected an A will feel that they failed to accomplish what they should have).

People approach achievement situations differently depending on the makeup of their achievement motivation. Atkinson noted that two key components of achievement motivation are motivation to succeed and motivation to avoid failure. Motivation to succeed is determined by the strength of one's overall need for achievement, one's estimate of the probability of succeeding on the task at hand, and the degree to which one values the rewards that such success would bring. Counterbalancing these components of motivation to succeed are the parallel components of motivation to avoid failure: the strength of one's overall need to avoid failure, one's estimate of the probability of failing the task, and the degree to which one fears the negative outcomes that such failure would bring (e.g., private disappointment, public embarrassment).

Individual differences in approach to achievement situations are predictable from the relative strengths of people's motivation to succeed and their motivation to avoid failure. When our motivation to succeed is stronger, we engage in the task willingly. When our motivation to avoid failure is stronger, we seek to avoid the task. If we cannot avoid it, we seek to engage in it in such a way as to minimize the likelihood of failure. Atkinson and Litwin showed this in an experiment in which people played a ring-toss game. They were free to stand anywhere from 1 to 15 feet from the target peg. Those whose motivational patterns emphasized seeking success tended to toss their rings from 9 to 11 feet away. This was a moderate-difficulty, optimal-challenge distance: far enough away to challenge them (they would be successful only about half the time), but not so far away that success depended more on luck than skill.

In contrast, people who were more concerned about avoiding failure tended to respond in either of two contrasting ways. Some stood very close to the peg, so that most if not all of their tosses would be successful. These people ensured a high probability of success but their frequent "successes" were not significant accomplishments. Other people who sought to avoid failure were less obvious about it. In fact, they tossed the rings from the maximum distances of 12 to 15 feet away. This enabled them to give the appearance of taking risks and accepting challenges without really doing so.

By standing so far away, they converted a skill task into a luck task. Any successes they achieved were causes for celebration but their frequent misses were not considered embarrassing failures because most tosses from 12 to 15 feet away were expected to be misses.

Other work by achievement motivation theorists confirmed these early findings. People who focus on achieving success tend to approach achievement situations willingly, to prefer tasks that are moderately difficult for them, and to engage in those tasks with emphasis on developing their skills. In contrast, people who focus on avoiding failure tend to fear achievement situations and thus to avoid them when possible. When required to engage in them, they do so in ways that minimize their risk of failure. One way is to stick with easy tasks and avoid risks. Another is to set goals so high that failure is virtually certain but does not carry the stigma that would be attached to failure to accomplish more realistic goals.

Attempts to draw teaching implications from early studies on achievement motivation are hampered by contrasts between the situations facing the people in those studies and the situations facing students in classrooms. The experiments often involved informal or play settings and engagement in physical activities such as ring toss games. Under these conditions, success seekers' achievement motivation was maximized when their probability of success on the task was 50% (rather than either lower or higher). This does not mean that students' motivation will be maximized when classroom tasks produce a 50% success rate, however, for several reasons.

First, most classroom tasks involve cognitive rather than physical work, so a higher success rate is not merely preferable but necessary. Learning proceeds most smoothly when it involves continuous progress achieved through small, easy steps with consistent success all along the way. Novelty and challenge are important, but overly difficult tasks produce confusion and discouragement. The degree of cognitive strain that would be produced by classroom tasks that allowed students only a 50% success rate would be so great as to discourage most students and make learning unduly difficult for the rest.

Also, later work clarified that the 50% figure refers to the person's subjective estimate of the probability of attaining his or her own goal, not to a score of 50% on some absolute scale. Thus, theoretically, teachers could maximize students' achievement motivation by inducing them to set performance goals at levels that the students believed they had 50% chances to attain. The absolute levels of performance corresponding to these subjective estimates of 50% chance of attainment would vary with individual students.

However, even this idea only takes into account success seeking; it does not consider fear of failure. Individuals who are driven more by fear of failure than by a desire to achieve success try to avoid achievement situations in which their chances of success hover around 50%. Instead, they seek situations in which the probability of success is either much higher, near 100%, or much lower, near zero (so that failure is not "real," because success is not really expected anyway). In the classroom, where activities are compulsory, performance is often public, and failure has a variety of negative consequences, few if any students are likely to be optimally motivated in situations in which they believe they have only a 50% chance of succeeding. Most will prefer a much higher success probability.

Expectancy Aspects of Motivation

Research on people's thinking and behavior in achievement situations has continued, but its emphasis has shifted from achievement needs to achievement goals. Also, it has broadened from recreational tasks and settings to include learning tasks in classrooms. Finally, it has broadened from a focus on the difficulty levels of goals to consider the qualitative aspects of goals and related task engagement strategies.

Achievement motivation research initially established that effort and persistence on achievement tasks are greater in people who set goals of moderate difficulty (neither too hard nor too easy for their current abilities), who seriously commit themselves to pursuing these goals rather than treat them as mere "pie-in-the-sky" hopes, and who concentrate on trying to achieve success rather than on trying to avoid failure. As this work extended to include more cognitive factors, information was developed about the role of the following perceptions and concepts:

— *Effort–outcome covariation.* Effort and persistence are greater when people perceive a continuing connection between the level of effort they invest in a task and the level of mastery that they achieve.

— *Internal locus of control.* Effort and persistence are greater when people believe that the potential to control outcomes (e.g., achieve success on the task) lies within themselves rather than in external factors that they cannot control.

— *Concept of self as origin rather than pawn.* Effort and persistence are greater when people believe that they can bring about desired outcomes through their own actions (act as origins) rather than feeling that they are pawns whose fate is determined by factors beyond their control.

Recent work on the expectancy aspects of motivation includes these and many other cognitive features. Three lines of work have been especially productive: research on implicit theories of ability, causal attributions, and self-efficacy perceptions.

Implicit Theories of Ability

Carol Dweck and her colleagues have explored the connections between people's goal setting and behavior in achievement situations and their implicit theories of ability. Their work began with description of the contrasting ways in which two groups of children responded to an experimental concept-formation task that allowed them to succeed on the first eight problems but then presented four problems that were too difficult for them. The children were asked to think out loud as they worked on the problems. Soon after the onset of the more difficult problems, helpless children began to define themselves as having failed and to give reasons for their failure, typically attributing it to limited ability. Besides denigrating their abilities, they began to express negative affect toward the task, to make pessimistic predictions about their future performance, and to show declines in the sophistication of their strategies. In summary, helpless children quickly perceived themselves to be failing, construed these failures as indicators of limited ability, and "became mired in them as past and future successes seemed to recede from their grasp".

Mastery-oriented children responded to this task much more productively. When they encountered the more difficult problems, they did not become upset or talk about how they were failing. Instead, they redoubled their concentration on the task and began issuing more self-instructions—verbalizing plans and strategies designed to overcome their difficulties. Also, instead of losing confidence and beginning to predict continued failure, they maintained positive affect and spoke of meeting the challenge of mastering the more difficult problems. Most maintained or even increased the sophistication of their strategies.

The next stage in the research was aimed at understanding why helpless children react to failure as though their ability is being assessed and discredited, whereas mastery-oriented children react to it as an opportunity for learning. Elliott and Dweck showed that these contrasting response patterns were linked to contrasting goals. Children who established learning goals focused on learning something new or mastering the task. Consequently, they processed information in terms of its relevance for problem solving and they responded to errors as indications that they needed to adjust their strategies. In contrast, children who set performance goals were more concerned about gaining favorable judgments of their competence than about learning something new. Consequently, they processed information primarily in terms of its relevance for assessing their ability. This made them vulnerable to the helpless pattern because when they encountered failure, they tended to view it as calling their ability into question. Once this occurred they were prone to lose confidence, become upset, and begin to use less sophisticated strategies.

At this point, Dweck and her colleagues had shown that children with comparable ability levels may respond very differently in achievement situations. Those who set learning goals tend to adopt a mastery orientation and focus on improving their ability, whereas those who set performance goals tend to focus on displaying their ability and are prone to adopt a helpless orientation if they fail to do so. To explain why children might follow such contrasting patterns, Dweck suggested that children with different goals have different conceptions of ability—different implicit theories about its nature. Two contrasting theories are the entity theory and the incremental theory.

Children who subscribe to the entity theory think of ability as a fixed entity over which they have no control. In contrast, children who hold an incremental theory believe that ability can be increased incrementally through effort. Entity theorists are more likely to set performance goals and develop helplessness in achievement situations, whereas incremental theorists are more likely to set learning goals and persist in their efforts to attain them. Fortunately, most people are incremental or mixed theorists (holding different beliefs about different domains) rather than entity theorists. The classroom implications of her work are straightforward. As a teacher, encourage your students to adopt incremental theories rather than entity theories of ability, to set learning goals rather than performance goals, and to adopt a mastery orientation rather than a helpless orientation to achievement situations.

This will focus your students' attention on self-improvement rather than comparisons with classmates. It also will lend credibility to your efforts to counter whatever ego-protective behavior that does occur by reminding students that mistakes are part of learning, that ordinarily we move toward mastery through successive approximations rather than attain it quickly in one or two giant steps, and that we are in the classroom to learn, not to compete.

You can encourage the incremental theory of ability and a mastery orientation toward learning activities by portraying these activities as opportunities to acquire (not just to display) knowledge or skill and by giving feedback to students in ways that reinforce this idea.

When giving feedback to the class as a whole or to individuals, phrase your comments so as to stimulate appreciation of accomplishments to date and imply confidence that ultimate goals will be attained ("You've done a good job of establishing your purpose in the first paragraph and structuring each paragraph around a main idea. However, the idea flow across paragraphs is a little choppy. As you revise [or, in your next composition], take time to outline the flow of ideas so that your argument builds step-by-step from start to finish, and use this outline to sequence your paragraphs. Then you'll have a nicely constructed argument!"). Notice that nothing in this example says anything directly about the students' abilities or the teacher's confidence that they will be successful.

Dweck herself recommends avoiding generic evaluative comments and instead providing more specific feedback when reacting to students' work. In particular, she cautions against praising their ability or intelligence (which conditions them toward global self-assessment and eventual entity theorizing). Instead, she suggests focusing feedback on the care, concentration, or effort that students put into the work or on their development of effective strategies for accomplishing it. Useful alternatives to direct feedback include asking questions that show appreciation for the work and initiating discussion of what was learned.

Causal Attributions

Bernard Weiner and other attribution theorists have focused on the causal attributions that people make in achievement situations—the explanations we generate to explain our behavior. Some causal attributions address task value aspects of motivation (What benefits do I expect to derive from engaging in this task?). However, attribution theorists have focused on causal attributions for the level of performance achieved on a task (Why did I fail that math test?), and the implications of these attributions concerning expectations about future performanc. People are most likely to engage in attributional thinking when what occurs is different from what they expected, and especially when their performance falls below their expectations.

Causal attributions generated during or after a performance are likely to affect subsequent motivation in that situation and others like it. The effects will depend on the n ature of the causes to which the performance is attributed. Causal attributions have been distinguished according to whether they are used to explain perceived success or perceived failure. Furthermore, both success attributions and failure attributions have been classified according to whether the attributed causes are internal or external to the person, controllable or uncontrollable by the person, and stable or unstable across situations.

Research on causal attributions for performance has shown that effort and persistence are greater when we attribute our performance to internal and controllable causes rather than to external or uncontrollable causes. Concerning explanations for successful performance, optimal patterns of motivation are associated with attributions of successes to the combination of sufficient ability and reasonable effort. "Sufficient" ability implies that we entered the achievement situation already possessing whatever abilities were needed or that we were able to develop those abilities in the process of responding to the task. "Reasonable" effort implies that we had to apply ourselves in order to succeed, but we did not have to extend ourselves to the limits of our capacities. That is, we were able to succeed through relatively normal levels of effort that we would expect to apply in any achievement situation, rather than only through heroic efforts that we would not be able to sustain on a daily basis.

Attributing a successful performance to internal and mostly stable and controllable causes gives reason to believe that we will continue to succeed on this and similar tasks in the future. We would have less reason for confidence if we attributed our success to more external, less stable and controllable causes (e.g., we were successful because this task happened to be an easy one; we lucked into the solution; we got unexpected help that we probably would not get the next time).

Concerning explanations for unsuccessful performance, effort and persistence are greater when we attribute our failures to internal but controllable causes such as insufficient knowledge (of task-relevant information or response strategies) or insufficient effort (if we did not prepare or concentrate as much as we should have). These failure attributions provide a basis for believing that we can improve performance and ultimately achieve success (by acquiring the needed knowledge or by increasing our level of effort). We would have less basis for confidence in improved performance if we attributed our failure to external causes. Worse yet, we would establish a basis for continued failure expectations if we attributed our failure to the internal cause of low ability, especially if we viewed this cause as stable and uncontrollable (i.e., if we held an entity theory of ability).

Attributions also affect our emotional responses to successes and failures. Successes attributed to internal causes, for example, are likely to result in feelings of pride in accomplishment and enhanced self-esteem, whereas failures attributed to internal causes are likely to result in feelings of guilt (if attributed to lack of effort) or shame (if attributed to lack of ability). In contrast, successes attributed to external causes (such as extra help from a teacher) are likely to result in feelings of gratitude, whereas failures attributed to external causes (such as a teacher not caring enough to explain clearly or respond to a request for help) are likely to result in feelings of anger and blame.

Again, implications for the classroom seem straightforward. As a teacher, help your students learn to attribute their successes to the combination of sufficient ability and reasonable effort, and to attribute their failures to (temporary) lack of task-relevant information or response strategies (or to lack of effort, where this has been the case). At the same time, avoid leading students to infer that their failures are due to fixed ability limitations that are beyond their control. This kind of socialization requires subtlety, because teachers' communications to students ordinarily should focus on building understandings and providing informative feedback, not making performance attributions.

Success attributions ordinarily should be implied rather than stated directly, so as to avoid calling students' attention to self-worth issues. However, at least occasionally you might wish to give feedback that expresses appreciation for effort and reinforces confidence in abilities. Failure attributions ordinarily should be expressed only privately with individuals rather than publicly with the class, unless the class as a whole has performed poorly on an assignment or test.

Individual students may verbalize attributions to low ability either spontaneously or in response to your questions about why they "blew" an assignment or test. When this occurs, gently but firmly refuse to accept this explanation. Instead, suggest that the student has the ability to succeed but failed to do so because he lacked key knowledge or addressed the task using an ineffective strategy (or if relevant, because he failed to put forth serious efforts to attain the task's goal). If possible, cite direct evidence that the student possesses the needed ability (e.g., successful performance on similar tasks in the past). Otherwise, construct a suc-cess scenario that includes this implication (e.g., based on your general experience at the grade level and your personal observations of this student, you know that he will soon be successful if he trusts you and makes an honest effort to do what you ask him to do). If you are unable to "turn around" such a student immediately, at least make it clear that you have confidence in his abilities and do not accept his low estimation of them.

Self-Efficacy Perceptions

Over the last three decades, Albert Bandura has conducted and inspired a great deal of research on self-efficacy perceptions, which he defines as "beliefs in one's capabilities to organize and execute the courses of action required to produce given attainments". People who enter achievement situations with self-efficacy perceptions believe that they can accomplish what the situation calls for, whereas people who lack these perceptions are unsure that they can or even convinced that they cannot. Self-efficacy perceptions are usually defined and assessed with reference to the capabilities needed to succeed in particular achievement situations, so the term has more specific meaning than terms such as confidence or academic self-concept. Even so, educational researchers have studied the role of self-efficacy perceptions in contexts ranging from a single lesson taught to elementary students to college students' choices of majors and careers.

Perceptions of self-efficacy are most commonly acquired through mastery experiences in which success is attributed to internal and controllable causes (we had what it took to do it this time, so we have good reason to believe that we can do it again in the future). However, they also can be acquired through vicarious learning (by watching the task performed successfully by people whom we view as similar to ourselves) or through persuasion (in which a trustworthy source convinces that we can accomplish the task if we apply reasonable effort).

Self-efficacy perceptions can influence task choice and the quality of task engagement. When their self-efficacy perceptions are high, people are likely to approach achievement situations with confidence and engage in them willingly and persistently. However, if they doubt their capabilities for succeeding, they are likely to try to avoid the situation, or if this is not possible, to give up easily when they encounter frustration or failure. In these and other respects, the implications of high versus low self-efficacy perceptions are similar to those for mastery versus helpless orientations and for attributing performance outcomes to internal and controllable causes versus external or uncontrollable causes.

Self-efficacy theorists have been especially active in identifying ways that teachers can support their students' self-efficacy perceptions, and in the process optimize their motivation and task engagement patterns. Studies have shown that increases in self-efficacy perceptions, in task effort and persistence, and in ultimate performance levels can be achieved by

(1) encouraging students to set specific and challenging but attainable goals;
(2) modeling and cueing effective task response strategies;
(3) providing feedback that helps students to achieve success, and
(4) making attributional statements that help them to appreciate that they are developing their abilities by accepting challenges and applying consistent effort.

Integration of Expectancy-related Concepts

Some refer to general dispositions, while others refer to thinking or behavior in specific situations. Some refer to perceptions, some to cognitive inferences, some to affective experiences, and some to strategies for accomplishing goals or solving problems. All of them, however, refer to the expectancy (rather than the value) aspects of motivation in achievement situations that call for striving to accomplish goals. Taken together, they compose a rich portrait of adaptive versus maladaptive patterns of response to these achievement situations. Experiments involving attempts to improve students' motivation have begun to combine elements drawn from different theoretical traditions into more complete and powerful packages that simultaneously address several of its expectancy-related aspects. For example, Bell and Kanevsky blended motivational instruction into a series of mathematics lessons taught to second graders. The motivational instruction incorporated three components: learning goal, nature of learning, and attribution training. Instruction relating to the learning goal emphasized the importance of persistence in putting forth effort ("that you don't give up and that you practice until you learn"). Instruction relating to the nature of learning was designed to develop appropriate expectations about time and effort and inoculate students against becoming overly frustrated by initial failures ("It often takes lots of hard work and lots of tries and lots of time and lots of mistakes before something is learned."). Attribution training sought to develop students' awareness that learning results from their own efforts. It was supported by a poster summarizing the four parts in a self-attribution strategy developed to help students sustain their learning efforts:

Shawaker and Dembo incorporated a five-element motivational component into reading comprehension instruction for middle-school students. The five elements were as follows:

1. *Task analysis.* Students were taught a four-step procedure that involved first reading the entire paragraph reflectively, then identifying its main idea, then deciding what type of paragraph it was (concept, generalization, sequence, process, or comparison), and finally marking evidence within the paragraph that supported these decisions.
2. *Proximal goal-setting.* Students were taught to work through the task analysis sequence one step at a time, using the steps as proximal goals to guide their information processing.

3. *Reciprocal teaching.* Students took turns with the teacher or with other students in modeling task processes, thinking aloud while doing so.
4. *Attribution training.* Attributional statements were incorporated into the feedback given to students, frequently reinforcing the notion that they had the ability to succeed on the task if they applied themselves toward doing so.
5. *Self-talk reminders.* Students occasionally were reminded to use their own self-talk to guide their behavior ("Talk yourself through the steps and be sure to compliment yourself when you work hard.").

Supporting Students' Confidence as Learners

As a teacher, you will want to help your students to maintain their confidence as learners and approach learning activities with productive goals and strategies.

Program for Success

The simplest way to ensure that students expect success is to make sure that they achieve it consistently so that they can adjust to each new step without much confusion or frustration. However, two points need to be made about this strategy to clarify that it does not mean assigning mostly underchallenging busywork.

First, "success" here means gradual mastery of appropriately challenging objectives, not quick, easy successes achieved through "automatic" application of overlearned skills to overly familiar tasks. You should pace your students through the curriculum as briskly as they can progress without undue frustration. Programming for success is a means toward the end of maximizing your students' ultimate achievement, not an end in itself.

Second, keep in mind your role as the teacher. Potential levels of success depend not only on the difficulty of the task itself, but also on the degree to which you prepare students through advance instruction and scaffold their learning efforts through guidance and feedback. A task that would be too difficult for students left to their own devices might be just right when learned with your help. In fact, learning theorists believe that instruction should focus on the zone of proximal development, which refers to the range of knowledge and skills that students are not yet ready to learn on their own but can learn with help from their teachers.

Programming for success involves continually challenging students within their zones of proximal development, yet making it possible for them to meet these challenges by providing sufficient instruction, guidance, and feedback. You may need to provide extra instruction to slower students, to monitor their progress more closely, and to give them briefer or easier assignments if they cannot handle the regular ones even with extra help. Even so, it will be important to continue to expect these students to put forth reasonable effort and progress as far as their abilities will allow. Don't give up on them or allow them to give up on themselves.

One paradoxical feature of the success expectancy aspects of student motivation is that self-efficacy perceptions are optimized when they are not at issue at all. That is, learning tends to proceed most smoothly when students are concentrating on the task rather than on evaluating their performance, even successful performance. In effect, then, student motivation is optimized not only by teacher techniques traditionally recognized as promoting such motivation, but also by techniques traditionally considered instructional rather than motivational: clarity and specificity of explanation and demonstration, modeling of task performance strategies, and provision of informative feedback. Of these, modeling of task-related thinking and problem-solving strategies is especially important, because so many school tasks are primarily cognitive rather than physical (so that the processes used to accomplish them cannot be observed directly).

By thinking out loud while modeling use of a strategy, a teacher makes overt the otherwise covert thought processes that guide its implementation. Such modeling provides learners with first-person language ("self-talk") that they can adapt directly when using the strategy themselves. This eliminates the need for translation that is created when instruction is presented in the impersonal third-person language of explanation or even the second-person language of coaching. Learners can focus directly on the processes to be learned, with minimum strain on their cognitive capacities. Theoretically, any task that lies within a student's zone of proximal development is appropriate for that student. In practice, however, the difficulty level of a task is determined not only by the task itself but by your success in providing clear and complete instruction. If you present instruction that students can understand and follow with ease, successful performance and perceptions of efficacy are likely to follow. However, low efficacy perceptions and feelings of anxiety and frustration would emerge if you explained the same task so poorly so that your students experienced difficulty with it. This would be true even if you kept reassuring the students that the task was well within their abilities. This is just one example showing how instructional and motivational strategies are intimately linked and need to be mutually supportive in order to be effective.

Teach Goal Setting, Performance Appraisal, and Self-Reinforcement

Students' reactions to their own performance depend not just on the absolute levels of success they achieve but also on their perceptions of what this means. Some students may not fully appreciate their accomplishments unless you help them to identify and use appropriate evaluation standards. You can provide such help in your everyday teaching, especially when introducing assignments and when providing students with feedback about their performance.

Goal Setting

The process begins with goal setting. Setting goals and making a commitment to trying to reach these goals increase performance levels. Goal setting is especially effective when goals are proximal rather than distal (they refer to a task to be attempted here and now rather than to some ultimate goal for the distant future), specific (e.g., complete a page of math problems with no more than one mistake) rather than global (e.g., do a good job), and challenging rather than too easy or too hard.

For example, suppose that you have given a mathematics assignment that involves 20 problems of varying difficulty. If some of your students have been struggling in mathematics, it may not be realistic to expect them to solve all of the problems correctly on their own. Therefore, you might ask them to adopt the goals of making a serious attempt to solve each problem and persisting until confident that at least 15 of the problems have been solved correctly. This is likely to lead to more persistent and higher quality problem-solving efforts than asking them to "do the best you can" or "do as many as you can." These suggestions are too vague to function as specific challenges toward which students can work as goals.

For a brief assignment, meeting the instructional objective is the appropriate goal. On more comprehensive assignments or tests, however, perfect performance is not a realistic goal for many students, and these students may need help in formulating challenging but reachable goals. In the case of a long series of activities that ultimately leads to some distal goal, establish proximal goals for each successive activity. Then, as students accomplish these goals, make them aware of the linkages between successive advances and their eventual achievement of the ultimate goal. Proximal goals usually seem attainable with reasonable effort even to students who doubt their capacities for attaining ultimate goals, and "keeping your eye on the prize" (bearing in mind that what you are doing now is another step toward an important ultimate goal) can help people persist through frustrations. Thus, if you keep struggling students moving forward (acquiring more knowledge and skill in a domain) as they pursue proximal goals, eventually they will attain ultimate goals as well.

Along with establishing expectations about reasonable levels of challenge, goal setting can include specifications of the characteristics of desired outcomes that can help learners develop subgoals and assess their work. For example, Page-Voth and Graham used a goal-setting treatment with junior high students learning to write argumentative essays. All of the students received similar instruction describing the features of good essays and imparting strategies to follow in planning and writing them. In addition, the experimental students were asked to adopt goals of increasing the number of reasons given to support the essay's premise, the number of counterarguments refuted by the writer, or both, and to talk about how they would seek to realize these goals. These students wrote longer and better essays than the others. The authors concluded that setting specific goals helps learners in at least three ways: The goals focus attention on important aspects of the task; they help motivate and sustain task mastery efforts; and they serve an information function by arming learners with criteria that they can use to assess and if necessary adjust their strategies as they work.

Goal setting is not enough by itself; students must show goal commitment by taking goals seriously and committing themselves to trying to reach them. You may need to negotiate goal setting with some students, or at least provide them with guidance and stimulate them to think about their performance potential. One way is to list potential goals and ask students to commit themselves to a particular subset (and to associated levels of effort). Another is performance contracting, in which students formally contract for a certain level of effort or performance in exchange for specified grades or rewards. This method is time consuming and may call more attention to rewards than is desirable, but it does ensure active teacher–

student negotiation about goal setting and require students to formalize their commitments to goals. Students are more likely to follow through on these commitments when they have had a voice in establishing them.

Performance Appraisal and Feedback

Students also are more likely to follow through when they know that their performance will be monitored and evaluated. Unless students are held individually accountable for following through on commitments and making progress toward curricular goals, goal setting may not have performance enhancement efforts. Furthermore, unless the monitoring leads to provision of feedback that is useful to those who need it, some learners may fail to accomplish key goals even though they may be highly motivated to do so.

Feedback must be "useful" because some forms of feedback are ineffectual or even counterproductive. In a meta-analysis of feedback intervention studies, Kluger and DeNisi found that although feedback interventions improved performance on average, they reduced performance in more than a third of the cases. Unhelpful feedback merely informs learners about how well they did, whereas informative feedback identifies which aspects of their performance were unacceptable and what they will need to do to improve. With most forms of learning, but especially complex learning that takes time to develop, both goal setting and feedback are likely to be most effective if they focus on the processes or strategies needed to accomplish the task rather than the ultimate end product, especially during earlier stages in the learning..

Teachers sometimes fail to provide students with needed feedback (or provide misleading feedback) because of misguided concerns about protecting their students' self-esteem. Pajares and Graham illustrated this in a study of middle school language arts teachers and their students. The teachers were presented with the following vignette:

An eighth grade language arts teacher is interested in students learning to be poetically expressive. S/he assigns them the task of composing a free verse poem. A 13-year-old boy submits the following:

Most teachers said that they would not answer the student's question in a direct and honest fashion, because they endorsed one or more of the following beliefs: You should always find something good to say about a student's work and generally offer positive feedback; regardless of a poem's merits, you should praise the poet for effort and creativity; criticism will crush students' creative propensities and turn them off to writing; teachers should not answer such questions directly but rather redirect the question to the student; and the value of poetry is relative and thus cannot be judged in any case. Ironically, these teacher views were endorsed, respectively, by only 7%, 3%, 2%, 3%, and 5% of the students. Instead, the vast majority of the students believed that the teacher should answer such questions with informative feedback, identifying what is good and why, as well as what needs to be improved and how. Many students did say that the teacher should be respectful of the students' feelings and keep criticism constructive, but they valued informative feedback, not gratuitous praise. Teachers interpreted caring as helping students feel good about their work independent of its merits, whereas students interpreted caring as providing them with whatever academic assistance they needed to enable them to meet learning goals.

Straub reported similar findings in a study of students' reactions to teacher comments on written compositions. The students expressed strong preferences for specific and detailed comments over vague or generic comments. Although they resented gratuitous attacks on themselves or their ideas, they welcomed constructive criticism that called for better argumentation in support of their conclusions, clearer rendering of their arguments, and so on.

In giving feedback, help students to use appropriate standards for judging levels of success. In particular, teach them to compare their work with absolute standards or with their own previous performance rather than with the performance of classmates. Provide accurate feedback about specific responses (errors will need to be labeled as such if they are to be recognized and corrected), but also provide encouragement in your more general evaluative comments (e.g., "You've shown good understanding of the events that led up to the Revolutionary War, but not the reasons why the colonies were able to win it. Go over those reasons again and discuss them with your study partner until you're sure that you know them."). You might note levels of success achieved in meeting established goals or describe accomplishments with reference to what is reasonable to expect rather than with reference to absolute perfection.

Some students need specific, detailed feedback concerning both the strengths and weaknesses of their performance. Those who have only a vague appreciation of when and why they have done well or poorly will need feedback that includes concepts and language that they can use to describe their performance with precision. This is especially true for compositions, research projects, laboratory experiments, and other complex activities that are evaluated qualitatively.

Concerning compositions, for example, you might comment on the relevance, accuracy, and completeness of the content; the organization and sequencing of the content into a coherent beginning, middle, and end; the structuring of paragraphs to feature main ideas; the appropriateness of the style and vocabulary; and the mechanics of grammar, spelling, and punctuation. To the extent that performance is unsatisfactory, provide additional instruction and opportunities for improvement, along with continued encouragement that realistic goals will be achieved if the student continues to put forth reasonable effort.

Self-reinforcement

Students who have been working toward specific proximal goals and who have the concepts and language needed to evaluate their performance accurately are in a position to reinforce themselves for their successes. Many do this habitually, but others will need encouragement to check their work and to take credit for their successes (that is, to attribute these successes to the fact that they had the ability and were willing to make the required effort). If necessary, compare the students' current accomplishments with performance samples from earlier in the year or have them keep portfolios, graphs, or other records to document their progress. Schunk found that arranging for students to periodically assess their progressively improving performance capabilities has positive effects on their motivation and learning.

In monitoring performance and giving feedback, focus on mastery. Stress the quality of your students' task engagement and the degree to which they are making continuous progress toward mastery rather than comparisons with how their classmates are doing. Treat failures as indicators of a need for additional instruction and learning opportunities, not as evidence of lack of ability in the domain. For additional information about giving feedback to students.

Help Students to Recognize Effort–Outcome Linkages

Blend motivational elements into your everyday teaching that will help your students to appreciate the connections between learning efforts and learning outcomes. The following strategies are useful for developing an internal locus of control and a sense of efficacy in students and helping them to recognize that they can achieve success if they put forth reasonable effort.

First, model beliefs about effort–outcome linkages when talking to students about your own learning and when demonstrating tasks by thinking out loud as you work through them. When you encounter frustration or temporary failure in performing everyday classroom activities, model confidence that you will succeed if you persist by searching for a better strategy or for some error in your application of strategies already tried.

Also, stress effort–outcome linkages when socializing your students or giving them feedback. Explain that your curriculum goals and instructional practices have been established to make it possible for them to succeed if they apply themselves. If necessary, reassure certain students that persistence (perhaps augmented by extra help) eventually pays off. Some students may need repeated statements of your confidence in their abilities to do the work or your willingness to accept slow progress so long as they consistently put forth reasonable effort.

Extra socialization will be needed with low achievers when grades must be assigned according to fixed common standards or comparisons with peers or norms rather than according to the degree of effort expended or the degree of success achieved in meeting individually negotiated goals. You may need to socialize low achievers to take satisfaction in receiving Bs or Cs when such grades represent, for them, significant accomplishments. When this is the case, express to these students (and their parents) recognition of their accomplishments and appreciation of the progress they are making.

Acknowledge that learning takes effort, but portray effort as investment rather than risk. Make your students aware that learning may take time and involve confusion or mistakes, but that persistence and careful work eventually yields knowledge or skill mastery. Furthermore, help them to appreciate that such mastery not only represents success on the immediate task but also provides them with knowledge or skills that will make them more prepared to handle higher level tasks in the future. If they give up on a task because of frustration or fear of failure, they cheat themselves out of this growth potential.

In characterizing students' achievement progress, portray skill development as incremental and domain-specific. Help your students to appreciate that their intellectual abilities are open to improvement rather than fixed and that they possess a great many such abilities rather than just a few. Difficulties in learning usually occur not because students lack ability or do not make an effort but because they lack experience with the type of task involved. With patience, persistence, and help from you, your students can acquire knowledge and skills specific to the domain that the task represents. Development of such domain-specific knowledge and skills will enable them to succeed on this task and others like it. Difficulty in learning mathematics need not imply difficulty in learning other subjects, and within mathematics, difficulty in learning to graph coordinates need not mean difficulty in learning to solve differential equations or to understand geometric relationships. Even within a domain that is difficult for them, students can expect to build up knowledge and skills gradually if they persistently apply themselves, accept your help, and do not lose patience or give up whenever success is not achieved easily.

INFORMATIVE FEEDBACK—INTEGRAL PART OF LEARNING PROCESS.

Even if it were not required for report card purposes, testing and other assessment of students' progress would be necessary to provide needed feedback, both to you as the teacher and to your students as learners. Therefore, help your students to understand that getting and following up productively on informative feedback is an integral part of the learning process.

If assessment methods are goal-oriented and integrated within a larger program of curriculum and instruction, they can provide valuable information to students. When students are clear about what they are expected to learn and how this learning will be evaluated, they can guide their learning efforts accordingly. After they engage in an evaluation activity and get the feedback it generates, both you and they will have a clearer picture of areas of strength in which they have progressed nicely as well as areas of weakness in which they need follow-up instruction and learning activities. Certain mistakes (minor factual or computational errors) may require only brief correction, but others (that suggest misunderstanding of basic concepts or principles) may require more sustained follow up.

Unfortunately, classroom evaluation and grading systems also have the potential to undermine students' motivation and learning strategies. To the extent that they are perceived as controlling students by placing extrinsic pressures on them to study or do homework, they are likely to erode the students' intrinsic motivation. To the extent that test content is confined to matching or fill-in-the-blank items, students are likely to emphasize surface-level memorizing strategies rather than deeper level information processing strategies as they study the material. To the extent that you have been overly specific in specifying the nature and content of test items, students may narrow their focus to preparing to answer the kinds of questions they expect on the test, rather than engaging in more integrative learning.

Finally, to the extent that the demands of tests are not well matched to the knowledge and skill levels of some of your students, the desired covariation between effort and outcome (grades) will be missing. Some students will learn that they can get high grades without exerting much effort, and others will learn that they cannot get high grades no matter how hard they try. However, motivational theorists and researchers have developed suggestions to help you to maximize desirable effects and minimize undesirable effects of your evaluation and grading strategies.

Uses and Forms of Assessment

Think of assessment as part of your larger program of curriculum and instruction—a set of tools to help your students reach your instructional goals. Viewed in this light, assessment is important as a way for you to keep track of the progress of the class as a whole and alert you to the need for adjustments in your instructional plans, not just as a way to provide a basis for grading individual students.

Closed-ended, "one right answer" questions may be needed to test mastery of certain basic knowledge and skills (e.g., spelling, multiplication tables). Also, some use of matching or fill-in-the-blank items may be appropriate for testing basic vocabulary knowledge in English, foreign languages, science, or social studies. Unfortunately, however, studies of teacher-made tests and the tests supplied with publishers' instructional materials indicate widespread overreliance on these low-level recognition or memory reproduction items. Assessment information will be most useful to you and to your students if it reflects progress made toward major instructional goals. Ordinarily, this will mean emphasizing authentic tasks that require students to integrate and apply what they are learning, not just to recognize or retrieve miscellaneous items of information.

Tests ought to sample from the full range of content taught and include enough items to allow reliable measurement. Sampling from all content taught helps to ensure that you become aware of areas of weakness and that your students are held accountable for learning all of the material. It also helps to ensure that your students will view the test as fair. They may not view it as fair if it emphasizes only a small portion of what was taught in a unit, especially if they thought this material was relatively unimportant and therefore concentrated their study efforts on other material.

Grant Wiggins offered detailed suggestions on ways for teachers to make assessment both more fair and more authentic. He recommended: (a) Use assessments that feature worthwhile tasks that are educative and engaging; (b) instead of being secretive about grading standards, clarify to students what constitutes exemplary performance and provide models for them to emulate; (c) use methods that allow students the time to produce thoughtful and complete work; and (d) follow up with opportunities to improve on areas of weakness and ultimately produce products in which the students can take pride.

"Assessment" and "evaluation" are much broader terms than "testing," and should not be equated with it. Ordinarily, daily lesson participation and work on assignments, especially work on significant projects, should be used at least as much as tests to provide a basis for assessing progress and grading students. This is especially the case in the elementary grades, where limitations in the students' cognitive developmental levels and academic skill repertoires limit the kinds of tests that can be used productively. Even in the secondary grades, overreliance on tests is likely to lead to memorizing and forgetting instead of integrated learning.

Increasingly, portfolio assessment is being recommended as an alternative that is better suited than testing as a way to meet students' informa-tional and motivational needs. Portfolios are organized sets of student work that illustrate their progress over time. Students have opportunities to exercise a degree of choice in deciding what to include in their portfolios, and to revise and improve the items in response to feedback from the teacher or their peers. The portfolio approach reflects several motivational principles by focusing attention on quality standards rather than just grades or scores, by incorporating the use of assessment data as informative feedback, by encouraging students to become more reflective about their work and more oriented toward self-improvement over time, and by allowing them to assemble a collection of their best work that they can share with parents and other family members.

Helping Students Prepare for Assessment

In talking about assessment generally, and in preparing students for any particular assessment experience, emphasize the role of assessment in providing informative feedback about progress, not its role in providing a basis for grading or a means to pressure students to keep up with study assignments. Portray tests as opportunities to find out how "we" are doing and portray projects as opportunities to apply what "we" are learning. Express confidence that students will succeed if they apply themselves to lessons and learning activities.

Also, portray yourself as a helper and resource person who assists your students in learning and preparing for assessment, not as a remote evaluator. Encourage students to you as allied with them in preparing for tests, not as allied with the tests in pressuring or threatening them.

Clarify your goals and assessment criteria in ways that will help students to understand what they need to learn and what strategies are likely to be most useful for enabling them to do so. At least in general terms, let them know how their learning will be assessed. However, avoid overspecificity that might tempt certain students to focus only on what is needed to pass the test and thus fail to develop more integrated learning.

Follow-Up Feedback and Grading

In addition to (or instead of) letter, number, or percentage grades, provide students with informative feedback designed to help them appreciate their accomplishments but also recognize areas of weakness and commit themselves to making needed improvements. Deliver such feedback privately and emphasize students' progress relative to their own prior accomplishments rather than comparisons with other students. Some of your best opportunities for encouraging incremental theories of ability and desirable performance attributions and efficacy perceptions occur when you are giving feedback to students following tests or other assessment experiences.

Although Thomas questioned the practice, most motivational researchers advise teachers to include "safety nets" for failing students as part of their assessment follow-up and grading system. That is, students who have failed to earn satisfactory grades are given the opportunity to do so by taking an alternative test following a period of review and relearning. Or, they are allowed to earn extra credit by engaging in learning activities and producing some kind of product to indicate that they have overcome the deficiencies identified in their test performance. By making the extra effort to provide such safety nets, you can encourage struggling students to make the extra effort needed to accomplish your instructional goals.

If the cumulative level of performance that would earn a report card grade of A is not a realistic goal, help students to identify and commit themselves to realistic goals that, if reached, would yield grades of B or C. In doing so, you might use a strategy emphasized in Mastery Learning programs: Provide a list of potential goals (graduated in terms of the effort required to meet them and the grades earned if success is achieved) and ask the students to commit themselves to particular goals and associated levels of effort. Whatever you do, be sure to arrange conditions so that every student who consistently puts forth reasonable effort can earn report card grades of C or better. If you fail to do this, your struggling low achievers will have little incentive to keep trying and your efforts to motivate them will not have much chance to succeed.

The principle of emphasizing informative feedback over peer comparisons applies to report card grades as well as to feedback regarding individual tests and assignments. Wlodkowski and Jaynes suggested that a well-designed report card informs students about their progress in learning and encourages their continuing motivation to learn. This is accomplished more through qualitative comments than letter or number grades. Separate sets of comments can be made for the students' achievement progress, effort and persistence in learning, noteworthy academic strengths and talents, areas needing improvement, and social development (cooperation, maturity, classroom participation). Where weaknesses are identified, the comments should emphasize the kinds of improvements needed rather than criticism of the student.

Reducing Test Anxiety

To the extent that you use tests or other formal evaluation methods, you may find that certain students show symptoms of text anxiety. They may learn effectively in informal, pressure-free situations but become highly anxious and perform considerably below their potential on tests or during any testlike situation in which they are aware of being monitored and evaluated. Test anxiety problems are most likely to be observed among low achieving students, but they occur in average- or high-achieving students as well. Several strategies have been developed for minimizing test anxiety problems.

The most widely recommended of these strategies are the following:

1. Rather than "spring" a test on students, let them know well in advance the date of the test, its general scope and nature, and how they can best prepare for it.
2. Be friendly and encouraging when administering the test, avoiding behavior that would make the testing situation any more threatening to students than it needs to be.
3. Avoid time pressures unless they are truly central to the skill being taught.
4. Stress the feedback functions rather than the evaluation or grading functions of tests when discussing the tests with your students.
5. Portray tests as opportunities to assess progress rather than as measures of ability.
6. Where appropriate, tell your students that some problems are beyond their present achievement level (so that they will not become upset if they fail to solve these problems).
7. Give pretests to accustom students to "failure" and provide base rates for comparison when you administer posttests later.
8. Teach your students stress management skills and effective test-taking skills and attitudes.
9. Help your students to understand that the best way for them to prepare for tests is to concentrate their energies on learning what they need to know, without spending much time worrying about what will be on the test or how they will cope with anxiety in the test situation.

Expectancy concepts are especially relevant to achievement situations that require people to perform some goal-oriented task knowing that their performance will be evaluated. Early work on achievement motivation indicated that people focused on motivation to succeed tend to approach achievement situations willingly, to prefer tasks that are moderately difficult for them, and to engage in these tasks with emphasis on developing their skills. In contrast, people focused on avoiding failure tend to fear and seek to avoid achievement situations. When required to engage in them, they seek to minimize risk of failure by setting goals either very low or impossibly high.

More recent work on people's thinking and behavior in achievement situations has shown that effort and persistence are greater when people perceive effort–outcome covariation, believe that the potential to control outcomes lies within themselves rather than in external factors that they cannot control, view themselves as origins rather than pawns, possess an incremental rather than an entity theory of intelligence, attribute their performance to internal and controllable causes, and possess a sense of efficacy or competence. In addition, people who possess these desirable dispositions are likely to engage in achievement situations with an emphasis on learning goals and to process information using deeper level strategies rather than surface-level memorizing.

Research findings on the expectancy aspects of motivation underscore the importance of supporting your students' confidence as learners, helping them to focus on learning what the task teaches rather than on worrying about potential failure or embarrassment. You can do this through your curriculum (teaching students in their zones of proximal development and helping them to achieve success), your instruction (including instruction in goal setting, performance appraisal, and self-reinforcement along with instruction in the formal curriculum and helping your students to recognize effort–outcome linkages), and your assessment (using sources of assessment that promote accomplishment of your instructional goals, emphasizing informative feedback over categorizing or comparing students, and taking steps to minimize test anxiety).

References

Atkinson, J. (1964). *An introduction to motivation.* Princeton, NJ: VanNostrand.

deCharms, R. (1976). *Enhancing motivation: Change in the classroom.* New York: Irvington.

Dweck, C. (1999). *Self-theories: Their role in motivation, personality, and development.* Philadelphia: Taylor & Francis.

Reeve, J. (1996). *Motivating others: Nurturing inner motivational resources.* Boston: Allyn & Bacon.

Tharp, R., & Gallimore, R. (1988). *Rousing minds to life: Teaching, learning, and schooling in social context.* Cambridge, England: Cambridge University Press.

4

Goal Theory of Motivation

It is widely acknowledged that an issue of great concern to educators is developing and maintaining students' optimum motivation. Particularly during adolescence, many students experience a lack of motivation to engage in academic activities and fail to reach their academic potential. Consequently, the motivation of adolescents has been the focus of much research. Although there has been a range of theories developed to better understand why students choose to engage in learning activities, over the last 20 years, goal theory has emerged as one of the most prominent theories of motivation.

Goal theory focuses on the mental representations of desired outcomes that initiate and direct behaviour. Although a range of goals influencing student motivation have been identified and investigated, the majority of research has focused on achievement goals which represent the "purposes students perceive for engaging in achievement-related behaviour", such as the desire to develop or demonstrate competence. Social goals and more recently, future goals have also been shown to influence students' motivation and engagement at school. A widely held view is that motivation is best understood by a multiple goals perspective, where motivation occurs through multiple goals working simultaneously.

Even though the research using goal theory to investigate the motivation of adolescents has been plentiful, there are emerging issues that still require investigation. Firstly, much goal focused research has examined particular goals (such as achievement goals), sometimes in isolation, and often with predetermined assumptions about what goals might reflect students' motivation to achieve at school. Such research typically uses deductive methods, which can reduce potential for understandings about other goals (and multiple goals) to be developed by limiting students' opportunities to spontaneously articulate their own goals. Only a few recent studies have used inductive measures and considered the range of goals that may influence students' desire to achieve. Secondly, there is some evidence that goals may differ across contexts and, for example, according to culture and ethnicity. Thus questions emerge about how goal emphasis may vary in different countries and educational contexts.

Development of Goal Theory

Investigators studying motivation in education began investigating the motivational implications of school as an institution and classrooms as learning communities featuring ongoing interpersonal relationships. Much of this was fueled by concerns about findings indicating that although most students begin school eager to learn, this motivation tends to drop steadily as they progress through the grades. John Nicholls, for example, noted that most children initially assume that ability flows from effort (i.e., that one can increase one's ability in a domain by engaging in learning activities in that domain), but many later shift to the idea that ability and effort are related inversely (i.e., that if you have high ability in a domain you can handle tasks in that domain with relative ease, whereas if you have to expend noteworthy effort to complete the tasks successfully, you lack ability in the domain).

Nicholls went on to suggest that once children understand that alternative theories of the relationship between ability and effort are possible, their tendency to favor one theory over the other may depend on the goals or definitions of success that they adopt in a given situation. This was similar to Dweck's ideas about implicit theories of ability, except that Dweck treated these implicit theories as general dispositions likely to affect goal setting in most situations, whereas Nicholls treated conceptions of the relationship between ability and effort more as situational states and as effects rather than causes of goal adoption.

Martin Covington emphasized classrooms' threatening aspects, especially their tendencies to create situations in which students are publicly revealed to be ignorant, confused, or unable to respond successfully, leading to embarrassment and other social costs. He developed a self-worth perspective on achievement motivation, suggesting that in classrooms where ability comparisons are often made or easily inferred, students may become more concerned with preserving their sense of self-worth than with mastering the curriculum. This can lead them to face-saving but ultimately counterproductive reactions such as pretending to understand when they do not, refusing to ask for help, or engaging in various self-handicapping strategies (such as not studying for a test) that position the students so that if they do poorly, they can blame their failure on something other than lack of ability. Related strategies include procrastinating until the last moment before studying for a test or doing an assignment and sandbagging by pretending to have less ability than one has or deliberately underestimating when making predictions about one's performance.

Carole Ames examined the reward structures operating in classrooms and identified three structures likely to have contrasting effects on students' motivation. In an individualistic structure, students work on their own and are rewarded (e.g., with grades) according to how much they achieve relative to absolute standards, regardless of what classmates might achieve. An individualistic structure tends to orient students toward personal achievement goals (i.e., they try to learn as much as they can, but focus in particular on any learning outcomes that the teacher has identified as major instructional objectives). A second possible reward structure is a competitive structure in which students are required to compete with their classmates for available rewards (because they will be graded on a curve). This structure tends to orient students toward interpersonal competitive goals, to the point that they may be more focused on competition than on learning and may avoid any form of collaboration with peers. Finally, in a cooperative structure, students work together in groups and are rewarded at least in part according to the quality of the products that their group creates. Cooperative reward structures orient students toward fulfilling their moral responsibilities to do their parts for their groups, perhaps even more so than meeting individual learning goals. In contrast to Dweck, who treated goals primarily as predictable from stable personal traits (entity vs. incremental theories of ability), Ames treated goals primarily as responses to the reward structures operating in the situation.

In 1960's, Edwin Locke put forward the Goal-setting theory of motivation. This theory states that goal setting is essentially linked to task performance. It states that specific and challenging goals along with appropriate feedback contribute to higher and better task performance. In simple words, goals indicate and give direction to an employee about what needs to be done and how much efforts are required to be put in. The important features of goal-setting theory are as follows:

a. The willingness to work towards attainment of goal is main source of job motivation. Clear, particular and difficult goals are greater motivating factors than easy, general and vague goals.

b. Specific and clear goals lead to greater output and better performance. Unambiguous, measurable and clear goals accompanied by a deadline for completion avoids misunderstanding.

c. Goals should be realistic and challenging. This gives an individual a feeling of pride and triumph when he attains them, and sets him up for attainment of next goal. The more challenging the goal, the greater is the reward generally and the more is the passion for achieving it.

d. Better and appropriate feedback of results directs the employee behaviour and contributes to higher performance than absence of feedback. Feedback is a means of gaining reputation, making clarifications and regulating goal difficulties. It helps employees to work with more involvement and leads to greater job satisfaction.

e. Employees' participation in goal is not always desirable.

f. Participation of setting goal, however, makes goal more acceptable and leads to more involvement.

g. Goal setting theory has certain eventualities such as:

    i. *Self-efficiency*: Self-efficiency is the individual's self-confidence and faith that he has potential of performing the task. Higher the level of self-efficiency, greater will be the efforts put in by the individual when they face challenging tasks. While, lower the level of self-efficiency, less will be the efforts put in by the individual or he might even quit while meeting challenges.

    ii. *Goal commitment*: Goal setting theory assumes that the individual is committed to the goal and will not leave the goal.

The goal setting theory is a technique used to raise incentives for employees to complete work quickly and effectively. Goal setting leads to better performance by increasing motivation and efforts, but also through increasing and improving the feedback quality.

Early Goal Theory Studies

As work by Ames, Covington, Nicholls, and others became established and work by Bandura, Dweck, Weiner, and others continued, a sizeable research literature accumulated around issues relating to people's motivation in achievement situations, especially in classrooms. Most of this work focused on the expectancy rather than the value aspects of achievement motivation and supported the conclusion that it is more desirable for people to be focused on mastering the tasks involved in these achievement situations than on competing with peers or worrying about how their performance will be perceived and judged by others. The obvious practical implication is that teachers should employ instructional and motivational practices that will focus learners' attention on the task at hand and avoid practices that encourage social comparisons and competition concerns.

Commenting on the growth of this knowledge base, reviewers commonly celebrated its rapid development but expressed concern about the unnecessary proliferation of terms that appear to mean essentially the same thing. Theorists associated with particular concepts (e.g., attributions, efficacy perceptions, theories of ability) sometimes argued for a synthesis of motivational theorizing built around their favorite concepts, but the field never coalesced around any single theorist's work. The proliferation of terms, definitions, and measures continued, causing a lot of confusion. There clearly was a need for synthesis, particularly with respect to achievement situations and implications for teachers.

A synthesis eventually emerged, but not because one established theory prevailed over the others. Instead, synthesis developed around the goal orientations emphasized in what has become known as achievement goal theory or simply goal theory. These goal orientations refer to students' beliefs about the purposes of engaging in achievement-related behavior. Students who approach the same lesson or activity with different goal orientations may engage in it quite differently and emerge with different outcomes.

Early goal theory research focused on two sets of contrasting goal orientations, variously called learning vs. performance goals, mastery vs. performance goals or task-involvement vs. ego-involvement goals. These studies found that students who approach academic activities with learning goals (also called mastery or task-involvement goals) focus on acquiring the knowledge or skills that the activities are designed to develop. They seek to construct accurate understandings by paraphrasing the material into their own words and connecting it to prior knowledge. When they encounter difficulties they are likely to seek help or if necessary to persist with their own self-regulated learning efforts, buoyed by the belief that these efforts are worthwhile and the confidence that they will pay off eventually.

In contrast, students who approach academic activities with performance goals (also called ego-involvement goals) treat these activities as tests of their ability to perform rather than as opportunities to learn. Their primary concern is preserving their self-perceptions and public reputations as capable individuals who possess the ability needed to succeed on the task. In striving to meet task demands and avoid failure, they may rely on rereading, rote memorizing, and other surface-level learning strategies instead of deeper level knowledge construction strategies, and their learning efforts may be impaired by fear of failure or other negative affect. They seek to avoid challenging tasks and tend to give up easily when frustrated because they believe that their abilities are limited, so they lack confidence that persistent efforts will eventually pay off. Rather than ask for help when they need it, they prefer to conceal their difficulties by leaving items blank, taking wild guesses, or perhaps copying from neighbors.

Note that what goal theorists mean by performance goals is different from the meaning suggested by informal use of the term. In everyday language, to say that people are operating from performance goals usually means they are striving to achieve some criterion-referenced standard, such as batting.300 or getting at least a B in a course. For goal theorists, however, operating from performance goals means seeking to display high ability for the task at hand, or at least to avoid being viewed as low in ability. The emphasis is on maintaining one's image rather than on accomplishment per se. Given this potential for confusion, it would have been better if performance goals had been called ego-protective goals, ability display goals, image preservation goals, relative ability goals, or some other term that more clearly communicated a preoccupation with looking good in social comparisons rather than with learning or personal improvement.

Goal theory made sense as a vehicle for synthesizing emerging research on the expectancy aspects of motivation in education, for several reasons. It fit well with recent shifts in emphasis from behavior to cognition, from quantitative to qualitative aspects of motivation, from traits to situations, and from individual to social purviews. It complemented theorizing based on needs or other motives by accommodating cultural and situational factors that influence behavior and the cognitive processes and subjective experiences that mediate or accompany goal striving. It also accommodated the concepts and research of the theorists cited previously, and it appealed to educators because it appeared to support straightforward guidelines for application.

As goal theory developed, some new studies continued to indicate that learning goals were associated with desirable correlates such as greater effort and persistence, more self-regulated learning using deeper processing strategies, and more positive attitudes toward school and oneself as a learner. Most of theses studies also continued to indicate that performance goals were associated with negative correlates such as an emphasis on rote memorizing and other surface-level processing oriented toward preparing for tests rather than necessarily learning material thoroughly, engaging in various forms of cheating, engaging in ego-protective behaviors such as self-handicapping or defensive pessimism (keeping one's expectations low so that one will not be so disappointed if one does not do well), and negative attitudes toward learning and oneself as a learner.

The findings reported so far came from studies of the goal orientations that students brought with them into their classes. Investigators measured them by asking students to endorse items such as "I want to show my teacher that I am smarter than the other students" (performance goal) or "The main reason I do my work is that I like to learn" (learning goal). These findings were supported by other studies in which investigators measured students' perceptions of the goal orientations that they found when they entered their classes, using items such as "In this school, we are encouraged to compete against each other for grades" (perceived performance focus) or "Our teachers want to really understand our work, not just memorize it" (perceived learning focus). These studies indicated that a perceived learning orientation in the classroom or school was associated with student tendencies to personally adopt learning goals, to use deep processing study strategies, and to have higher self-efficacy perceptions and more positive attitudes toward school. Meanwhile, perceptions of a strong performance orientation at school was associated with adoption of performance goals, use of shallow processing strategies, lower self-efficacy perceptions, greater self-consciousness at school, more cheating, more use of self-handicapping strategies, less willingness to seek help, and a generally more negative attitude toward school.

These studies suggested that, although students enter classes with already developed dispositions toward particular goal orientations, these orientations can be modified in response to the goal orientations emphasized by their teachers or their school as a whole. This hypothesis was confirmed in several experimental studies in which participants were induced to adopt either learning or performance goals. The latter studies also confirmed that learning goals were associated with a more positive pattern of outcomes than performance goals, although the relative advantage to learning goals varied with the motivational patterns of individuals and the nature of the task. The advantage to learning goals was greater for challenging and complex tasks than for easy or rote tasks, and greater for college students than for elementary students. Other studies suggested that learning goals had more positive effects on college students who were low in achievement motivation, but performance goals could have positive effects on competitive college students who were high in achievement motivation.

The 2 × 2 Goal Theory Model

Thus, goal theory research at first seemed to support the simple conclusion that learning goals are desirable and performance goals are counterproductive. As research continued, however, some investigators reported that performance goals were not always associated with negative outcomes, or even that they were associated with certain desirable outcomes. For example, based on responses to a questionnaire, Valle et al. identified groups of students who showed a predominance of performance goals, a predominance of learning goals, or a multiple goals pattern that included both of these goals plus social reinforcement goals. They found that students who emphasized performance goals but not learning goals were less likely to take task characteristics into account when planning strategies to use in the learning process, and showed lower persistence and less use of deep learning strategies. In contrast, students who emphasized learning but not performance goals did take task characteristics into account but did not attend as much to the evaluation criteria when deciding which learning strategies to use. Overall, the multiple goals group was the most successful, presumably because they were mindful of both the characteristics of the learning task and the evaluation criteria likely to be emphasized in the test.

Several studies done by Judith Harackiewicz, Andrew Elliot, and their colleagues suggested that at least in some circumstances, performance goals could complement mastery goals, especially if the performance goals were focused on achieving success rather than avoiding failure. These studies, conducted with college students enrolled in large introductory courses, indicated that although learning goals were more closely associated with interest in the subject matter, long-term retention of the content, and plans to take related courses in the future, performance goals were more closely associated with course grades and scores on short-term retention tests.

These findings led some investigators to distinguish between performance-approach goals that focus on achieving success and performance-avoidance goals that focus on avoiding failure, and to measure them separately in studies relating students' goal orientations to other variables. The new studies indicated that although performance-avoidance goals were associated with negative correlates such as low self-efficacy perceptions, high test anxiety, avoidance of help seeking, disorganized study strategies, and low test scores and grades, performance-approach goals were associated with a mixed pattern of correlates that included high need for achievement but also high fear of failure, strong needs to please parents, high effort and persistence in studying but with an emphasis on surface-level rather than deep-level processing, high competitiveness, and high grades and test scores. In some studies the evidence for relationships between performance approach goals and positive correlates was limited or nonexistent, but in others it extended to include variables such as task value or high academic self-concepts.

In a study of college students' reported emotions and behaviors related to exam preparation, McGregor and Elliot generated results that both typify and begin to explain the overall findings from recent goal theory research. They found that mastery goals predicted early preparation (time spent studying well in advance of the exam), a sense of challenge with respect to preparation for the exam, absorption during such preparation, and a sense of calmness at exam time due to good preparation. Performance-approach goals were predictive of high grade aspirations, perceiving the exam as both a challenge and a threat, and effortful but sometimes less optimal patterns of study (e.g., beginning to prepare later in the term and concentrating study in the days immediately prior to the exam). Finally, performance-avoidance goals were associated with low ability self-concepts, high test anxiety, desire to escape the exam, procrastination and disorganization in preparing for it, and feeling anxious and unprepared during the exam.

Such findings have led to expansion of goal theory into a 2 × 2 framework that considers goals not only with respect to the learning–performance distinction, but also with respect to the approach–avoidance distinction. Little is known about learning goals that are framed within an avoidance orientation (e.g., striving not to make mistakes or fail to learn in the short run, and striving not to lose one's accumulated skills in the longer run). So far, the learning goals studied in almost all of the relevant research have been approach goals, in which learners focused on gaining the knowledge taught in a lesson or learning the skills needed to complete a task successfully. Early work on learning-avoidance goals suggests that they are common in struggling students who are seeking to master the material but fear failure, and that their pattern of correlates is less positive than for students who emphasize learning-approach goals but not as negative as for students who emphasize performance-avoidance goals. As this literature develops, it will be interesting to learn more about learning-avoidance goals (e.g., whether they are common in students who are overly perfectionistic). For now, however, research findings on learning goals are focused almost exclusively on learning-approach goals, and the latter concept is implied whenever the term learning goals is used in this text.

The Value of Performance-Approach Goals

Learning goals are associated with positive correlates and performance-avoidance goals are associated with negative ones, but controversy over performance-approach goals continues. Midgley, Kaplan, and Middleton conceded that performance-approach goals have been associated with adaptive patterns of learning in some studies, but noted that other studies have shown these goals to be unrelated or negatively related to the same variables. They warned that any emphasis on performance-approach goals needs to be coupled with an emphasis on learning goals, arguing that performance-approach goals alone might help students mobilize to get high test scores in the short run, but also encourage them to avoid challenging tasks, compete rather than cooperate with peers, and cheat if they fear failure. In the longer run, students operating on performance-approach goals but not learning goals would be vulnerable to developing learned helplessness and shifting to performance-avoidance goals if they encountered failure.

In seeking to explain the conflicting findings concerning performance-approach goals, Midgley, Kaplan, and Middleton noted that performance-approach goals have more positive patterns of correlates for students higher in perceived competence than for students lower in perceived competence, for boys than for girls, and for older students in more competitive learning contexts than for younger students in less competitive learning contexts (age and context competitiveness were conflated in these studies). These differences are open to several interpretations. For example, if the relationships are causal, they imply that adoption of performance-approach goals is functional (i.e., leads to desirable outcomes) for some students in some learning contexts but not others. It also is possible, however, that at least some of the relationships are merely correlational. Thus, it may be that high achievers are more likely to state performance-approach goals than low achievers because they can do so with reasonable expectation of success (whereas low achievers who state performance goals have more reason to fear failure and thus are more likely to phrase these goals as performance-avoidance goals). If this is the case, the contrasting patterns of correlates observed for performance-approach and performance-avoidance goals may occur merely because they are part of a larger set of contrasts between high- and low-achieving students, and not because the students' stated goals have causal effects on their subsequent learning strategies or outcomes.

The conflicting findings also might be related to the ways that different investigators study and measure goal orientations. Elliot, Harackiewicz, and their colleagues tend to construct experiments in contrived settings, in which college students play pinball or work on hidden-figure puzzles. The students are alone in the experimental setting except for the experimenter who provides instructions about the task and later gives feedback telling them how well they (ostensibly) performed. There is no direct competition with known peers in the immediate situation. In contrast, investigators studying motivation in K–12 students tend to measure goal orientations through questionnaires distributed in classrooms, and the performance-goal items make reference to performance relative to known peers. This probably makes the social comparison aspect more real and salient in these studies than in the studies done with college students.

Another difference concerns operational measures. Much of the research suggesting that learning goals and performance-approach goals are compatible and mutually supportive comes from experimental studies in which goal orientations were induced. In these studies, goal induction was mostly implicit and the wording sometimes blurred the distinction between learning and performance-approach goals. In contrast, much of the research suggesting caution about recommending performance-approach goals comes from nonexperimental studies in which preexisting goal orientations were measured using items that contrasted the goals more explicitly and sometimes even forced a choice between them rather than allowing students to consider them separately. Under the circumstances, it is not surprising that these different approaches yielded contrasting findings.

Moving Beyond Achievement Goals

Learning and performance goals are similar in content (they both focus on achievement) but imply contrasts in the ways that achievement is defined and the processes used to pursue it. Recently, goal theorists have been expanding their purview on goal content, studying other kinds of goals besides achievement goals. These studies indicate that students often adopt other goals in addition to or instead of learning goals or performance goals.

Work-Avoidant Goals

Some of the most alienated or discouraged students do not show much evidence of either of these types of achievement goals and instead adopt work-avoidant goals: Rather than becoming cognitively engaged in learning activities, they seek to meet minimal requirements with minimal work investment through such behaviors as tuning out from lessons, copying the work of peers, frequently seeking teacher or peer help, or attempting to negotiate less demanding assignments. Besides being associated with cheating, work-avoidant goals correlate negatively with numerous indicators of motivation and performance, such as use of deep processing learning strategies, reading voluntarily for fun, positive attitudes toward the class or the subject matter, learning goals, and achievement test scores. Students operating from work-avoidant goal orientations are not striving to achieve anything in particular. Instead, they are trying to get away with putting in as little work as possible in the situation.

Social Goals

Along with achievement goals, students pursue social goals that focus on their relationships with others in the classroom. Social goals include such things as building friendships, maintaining one's reputation as a good and likeable person, assisting others, pleasing the teacher or peers, and enjoying social interactions. Students' setting of achievement goals can be affected by the nature of their social goals. They are likely to be more highly achievement oriented if their social goals include pleasing their teachers or parents or take the form of social responsibility goals that emphasize keeping interpersonal commitments, meeting social role obligations, and conforming to social rules and expectations. However, some students may focus less on social responsibility goals than on other social goals such as intimacy goals (maintaining close friendships with peers) or status goals (being admired by the peer group). For these students, the effects of social goals on achievement orientations will depend on the values of the peer group, and especially those of peers with whom the students share intimate friendships. Students sometimes might perform less than their best in order to maintain popularity or avoid hurting the feelings of friends.

Extrinsic Goals

Some investigators have assessed the degree to which students' achievement orientations focus on garnering extrinsic rewards. In the short run, extrinsic goal orientations focus on earning good grades and related contingencies (maintaining eligibility for extracurricular activities, money from parents, prizes from the teacher, etc.). In the longer run, they include such things as opportunities to win scholarships, gain admittance to good colleges, or qualify for good jobs. Unlike learning goals, which focus on satisfying curiosity or interest, responding to challenges, or developing understandings (i.e., the learning process itself), extrinsic goals focus on rewards associated with displays of successful learning. However, extrinsic goals are not the same as performance goals because they do not involve desires to display high ability relative to peers.

Research on extrinsic goals has yielded a mixed pattern of findings. Those goals help mobilize learners to put forth the effort and persistence needed to earn good grades, but they also tend to be associated with less desirable correlates such as cheating or relying primarily on shallow rather than deeper information-processing strategies. Lin and McKeachie found that college students with medium levels of extrinsic motivation were more likely to earn good course grades than students with either low or high levels. Those who combined high levels of intrinsic motivation with medium levels of extrinsic motivation were the most successful achievers.

Harackiewicz and Elliot distinguished between higher level purpose goals that frame the activity by representing the reason for task engagement or what the person is trying to accomplish in the situation, and task-specific target goals that represent concrete guidelines for particular actions that guide the person's behavior throughout task performance. In other words, purpose goals suggest the "why" for performing a behavior and target goals provide the "how." People are more likely to enjoy an activity (i.e., to have intrinsic motivation to engage in it) when their target goals are well matched to their purpose goals. As the target goals become accomplished, people not only feel more competent at the task but value that competence and seek to continue building it, because it serves their longer run purposes. One implication of this is that performance target goals are more optimal than mastery target goals in performance purpose goal contexts.

Investigators who have interviewed students about the goals they pursue in classrooms have elicited responses that line up only partially with the goals emphasized by goal theorists. For example, Lemos interviewed Portuguese sixth graders and found that seven types of goals were mentioned frequently:

— *Working goals* (29%): Engaging in academic work in order to "get it done" or "finish it and go on to the next one."

— *Evaluation goals* (21%): Working in order to garner positive evaluations or avoid negative ones. This is similar to the extrinsic goals described above.

— *Learning goals* (19%): Seeking to learn, to know more about, to find out how, etc.

— *Complying goals* (17%): Seeking to meet student role requirements successfully by adapting to the pace of the class, doing what the teacher says, following the rules, paying attention, etc.

— *Interpersonal relationship goals* (6%): Desire to develop positive relationships with teachers or peers.

— *Enjoyment goals* (5%): Engaging in activities for pleasure, enjoyment, or fun.

— *Discipline goals* (3%): Wanting to engage in ethical behavior and avoid getting into disciplinary trouble.

Note that although learning goals were represented, performance goals were not (students talked about getting good grades but not about displaying ability or looking good in comparisons with classmates). Also, the most commonly mentioned goal, simply completing the work, has not been studied by goal theorists.

Goal Coordination

Recent work on extrinsic goals, social goals, and other alternatives to achievement goals underscores the fact that students in classrooms, like anyone in any social situation, typically seek to optimize multiple goals and agendas simultaneously. They want to please teachers and parents by earning good grades, but also to maintain their self-esteem and their social reputations and friendships. This requires them to coordinate their goal striving by taking advantage of opportunities to pursue more than one goal simultaneously and trying to avoid getting caught in situations where the things they feel they must do to satisfy one goal will interfere with their attempts to satisfy another. Goal coordination can get complicated quickly. For one thing, investment in any goal implies commitments to whatever efforts are required to accomplish it, often accompanied by worry about the consequences of failure to do so. Also, some goals are much closer than others to individuals' core values and developing interests, so they will be assigned higher priorities.

Goal coordination in classrooms is especially difficult for struggling students, because maintaining commitment to learning goals will require them to work harder than their peers. Even then, their work may still result in reduced payoff (i.e., lower grades) if teachers grade on a curve or hold all students to identical high standards that make it difficult for struggling students to succeed.

Applying Goal Theory

In talking about classroom applications, most goal theorists emphasize managing classrooms in ways that encourage students to adopt learning goals (and if relevant, performance-approach goals) rather than performance-avoidance goals, work-avoidant goals, extrinsic goals, or other goals that would distract from a focus on learning. They all warn against two particularly counterproductive practices: harsh grading standards that make it unduly difficult for students to be successful (and tend to create a preoccupation with and anxiety about grades) and grading on a curve, heavy emphasis on public comparisons, and other practices that focus attention on social comparisons rather than one's own trajectory of progress. These practices make it difficult for learners to establish and maintain focus on learning goals, and also make it more likely that any performance goals they adopt will be performance-avoidance goals.

Even theorists who emphasize that performance-approach goals can complement learning goals tend to qualify their recommendations about performance-approach goals when talking about implications for practice. Pintrich suggested that performance-approach goals can be helpful but primarily as complements rather than alternatives to learning goals, adopted within classrooms featuring emphasis on learning rather than performance orientations. He added that habitual adoption of performance-approach goals but not learning goals is likely to be effective only so long as the students are successful, leaving them vulnerable to shifting to performance-avoidance goals and eventual learned helplessness if they begin to encounter failure consistently.

Harackiewicz, Barron, and Elliot noted that performance-approach goals can complement learning goals in certain contexts, especially highly competitive classes where student performance is graded on a curve, and particularly for highly competitive students. However, they also pointed out that even performance-approach goals can be counterproductive in neutral and especially learning-oriented contexts. For them, the key is an optimal match of goal to context: "Successful negotiation of academic life at the college level may require a performance orientation in some contexts, but a mastery orientation in others, and the wisdom to know which one to adopt when". Others would argue that a more fundamental principle is to avoid creating such highly competitive contexts in the first place and instead create learning communities that support continued focus on learning goals.

The TARGET Program

The most comprehensive classroom intervention rooted in goal theory is the TARGET Program, developed by Carole Ames. Ames began with Joyce Epstein's synthesis of research on family structures that influence children's developing motivational systems at home. Epstein organized her findings within six categories that are represented in the TARGET acronym: Task, Authority, Recognition, Grouping, Evaluation, and Time. Noting that these home structures have parallels at school, Ames blended in additional principles from goal theory research to develop TARGET into a program for managing these six facets of classrooms in ways that encourage students to engage in activities with a focus on learning rather than on their public performance and how it reflects on their abilities.

Tasks are selected so as to provide an optimal level of challenge and to emphasize activities that students find interesting and intrinsically engaging. Authority is shared with students and exercised with consideration of their needs and feelings. Recognition is provided to all students who make noteworthy progress, not just the highest achievers. Grouping is managed in ways that promote cooperative learning and minimize interpersonal competition and social comparison. Evaluation is accomplished using multiple criteria and methods, focusing on individualized assessment of progress rather than comparisons of individuals or groups. Finally, time is used in creative ways that ease the constraints of rigid scheduling and allow for more use of valuable learning activities that are hard to fit into 30 to 60 minute class periods.

TARGET is best viewed not as a fixed program but instead as a framework that is adaptable to different teaching situations and useful for building motivational considerations into your instructional plans.

After developing the TARGET program, Ames assessed its effectiveness by comparing data from at-risk students in 36 TARGET classrooms with data from at-risk students in 30 comparison classrooms. These data indicated that the TARGET students perceived their classrooms as more learning oriented and the comparison students perceived their classrooms as more performance oriented. Furthermore, students in the TARGET classrooms maintained their self-reported perceptions of competence, attitudes toward the classes, intrinsic motivation, and use of desirable learning strategies, whereas students in the comparison classrooms showed deterioration on all of these measures as the semester progressed.

Other investigators also have incorporated TARGET principles with good results. Fuchs et al. incorporated the task, authority, recognition, and evaluation components of TARGET into interventions in elementary mathematics teaching. They found that, compared to low-achieving students in control classrooms, low-achieving students in the treatment classrooms reported enjoying and benefiting from the intervention, chose more challenging and a greater variety of learning topics to address, and increased their levels of effort. In addition, there have been several experiments in physical education classes in which the TARGET program was used as a basis for creating task-involving and ego-involving climates. These studies indicated that students taught in task-involving climates tended to become more task-involved themselves, and students taught in ego-involving climates tended to become more ego-involved. The former students reported positive changes in their views of the motivational climate of the class, willingness to attempt more challenging tasks and persist longer at them, and in some cases, improvement of skills at a faster rate.

Maehr and Midgley extended Ames's TARGET model from the classroom level to the school level, reasoning that the motivational efforts of individual teachers will have more powerful cumulative effects on students if the school as a whole supports students' motivation to learn. Consequently, the schoolwide TARGET model calls for adjustments such as reinforcing the intrinsic value of learning by extending it through field experiences and other extracurricular participation, arranging for public recognition of students' accomplishments, creating opportunities for students to learn study skills and strategies for managing their own learning, and revising time schedules to allow for more flexible curricular planning. Implementing the model as a schoolwide program amounted to transforming the culture of the school, and teachers differed in their willingness to accept TARGET values and guidelines. Nevertheless, at the end of the 3-year intervention, students attending the TARGET middle school were more learning oriented, whereas students attending the comparison middle school were more performance oriented.

New Directions in Goal Theory

An optimistic summary of goal theory to date would go something like the following. Goal theory was the natural result of the realization that the aspects of human activity most in need of motivational explanation were not its energization or initiation aspects but its directional and quality aspects. This dictated a shift from needs or other general motives to the goals and associated strategies operating in particular situations. Early work led to an apparent synthesis built around the idea that learning goals are productive and performance goals are counterproductive, but this generalization broke down as it became clear that goal theory would have to include the approach–avoidance distinction as well as the learning–performance distinction. However, these distinctions are now in place, and goal theorists also are taking into account other kinds of goals such as work-avoidant goals, social goals, and extrinsic goals.

As a result, a new synthesis has emerged around a multiple goals perspective, in which learners match their goals to the contingencies of situations and coordinate their goal striving so as to pursue multiple goals efficiently and minimize the likelihood that they will find themselves working at cross purposes. They will pursue learning goals to the extent that they value the content and are taught in ways that encourage or at least allow deep-processing strategies and a focus on mastery; they will pursue performance-approach goals where an emphasis on competition and test preparation make this necessary to earn good grades; and they will coordinate these achievement agendas with social and other agendas so that they support or at least do not conflict with one another.

Although the newly emerging consensus around a multiple goals perspective resolves some of the problems inherent in the earlier learning vs. performance goals perspective, it introduces some new problems of its own. In a study of people engaged in volunteer efforts, Kiviniemi, Snyder, and Omoto found that those who volunteered in response to a single motivation reported more positive experiences and fulfillment than those who reported that their volunteering was in the service of multiple motivations. This suggests, for example, that even performance-approach goals can be counterproductive in neutral or learning-oriented classrooms. This same caution is supported by research on relationships between goal striving and attention allocation. Emmons and King showed that mobilizing to strive to accomplish particular goals involves focusing attention on what is relevant to accomplishing those goals and shutting out what is not relevant. Simultaneous attempts to accomplish multiple (and especially, conflicting) goals tends to reduce our capacities for mobilizing to focus on any one of them.

This point was demonstrated with respect to approach vs. avoidance goals by Coats, Janoff-Bulman, and Alpert, who showed that phrasing goals positively (e.g., try to be creative) tended to focus attention on progress toward the goals and produce more favorable self-evaluations and greater psychological well-being than phrasing goals negatively (e.g., try not to be uncreative), which tended to focus people's attention on indications of failure. Performance-avoidance goals reduce students' capacities for mobilizing to meet task demands, because they lead to "invasion" of concentration by concerns about possible failure. Other investigators have reported similar findings.

Another complication introduced by the multiple goals perspective is that although it includes convincing evidence of the value (at least in the short term) of matching goals to learning situations, it has shifted the focus of debate to the learning situations themselves. Goal theory has roots stretching back to the philosophy of John Dewey and several prominent goal theorists have advocated wholesale school reforms that would replace a system featuring competition for limited rewards with a system that makes it possible for all students who invest reasonable effort to earn comparable rewards by achieving individualized criterion-referenced attainment goals.

Confronted with data suggesting that performance-approach goals can complement learning goals, goal theorists of this persuasion view such findings not as indicating the need to shift to a multiple goals perspective, but as indicating a need to question the advisability of learning contexts that make such findings possible. As Kaplan and Middleton put it, "... instead of interpreting the finding that performance-approach goals contribute to achievement whereas mastery goals contribute to interest as indicating that the most desirable motivational orientation is high performance approach-high mastery, one might question the educational characteristics of a context in which a focus on mastering and understanding the material does not contribute to a higher grade". This comment reminds that disputes about desirable motivational practices often embody conflicting value-based positions on the purposes and nature of education, and thus are only partially resolvable through scientific evidence.

Besides exemplifying these philosophical differences, the quote from Kaplan and Middleton alludes to a persistent and troubling enigma in goal theory research: disappointing correlations between motivation measures and achievement measures. Overall, this body of research has produced widely replicated and theoretically pleasing findings showing relationships of motivational measures to one another and to measures of information processing and learning strategies. Furthermore, individual studies, such as that of Miller et al., occasionally show reassuringly robust correlations between goal measures, strategy measures, and achievement measures. However, the more typical findings show the expected relationships between goal measures and strategy measures, but much weaker and often not even statistically significant relationships between goal measures and achievement measures (and sometimes, even between strategy measures and achievement measures).

Something is clearly amiss when contrasting patterns of self-reported goals and learning strategies fail to correlate significantly with test scores or grades. The most likely explanations would seem to be that the self-report measures of goals and learning strategies are not as valid as goal theorists have assumed or that the tests or other bases for grades are not ideal as measures of learning (i.e., focused on memory for disconnected bits of information rather than on the ability to show comprehension and application of big ideas).

There are other complications as well. Some goal theorists have treated goal orientations as highly stable dispositions that learners take with them into any learning situation. Others have treated them as highly malleable, responsive to the reward contingencies and related social atmospheres operating in the learning situation. The success of laboratory experiments that involved inducing goal orientations suggests that they are easy to manipulate, but the relatively modest findings of school intervention studies suggest that students' goal orientations toward their actual classroom work may be much more difficult to change significantly. For example, there is evidence that some students, including high-achieving students, persistently report performance-avoidance goal orientations even in learning communities that de-emphasize competition and support learning goals.

Also, students in the same class can vary considerably in their perceptions of the reward structures operating there and the teacher's relative emphasis on learning vs. performance. Furthermore, some students show remarkably different goal orientations in different school subjects, being learning oriented in some but performance orientated in others. Finally, although goal theory research consistently produces coherent results when contrasting goal orientations are induced or when goal orientations are measured using self-report questionnaires, students ordinarily do not mention performance goals spontaneously when interviewed about what goals they are pursuing in their classes. They do mention learning goals and work-avoidant goals, but they also mention other goals that have received little or no attention in goal theory research, such as work completion goals and extrinsic goals.

References

Covington, M. (2000). Goal theory, motivation, and school achievement: An integrative review. *Annual Review of Psychology,* 51, 171–200.

Freitas, A., & Higgins, E. T. (2002). Enjoying goal-directed action: The role of regulatory fit. *Psychological Science,* 13,1–6.

Somuncuoglu, Y., & Yildirim, A. (1999). Relationship between achievement goal orientations and use of learning strategies. *Journal of Educational Research,* 92, 267–277.

Urdan, T. (1997). Achievement goal theory: Past results, future directions. In P. Pintrich & M. Maehr (Eds.), *Advances in motivation and achievement* (Vol. 10, pp. 99–141). Greenwich, CT: JAI.

Valle, A., Cabanach, R., Nunez, J., Gonzalez-Pienda, J., Rodriguez, S., & Pineiro, I. (2003). Multiple goals, motivation and academic learning. *British Journal of Educational Psychology*, 73, 71–87.

Wolters, C., Yu, S., & Pintrich, P. (1996). The relation between goal orientation and students' be-liefs and self-regulated learning. *Learning and Individual Differences*, 8, 211–238.

5

Students with Expectancy-related Motivational Problems

Educators across the world are frustrated with the challenge of how to motivate the ever increasing number of freshmen students entering college who are psychologically, socially, and academically unprepared for the demands of college life. Such students often exhibit maladaptive behavior such as tardiness, hostility towards authority, and unrealistic aspirations.

The standard approach is to address the problem as an academic issue through remedial or developmental instruction. Developmental education programs however do not address the whole problem. Lack of motivation is not limited to the academically weak student. Successful remedial and study strategies courses aimed at the underprepared student have demonstrated that students who really want to improve their skills can do so when motivated. However, even the best remedial instruction programs have failed to positively impact the student who is both underprepared academically and unmotivated. When students have both a lack of academic skills and lack motivation, the greater problem is motivation. Faculty often have neither the time or inclination to address difficult motivational issues in the classroom, consequently, the task of trying to effectively motivate such students often falls to academic advisors.

The problem of devising effective strategies that influence motivation relies initially on the identification of specific motivational factors. The histories of psychology and education are abundant with research on motivation and its effect on behavior. The study of motivation in education has undergone many changes over the years, moving away from reinforcement contingencies to the more current social-cognitive perspective emphasizing learners' constructive interpretations of events and the role that their beliefs, cognitions, affects, and values play in achievement.

Some of your students will achieve less than most of their classmates, even if you meet their individual needs effectively and they progress as rapidly as it is reasonable to expect. Even so, these students may need additional motivational support. Also, many of them will bring into your classroom expectancy-related motivational problems that they have developed through prior experiences with failure and its consequences. These problems may continue unless you address them effectively.

1. students with limited ability who have difficulty keeping up and develop chronically low expectations and numbed acceptance of failure;
2. students whose failure attributions or ability beliefs make them susceptible to learned helplessness in failure situations;
3. students who are obsessed with self-worth protection and thus focus on performance goals but not learning goals; and
4. students who underachieve due to a desire to avoid responsibilities.

Students who do not put forth much effort because they do not find school very meaningful or worthwhile also require special motivational attention.

In a study of academically prepared and underprepared freshmen orientation students, Howey found clear motivational differences between academically prepared and underprepared community college freshmen orientation students. Specifically, underprepared students are more extrinsically motivated, see more value in study strategies offered in the course, have low self-efficacy beliefs, and suffer more from test anxiety. Academically prepared students, on the other hand, have more internalized locus of control beliefs, greater self-efficacy, and are less affected by test anxiety. Academically prepared students may be better served by emphasizing goal orientation (major selection) and related career information, critical thinking, leadership training, or service learning opportunities. Implications are that due to identified differences in the motivational constructs of expectancy, value, and affect, college administrators may want to consider more homogeneous grouping, based on academic readiness, of freshmen orientation students in order to better address individual motivational differences.

Early intervention is critical to improving the success rate and retention of at-risk students. In addition to providing an opportunity for timely intervention, freshmen orientation course material and textbooks are typically designed specifically to address motivation and study strategies. Clearly one venue with high potential to positively impact student motivation to succeed in college is through a customized and targeted freshman seminar course.

Strategies to Help the Low Achievers

Some students continuously struggle to keep up with their classmates due to limitations in academic ability or learning disabilities that impede their progress. For example, they may be able to decode text, yet not understand and remember what they read well enough to learn efficiently through independent study. Or, they may know basic number facts but have difficulty understanding and generating solutions to application problems. To the extent that these students fall behind, it becomes more difficult to teach them using instructional materials and methods developed for the grade level. Some of them may be able to keep up with the class if provided with tutoring or other forms of special help, but others may begin to require individualized materials and instruction.

If you are able to provide them with sufficient instructional support, slow learners can make steady progress and achieve enough to satisfy both you and themselves, even though they may remain at or near the bottom of the class in overall achievement. However, if they often become frustrated because they cannot handle tasks or get help when they need it, or if they frequently feel humiliated because they are not keeping up with their classmates, they may begin to show failure syndrome symptoms. That is, they may lose their motivation to persist with learning efforts and instead begin to give up quickly at the first sign of failure. Or, they may become more concerned with covering up their confusion than with learning what the activity is intended to teach. Some may begin to withdraw into passivity rather than participate in lessons, to leave items blank or simply guess at answers instead of seeking help, or to become behavior problems. At this point, low achievement due to limited academic ability becomes compounded by underachievement due to motivational problems.

Theorists and researchers who discuss strategies for teaching low achievers tend to disagree about what can be expected from these students and how much effort should be devoted to their needs relative to the needs of the rest of the class. However, reviews of this literature do converge on certain strategies, especially the strategies of providing tutorial help to low achievers and individualizing their assignments.

For example, McIntyre culled four sets of suggestions from a variety of sources. The first set focused on individualizing activities and assignments: Reduce the length and difficulty levels of the tasks that you assign to struggling students; use multisensory input sources to reduce their need to learn by studying texts; build assignments around their interests; make sure that assignments are well structured and within the range of their ability level; and make sure that the first part of the assignment is easy or familiar enough to provide initial success experiences.

The second group of suggestions focused on providing directions to structure tasks for low achievers. These included the following: Have them repeat the instructions to you to make sure that they know what is supposed to be done; model task performance for them by thinking out loud as you perform demonstrations; train them in methods of self-instructional guidance; outline exactly what must be done to achieve the desired level of accomplishment; and set time limits within which the work should be done, preferably longer limits than necessary to allow these students to "beat the clock."

A third set of suggestions focused on providing task assistance or tutoring. This might be done either by yourself or by an aide, adult volunteer, older student, or classmate. Specific suggestions included: Rephrase questions or provide hints when these students are unable to respond; praise them when they respond acceptably; have them revise work that is unacceptable; reassure them that help is available if needed; sit them among average (not superior) classmates with whom they enjoy friendly relationships, and ask these classmates to help keep the low achievers "on track" by providing task assistance and reminders of assignments and due dates; and set up a "study buddy" system to encourage low achievers to collaborate with a neighborhood friend during study sessions at their homes.

The fourth set of strategies focused on maintaining motivation. These included: Provide encouragement and positive comments on papers; help low achievers to establish realistic goals and evaluate their accomplishments; call attention to their successes and send positive notes home; encourage them to focus on trying to surpass their previous day's or week's performance rather than to compete with classmates; use performance contracting methods; and give marks and report card grades on the basis of effort and production rather than in relation to the rest of the class.

Abbott published a similar collection of strategies. Along with many of those mentioned by McIntyre, she included the following: Keep directions simple, if necessary by dividing the task into parts rather than providing lengthy directions that the student may not be able to remember; seat the student toward the front of the class and maintain frequent eye contact; provide extra assignments that address learning needs and allow the student to earn extra credit toward grades; and keep in close communication with anyone who tutors the student, to make sure that the tutoring focuses on his or her primary needs and that you keep abreast of progress and problems.

Low achievers may benefit from strategies used in mastery learning approaches: Make success likely by giving them tasks that they should be able to handle, provide them with individualized tutoring as needed, and allow them to contract for a particular level of performance and to continue to study, practice, and take tests until that level is achieved. By virtually guaranteeing success, this approach builds confidence and increases discouraged students' willingness to take the risks involved in seriously committing themselves to challenging goals.

Good and Brophy reviewed research indicating that low achievers need frequent monitoring and supplementary tutoring from their teacher (or an adequate substitute), not just exposure to so-called individualized instructional materials. Too many of these materials are restricted to low-level repetitive tasks that amount to busywork rather than truly remedial instruction. Also, low achievers often need to be retaught using varied and enriched forms of instruction, not just to be recycled through the original instruction followed by additional drill and practice.

Other strategies identified in their review included the following: collect books and instructional materials that address content taught at your grade but are written at easier reading levels; tutor slow learners in independent reading and study skills, not just in subject-matter content; provide them with study guides and related learning supports; and combine empathy for these students with determination to see that they meet established learning goals, not just that they are happy in school.

In a recent a study, 98 experienced teachers working in Grades K–6 were interviewed in depth concerning their strategies for working with 12 categories of students who present chronic achievement, motivation, or behavior problems. Half of these teachers had been rated as outstanding in their ability to teach such students effectively, whereas the other half had been rated as average or typical. Analyses focused on common themes in the teachers' responses, especially those of the higher rated teachers.

Concerning low achievers, most of these teachers' responses centered around the following set of principles: Focus on providing academic help; supplement this with counseling or motivational support if needed; provide extra monitoring, feedback, and tutoring; enlist help from peers, parents, or other students or adults; and view low achievers as challenges to your professionalism as a teacher rather than as candidates for retention in grade or transfer into special education.

At first, the higher rated teachers placed more emphasis on providing low achievers with academic help than with motivational support. However, follow-up analyses indicated that much of the intended motivational support reported by lower rated teachers amounted to ineffectual attempts at encouragement. The difference is illustrated in the following examples of two teachers' handling of a situation in which a student is "stuck" on a math problem.

Here is how the situation might be handled effectively:

STUDENT: I can't do Number 4.

TEACHER: What part don't you understand?

STUDENT: I just can't do it, it's too hard!

TEACHER: I know you can do part of it because you've done the first three problems correctly. The fourth one is similar, but just a little more complicated. You start out the same way, but there's one extra step.

Compare this with the following less effective scenario:

STUDENT: I can't do Number 4.

TEACHER: You can't! Why not?

STUDENT: I just can't do it, it's too hard!

TEACHER: Don't say you can't do it—we never say we can't do it. Did you try hard?

STUDENT: Yes, but I can't do it.

TEACHER: You did the first three; maybe if you worked a little longer you could do the fourth.

The first teacher communicated positive expectations and provided a specific suggestion about how to proceed, yet did not give the answer or do the work. In giving feedback about performance on the first three problems, she was more specific in noting that the answers were correct and in attributing this success to the student's knowledge and abilities, thus supporting the student's self-efficacy beliefs. She also provided some instructional assistance, and in the process, embedded some desirable socialization of the student's expectancy-related beliefs. The second teacher provided neither useful instructional guidance nor a credible basis for encouragement. Instead, she communicated half-hearted and somewhat contradictory expectations, leaving the student with no reason to believe that further effort would succeed.

In elaborating on principles culled from the research literature and from interviewing experienced teachers, we would stress the following suggestions for teaching low achievers. First, accept the situation and make the best of it. Identify the most essential (although not necessarily low-level or easily attained) objectives of each curriculum unit and make sure that low achievers master these, even if this means skipping other things. Also, help them to view their situation realistically, yet still try to progress as best they can. Let them know that their work is acceptable to you so long as they apply themselves, even if they are unable to keep up with most of their classmates. Elicit their commitment to establishing and working on feasible goals. Explain that extra practice may be necessary for them, even if it is not enjoyable. You empathize, but you want to them learn, too.

Low achievers need extra help, especially individualized help provided during tutoring interactions. However, their helpers will need to be patient and caring. If you use peer or cross-age tutors, make sure that the tutors understand this. Also, arrange for low achievers to tutor peers or younger students. This will help them to master material more thoroughly and also avoid making them always the receivers but never the givers of help.

As soon as possible after settling your class into assignments, give personal attention to low achievers to make sure that they understand what to do and get off to a good start. Don't let them "practice errors" or end up turning in completed papers that are "all wrong." If they are not ready for extended independent work, build toward it through successive approximations. If they don't read well, help them learn to do so. At other times, engage them in worthwhile learning activities that do not require significant reading skills or that can be explained to them orally. In mathematics, use concrete manipulables and other specialized instructional materials designed to help them grasp basic concepts. In language arts and the content subjects, ask them questions that focus on key ideas and require them to compose thoughtful oral or written responses, then provide feedback focused on their grasp of the key ideas rather than on the formal correctness of their language or writing.

In effect, "cut a deal" with low achievers: It's OK if they can't keep up with the rest of the class, because you have special goals and activities for them. You will be pleased if they accomplish these goals and are prepared to help them do so, but they will have to work persistently and hold up their end, too. You are demanding effort and progress, but not necessarily the attainment of grade-level norms or the performance of the class as a whole.

Mastery Learning

Mastery learning adjusts whole-class pacing by allowing slower students more time, and usually providing them with tutoring or other special assistance, to enable them to learn material that classmates have mastered more quickly. Originally mastery learning emphasized individualized tutoring, but the approach has since been adapted for use in tandem with whole-class or group-based instruction.

Mastery learning principles are often used with curricula that feature clearly specified learning objectives, preset mastery performance standards, and frequent assessment using criterion-referenced tests. The heart of mastery learning is the cycle of teaching, testing, reteaching, and retesting. Students are informed of the unit's objectives and then receive instruction designed to enable them to master those objectives. Upon completion of instruction and related practice activities, the students take tests designed to assess their mastery. Those who achieve preset performance standards (usually, passing at least 80% of the items) are certified as having mastered the unit and are not required to do further work on it. These students then move on to the next unit, or more typically, work on enrichment activities or activities of their own choosing until the entire class is ready to move on. Meanwhile, students who do not meet mastery criteria receive corrective instruction and additional practice before their mastery levels are assessed again. Theoretically, cycles of assessment and reteaching would go on indefinitely until all students reached mastery, but in practice, attempts to bring students to mastery usually cease after the second test, and the class then moves on to the next unit.

Mastery Learning methods increase, often dramatically, the percentage of students who master basic objectives. They benefit low achievers by providing extra time and instruction to enable them to master more content than they would otherwise, and this additional mastery is likely to bring motivational benefits as well. However, the approach is time consuming and often viewed as impractical by teachers.

Also, its potential benefits for slower learners may be counterbalanced by deficits to faster learners, unless the needs of all students in the classroom are taken into account in designing the system. Activities planned for faster learners should be selected for sound pedagogical reasons and not as mere time fillers to give them something to do while they wait for slower students to catch up. A feasible adaptation of the mastery learning approach may be to identify those learning objectives that seem most essential and that all of your students master them, while tolerating more variable performance on objectives that are less essential. You then can supplement the basic curriculum with enrichment opportunities that classmates work on individually or in groups during times when you are busy teaching a remedial or enrichment lesson to a small group of students.

How Some Teachers Communicate to Their Low Achievers

Like some students who have become discouraged by repeated academic failures, some teachers become discouraged by repeated instructional failures and begin to show the same kinds of symptoms: lowered self-efficacy perceptions, reduced expectations for future success, attribution of failure to external and uncontrollable causes, and a shift from persistent and adaptive problem-solving strategies to half-hearted and maladaptive ones. In extreme cases, teachers "burn out" and display such behavior most of the time with most of their students. More typically, however, teachers develop learned helplessness in teaching certain students, particularly low achievers who continue to struggle to keep up with the rest of the class. Some teachers redouble their efforts and make the best of the situation, but others gradually give up and begin just going through the motions with these students, communicating their low expectations in the process. For example, most teachers know that low achievers need patience and encouragement. However, Brophy and Good observed teachers who were not practicing these seemingly obvious strategies, at least not toward the end of the school year, when the observations were made. Consider these teachers' behavior when they called on a student to answer a question and the student made no response, said "I don't know," or answered incorrectly. At these times, the teachers could either stay with the student by repeating the question, giving a clue, or asking a new question, or else give up on the student by giving the answer or calling on someone else. Observations indicated that these teachers were twice as likely to stay with high-achieving students as with low-achieving students.

There also were differences in the teachers' rates of praise and criticism of students' responses. Good answers from high achievers were praised 12% of the time, but good answers from low achievers were praised only 6% of the time. Meanwhile, 6% of the high achievers' response failures yielded teacher criticism, whereas this occurred 18% of the time with low achievers. Thus, the students who most needed patience and encouragement often were treated with impatience when they struggled to respond. They also were less likely to be praised when they responded correctly (even though this happened less often), and more likely to be criticized when they were unable to respond correctly (even though this happened more often). Clearly, these teachers had drifted into counterproductive patterns of interacting with their low achievers.

Subsequent research has shown that some teachers do provide their low achievers with patience, encouragement, and other supportive treatment that helps these students to work up to their potential. Other teachers, however, drift into maladaptive patterns that feature low expectations and counterproductive modes of interacting with their low achievers. Examples that have been documented in various studies include the following:

1. waiting less time for low achievers to answer a question (before giving the answer or calling on someone else)
2. giving answers to low achievers or calling on someone else rather than trying to improve their responses by giving clues or repeating or rephrasing questions
3. inappropriate reinforcement: rewarding inappropriate behavior or incorrect answers by low achievers

4. criticizing low achievers more often for failure
5. praising low achievers less often for success
6. failing to give feedback following the public responses of low achievers
7. generally paying less attention to low achievers or interacting with them less frequently
8. calling on them less often to respond to questions, or asking them only easier, nonanalytic questions
9. seating them farther away from the teacher
10. generally demanding less from them (attempting to teach them less than they are capable of learning, accepting low-quality or even incorrect responses from them and treating them as if they were correct responses, substituting misplaced sympathy or gratuitous praise for sustained teaching that ultimately leads to mastery)
11. interacting with low achievers more privately than publicly, and monitoring and structuring their activities more closely
12. giving high achievers but not low achievers the benefit of the doubt in grading tests or assignments
13. being less friendly in interactions with low achievers, including less smiling and fewer other nonverbal indicators of support
14. providing briefer and less informative answers to their questions
15. interacting with them in ways that involve less eye contact and other nonverbal communication of attention and responsiveness (e.g., forward lean, positive head nodding)
16. less use of effective but time-consuming instructional methods with low achievers when time is limited
17. less acceptance and use of low achievers' ideas
18. limiting low achievers to an impoverished curriculum (low-level and repetitive content, emphasis on factual recitation rather than lesson-extending discussion, emphasis on drill and practice tasks rather than application and higher level thinking tasks)

Some of these differences are due at least in part to the behavior of the students. For example, if low achievers seldom raise their hands, it is difficult for the teacher to ensure that they get as many response opportunities as high achievers, and if their contributions to lessons are of lower quality, the teacher cannot accept and use their ideas as frequently. Also, some forms of differential treatment are appropriate at times and may even represent appropriate individualizing of instruction. Low achievers may require more structuring of their activities and closer monitoring of their work, for example, and under some circumstances it may make sense to interact with them more privately than publicly or to ask them easier questions. However, these differential patterns are danger signals, especially if the differences are large and occur on many dimensions rather than just one or two. Such differences suggest that a teacher is merely going through the motions of instructing low achievers, without seriously working to help them achieve their potential.

Failure Syndrome

Failure syndrome is one of several terms that teachers commonly use to describe students who approach assignments with very low expectations of succeeding and who tend to give up at the first sign of difficulty. Other such terms include low self-concept, defeated, and frustrated. Unlike low achievers, who often fail despite their best efforts, failure syndrome students often fail needlessly because they do not invest their best efforts. Instead, they begin tasks half-heartedly and simply give up when they encounter difficulty. Psychologists use more technical terms to describe these students, such as low self-efficacy, entity theorist, or attributes failure to internal, stable, and uncontrollable causes (i.e., low ability).

Psychologists also refer to learned helplessness, giving it a somewhat more restrictive and technical definition. Compared to students who develop more generalized failure syndrome patterns, students who develop learned helplessness reactions can be found at all levels of academic ability, and these reactions may appear only in particular achievement situations. Galloway and his colleagues, for example, found that many students showed learned helplessness symptoms in mathematics but not in English, or vice versa.

Students who are prone to learned helplessness reactions may not routinely develop high anxiety in response to evaluation cues or begin all tasks with failure expectations. As long as they do not question their ability to succeed, they may be able to handle even challenging activities smoothly and successfully. However, when they encounter serious frustration, they are prone to develop "catastrophic" reactions, followed by progressive deterioration in the quality of their coping once they have begun to fail.

Butkowsky and Willows noted the following tendencies in learned helplessness students confronted with challenging academic tasks:

1. They had low initial expectancies for success on the tasks.
2. They gave up quickly when they encountered difficulty.
3. They attributed their failures to lack of ability rather than to controllable causes such as insufficient effort or reliance on an inappropriate strategy.
4. They attributed their successes to external and uncontrollable causes (luck, easy task) rather than to their own abilities and efforts.
5. Following failure, they made unusually severe reductions in their estimates of future success probabilities.

Some students, especially in the early grades, show failure syndrome tendencies as part of a larger pattern of emotional immaturity that includes low frustration tolerance and avoidance, inhibition, or overdependency on adults as reactions to stress. These students may focus more on their dependency-related desires for attention from their teacher than on trying to learn what an academic activity is designed to teach.

However, most failure syndrome problems develop through social learning mechanisms centered around experiences with failure. Children usually nbegin school with enthusiasm, but many begin to find it anxiety provoking and psychologically threatening. They are accountable for responding to questions, completing assignments, and taking tests. Their performances are monitored, graded, and reported to their parents. These accountability pressures might be tolerable under conditions of privacy and consistent success, but they become threatening in classrooms where failure carries the danger of public humiliation. Learned helplessness reactions are especially likely to appear in classrooms where the teacher uses controlling (versus autonomy-supporting) strategies and the students have developed extrinsic (versus intrinsic) motivational orientations. Given these conditions, it is not surprising that some students, especially those who have experienced a continuing history of failure or a recent progressive cycle of failure, begin to believe that they lack the ability to succeed. Once this belief takes root, failure expectations and other self-conscious thoughts begin to disrupt their concentration and limit their coping abilities. Eventually they abandon serious attempts to master tasks and begin to concentrate instead on preserving their self-esteem in their own eyes and their reputations in the eyes of others.

Helping Students with Failure Syndrome

Students with failure syndrome problems need assistance in regaining self-confidence in their academic abilities and in developing strategies for coping with failure and persisting with problem-solving efforts when they experience difficulty. Over the years, reviewers of the literature in education and psychology have identified quite a collection of strategies for accomplishing these goals.

Wlodkowski suggested that teachers

- guarantee that failure syndrome students experience success regularly (by seeing that they know what to do before asking them to do it independently, providing immediate feedback to their responses, and making sure that they know the criteria by which their learning will be evaluated);
- encourage their learning efforts by giving them recognition for real effort, showing appreciation for their progress, and projecting positive expectations;
- emphasize personal causation in their learning by allowing them to plan and set goals, make choices, and use self-evaluation procedures to check their progress; and
- use group process methods to enhance positive self-concepts (activities that orient these students toward appreciating their positive qualities and getting recognition for them from their peers).

Swift and Spivack suggested most of these same strategies. In addition, they recommended exploring with these students which classroom situations they find comfortable and which anxiety-provoking, and why; helping them to gain better insight into and sense of control over their anxieties; and reassuring them of your willingness to help. Forms of help might include minimizing evaluation and competition, marking and grading with emphasis on noting successes rather than failures, using individualized instructional materials, and calling on these students only when they volunteer or are likely to be able to respond successfully (or alternatively, only when you have prepared them through advance warning and study suggestions).

McIntyre suggested reading and discussing with these students The Little Engine That Could; praising them for attempting difficult tasks as well as for whatever successes they achieve; requiring them to complete (or at least to make a serious attempt to complete) a certain portion of an assignment before asking you for help; pointing out the similarities between the present task and work completed successfully earlier; and allowing them extra time if necessary but insisting that their work be completed.

More specific and elaborated suggestions have emerged from research on particular theoretical concepts or treatment approaches. Many of these involve what Ames called "cognition retraining." Three prominent approaches to cognition retraining are attribution retraining, efficacy training, and strategy training.

Attribution Retraining

Attribution retraining involves inducing changes in students' tendencies to attribute their failures to lack of ability rather than to remediable causes such as insufficient effort or use of inappropriate strategies. Typically, attribution retraining treatments expose students to a planned series of experiences, couched within an achievement context, in which modeling, socialization, practice, and feedback are used to teach them to (a) concentrate on the task at hand rather than worry about failing, (b) cope with failures by retracing their steps to find their mistake or by analyzing the problem to find another approach, and (c) attribute their failures to insufficient effort, lack of information, or use of ineffective strategies rather than to lack of ability. Failure syndrome students are especially likely to benefit from exposure to programs that combine attribution retraining with training in strategies for accomplishing tasks.

Research on attribution retraining has led to significant advances over the commonsense idea of programming students for success. This work has shown that success alone is not enough—even a steady diet of success will not change an established pattern of learned helplessness. In fact, a key to successful attribution retraining is controlled exposure to failure. Rather than being exposed only to "success models" who handle tasks with ease, students are exposed to "coping models" who struggle to overcome mistakes before finally succeeding. In the process, they model constructive responses to mistakes as they occur (e.g., by verbalizing continued confidence, attributing failures to remediable causes, and coping by first diagnosing the source of the problem and then correcting the mistake or approaching the problem in a different way). Following exposure to such modeling, students begin to work on the tasks themselves. Conditions are arranged so that they sometimes experience difficulty or failure, but accompanied by coaching that encourages them to respond constructively rather than becoming frustrated and giving up.

These treatments reflect a growing recognition that successful socialization of students' motivational attitudes and beliefs includes attention to frustration tolerance, persistence in the face of difficulties, and related aspects of constructive response to failure. This is quite different from programming for success, especially if this idea is translated into attempts to enable students to avoid experiencing failure altogether.

Early attribution retraining programs stressed attribution of failures to insufficient effort. More recently developed programs stress attributing failure to using an ineffective strategy. This shift recognizes the fact that most students at least subjectively put forth their best efforts, so that failure results not so much from lack of effort as from a limited repertoire of relevant knowledge and coping strategies. That is, they do everything they know how to do but still don't succeed, and they don't know how to diagnose and overcome the problem on their own.

Efficacy Training

Efficacy training programs also involve exposing students to a planned set of experiences within an achievement context and providing them with modeling, instruction, and feedback. However, whereas attribution retraining programs were developed specifically for learned helplessness students and thus focus on teaching constructive response to failure, efficacy training programs were developed primarily for low achievers who have become accustomed to failure and have developed generalized low self-concepts of ability. Consequently, efficacy training helps students to set realistic goals and pursue them with the recognition that they have the ability (efficacy) needed to reach these goals if they apply reasonable effort.

Schunk identified the following practices as effective for increasing students' self-efficacy perceptions:

- cognitive modeling that includes verbalization of task strategies, the intention to persist despite problems, and confidence in achieving eventual success;
- explicit training in strategies for accomplishing the task;
- performance feedback that points out correct operations, remedies errors, and reassures students that they are developing mastery;

- attributional feedback that emphasizes the successes being achieved and attributes these to the combination of sufficient ability and reason able effort;
- encouraging students to set goals prior to working on tasks (goals that are challenging but attainable, phrased in terms of specific performance standards and oriented toward immediate short-term outcomes);
- focusing feedback on how students' current performance surpasses their prior attainments rather than on how they compare with other students;
- supplying rewards contingent on actual accomplishment (not just task participation).

Strategy Training

In strategy training, modeling and instruction are used to teach problem-solving strategies and related self-talk that students will need to handle tasks successfully. Strategy training is a component of good cognitive skills instruction to all students; it is not primarily a remedial technique. However, it is especially important to use with discouraged students who have not developed effective learning and problem-solving strategies on their own but who can learn them through modeling and explicit instruction.

Poor readers, for example, can be taught reading comprehension strategies such as identifying the purpose of the assignment and keeping it in mind when reading, activating relevant background knowledge, identifying major points and attending to the outline and flow of content, monitoring their understanding by generating and trying to answer questions about the content, and drawing and testing inferences by making interpretations, predictions, and conclusions. Poor writers can be taught strategies for planning, drafting, and revising text. Two keys to effective strategy instruction are that it includes attention not just to propositional knowledge (what to do) but also to procedural knowledge (how to do it) and conditional knowledge (when and why to do it), and it includes cognitive modeling (thinking out loud that makes visible the covert thought processes that guide problem solving).

Programs also have been developed for training students in general study skills and learning strategies. Cognitive elements of these programs include instruction in strategies such as rehearsal (repeating material to remember it more effectively), elaboration (putting material into one's own words and relating it to prior knowledge), organization (outlining material to highlight its structure and remember it), comprehension monitoring (keeping track of the strategies used and the degree of success achieved with them, and adjusting strategies accordingly), and affect monitoring (maintaining concentration and task focus, minimizing performance anxiety and fear of failure). The programs also contain affective management components similar to those used in attribution retraining and efficacy training programs, and they also are likely to be more successful when learners observe a coping model improve gradually than when they observe a success model perform flawlessly. A comprehensive cognition retraining program for failure syndrome students will include attention to both the cognitive and the affective aspects of task engagement and persistence.

Dweck and Elliott recommended that strategy training programs encourage incremental rather than entity views of ability. This involves: acting more as a resource person than a judge, focusing students more on learning processes than on outcomes, reacting to errors as natural and useful parts of the learning process rather than as evidence of failure, stressing effort over ability and individualized standards over normative standards when giving feedback, and attempting to stimulate achievement efforts through primarily intrinsic rather than extrinsic motivational strategies.

Failure syndrome students require patience and persistence, especially if their problems have been developing for years. You cannot quickly "cure" those who have become convinced that they lack ability by providing a few success experiences and words of encouragement. However, you can begin to undermine their certainty of failure and get them moving toward confidence by making sure that they are prepared to handle the challenges you present, teaching them needed task skills and more general learning and study strategies, and applying the principles involved in attribution retraining, efficacy training, and related treatment approaches.

Whether or not you undertake such treatments formally, you can include relevant socialization messages in your everyday interactions with failure syndrome students. Much of this socialization can be subtle and informal, as in the earlier example of effective handling of a student who was "stuck" on a math problem. Students treated in this manner every day should slowly but surely begin to gain confidence and become less prone to catastrophic reactions to failure.

Additionally, help these students learn to understand when they do or do not need help and to become willing to get help when they need it. Give them a set of procedures to follow when they encounter difficulties, starting with strategies for diagnosing possible causes of their problem and perhaps solving it on their own. If they cannot solve the problem on their own, they then should seek help.

Therefore, give these students one or more options to use to signal their need for help unobtrusively. Then, get to them as quickly as you can and provide the help that they need. In this regard, teach them to distinguish when they do and do not need help. If they have failed to engage the strategies you have taught them and thus have not yet determined whether they can handle the problem on their own, require them to engage these strategies before getting help. If they really do need help, provide it, but emphasize "instrumental" help (explanations, questions, or hints that will stimulate them to think about the problem and encourage them to work out the rest of it on their own) rather than "executive" help (giving them answers). Instrumental help scaffolds students' problem solving just enough to enable them to make needed connections and construct the knowledge or skill that the task was intended to teach, whereas executive help eliminates the need for further thinking and leaves them possessing correct answers but lacking key understandings.

Emphasising on Self-worth Protection

Struggling low achievers or students beset with failure syndrome problems are especially likely to focus on performance goals instead of learning goals. However, certain capable or even confident students also may emphasize performance goals over learning goals, especially as they approach adolescence and become more concerned about social comparison and reputation issues. Some may become predisposed toward learned helplessness in a steadily growing range of achievement situations. In other cases, the problem may be less extreme but still worrisome because self-worth preoccupations distract the students' attention from learning goals and cause them to engage in activities using less-than-ideal strategies.

Such students may attempt to escape being called on by scrunching down in their seats and avoiding eye contact with you (or by conspicuously waving their hands and projecting a confident demeanor, if they have discovered that this will make you less likely to call on them). If you do call on them and they are not sure how to answer, they may hesitate in the hope that you will help them. Or, they may offer a vague and rambling response in the hope that you will accept it and move on. During work times they may appear to be thinking when they are actually daydreaming or may appear to be working thoughtfully when they are actually just guessing at answers or perhaps copying from a neighbor. They may procrastinate in getting started and then hurry to finish as time runs out. They may skip items, do the minimum required, or in other ways perform marginally rather than accept the challenge of working up to their capabilities. Or, they may display unrealistic perfectionism by constantly rejecting their partially completed efforts and starting over (thus giving the appearance of commitment to high goals while actually not accomplishing much). These and related stratagems allow students who are obsessed with self-worth protection to go through the motions of achievement striving while actually avoiding acceptance of genuine challenges and arming themselves with excuses for potential failures.

Lehtinen et al. described the development of several of these mechanisms in a student named Heli whom they studied between third and sixth grade. Heli was a fluent decoder and viewed herself as one of the top students. However, she had great difficulties with text comprehension, restlessness, and lack of concentration, so her teacher rated her much lower. Fear of failure and symptoms of learned helplessness emerged whenever Heli encountered difficulty in her work or even picked up a cue from the teacher that the task was going to be difficult. She often complained that a new task was too long, too hard, or that she didn't like it. She would attempt to wheedle help through social dependence strategies (e.g., appealing for help, babyish chatting, or smooth-tongued questioning aimed at eliciting teacher guidance). If this did not succeed, she would escalate to passive avoidance strategies (e.g., absent-minded staring, averting her gaze from the task, or "silent treatment" of the teacher). At other times, she proceeded to more active or manipulative forms of avoidance (e.g., attempting to leave the classroom, engaging in stereotyped rituals or mannerisms, signaling tiredness, or resorting to intensive whining or tantrums).

Heli's symptomatic behaviors typically escalated as long as the stress continued, and sometimes carried over to the next activity. However, they typically disappeared and were replaced by a smiling, cooperative demeanor if the teacher gave up attempts to get more out of her. Over time, Heli perfected her techniques to the point that they were quite successful in limiting her teachers' (and her parents') willingness to persist in seeking to get her to work up to her abilities.

Some students do not usually fear failure and thus are not obsessed with protecting their self-worth, but they are frequently distracted from learning goals by social goals such as trying to please you as the teacher or trying to impress their peers (sometimes by displaying intelligence or task skills, but sometimes by showing off or acting "cool"). To the extent that students are distracted from learning goals by these social concerns, they are less likely to use optimal learning strategies that focus on constructing meaningful understandings and remembering them for later use in appropriate application situations.

Reducing Preoccupation with Self-Worth Protection

The most powerful strategies for dealing with such problems focus on prevention rather than cure. You can minimize your students' needs for self-worth protection by establishing your classroom as a learning community and consistently modeling, socializing, and instructing students in ways that orient them toward learning goals rather than performance goals.

Martin Covington has written at length about self-worth protection problems and experimented with methods for minimizing them. He recommended the following six general strategies:

1. *Provide students with engaging assignments.* Appeal to students' curiosity and personal interests that offer challenging yet manageable goals. To the extent feasible, allow them some choice of tasks and control over the level of challenge they face (but encourage them to increase levels of challenge in response to increases in their levels of expertise).
2. *Provide sufficient rewards.* Arrange the reward system so that all students (not just the brighter ones) can earn desired rewards. Also, dispense rewards in ways that reinforce students for setting meaningful goals, posing challenging questions, and working to satisfy their curiosity. Seek to make the act of learning itself a sought-after goal.
3. *Enhance effort-outcome covariation beliefs.* Help students learn to set realistic goals and develop confidence that they can be successful and earn rewards through reasonable (not superhuman) effort.

4. *Strengthen the linkage between achievement efforts and self-worth.* Help students learn to take pride in their accomplishments and their developing expertise, and to minimize attention to competition and social comparison.
5. *Promote positive beliefs about ability.* Help students to adopt multidimensional definitions of their abilities and to take an incremental rather than an entity view toward them.
6. *Improve teacher-student relations.* Emphasize your role as a resource person who assists these students' learning efforts, not your role as an authority figure who controls their behavior.

Other sources offer similar advice about minimizing or coping with self-worth protection problems. In addition to the suggestions advanced by Covington, these sources suggest the following strategies: Attempt to socialize the students' values and learning goals by helping them see the need for what they are learning in their present and future lives outside of school; teach them cognitive and metacognitive strategies for regulating their learning more effectively so that they will have less need for self-worth protection; encourage them to ask for help when they need it and make it possible for them to get such help without suffering public embarrassment; emphasize cooperative learning and avoid competition; and use individual criterion-referenced grading standards rather than absolute standards or grading on a curve.

We would add the following suggestions about socializing the attitudes and beliefs of students who are obsessed with self-worth protection. First, help these students to understand how this focus ironically limits their current performance and future development. Help them to appreciate that they develop their abilities only when they extend them by accepting new challenges: Sticking to what is easy and familiar minimizes risk but keeps them standing still while their classmates are moving forward.

Similarly, help them to understand that a focus on competing with peers is ultimately a losing game, even if they win most of the time. It distracts attention from learning efforts and is likely to create problems with peers (who usually do not appreciate overcompetitiveness). It also diverts energies that should be devoted to synthesizing their learning, appreciating its value, and remembering it with an eye toward using it in their lives outside of school. Portfolio assessment and related approaches for focusing students on progress over time can be helpful here.

Finally, take seriously these students' needs to look good in public situations. Don't dismiss their fears or suggest that they are groundless. Instead, ask if there are things you can do to help them feel more comfortable in your classroom and become more willing to accept genuine challenges. Follow through on any requests that are feasible. Make sure that your everyday interactions with these students are consistent with the notions that you care about them personally as well as about their achievement progress, that you would not want to embarrass them, and that you will try to provide any form of help they may need.

Supporting Committed Underachievers

Most students with problems in the expectancy-related aspects of motivation would like to achieve more than they do but are hampered by one or more of the problems described. However, you also may encounter a few "committed underachievers" who set low goals and resist accepting responsibility for their successes because they do not want to be expected to maintain a higher level of performance. These students need reassurance that they can attain consistent success with reasonable effort (i.e., not superhuman effort). They also may benefit from counseling designed to help them see that their deliberate under-achievement is contrary to their own long-run best interests.

McCall, Evahn, and Kratzer completed the largest study of under-achievers done to date, beginning when they were still in school but following them into adulthood. As students, these underachievers displayed such characteristics as low self-concept, low perception of abilities, unrealistic goal setting, lack of persistence, responding impulsively rather than thoughtfully to assignments, social immaturity and poor peer relationships, oppositional and aggressive response to authority, and a tendency to make excuses for continued underachievement rather than accept responsibility and make a serious commitment to change.

These school problems were part of a larger syndrome characterized by failure to persist in the face of challenge: Underachievers were less likely to complete college and to display job and marital stability than comparison groups, including a group that earned similar grades but had lower aptitude scores. Thus, there is no reason to believe that underachievement problems will take care of themselves once underachievers "find what interests them" or "leave school and enter the work world." This type of under-achievement syndrome tends to persist if left untreated.

McCall and his colleagues also reviewed the treatment literature and concluded that most programs had at least some success in remediating targeted symptoms. However, many programs failed to improve achievement because they targeted peripheral symptoms such as self-esteem or social relationships but not the core symptoms of low achievement motivation and the desire to avoid increased expectations and responsibilities. The best results are obtained with comprehensive programs that address the full range of observed symptoms and include treatment elements aimed at parents and teachers as well as students. The most common approach is teacher–parent collaboration in using behavior modification strategies.

A Confrontational Strategy

Mandel and Marcus described a strategy designed to pressure committed underachievers to stop generating excuses for their continued failure to apply themselves and instead begin to take responsibility for doing so. These authors argued that less confrontive strategies, such as providing a lot of encouragement or making the work easier or more interesting, will not lead to any fundamental change because these students are motivated to continue their underachievement pattern so as to avoid increased expectations and responsibilities. They claimed that their approach has been successful but warned that it requires being prepared to patiently work through the student's excuses and resistance strategies.

The first step is to ask whether the underachiever wants to get better grades in school (as opposed to announcing that you are going to help the student do so). For the overwhelming majority of students who respond positively to this initial question, the relationship has now been structured such that it is the responsibility of the student to set goals, whereas your role is to help the student achieve them. Step 2 involves taking detailed stock of current progress and problems in each subject, along with any plans that the student may have for addressing the problems. At this point, your role is to elicit information nonjudgmentally, without giving any interpretations or recommendations.

Step 3 involves focusing on specific problems and isolating the student's excuses for them. You ask what problems are getting in the way of better grades, probe for specifics when the student offers only vague generalizations, and if necessary, challenge questionable claims. For example, the student might claim to spend an hour every day studying, but specific questions about the last few days might establish that the real average is more like 10 or 20 minutes per day. Step 4 involves linking each excuse to its natural consequence by describing (or better yet, eliciting from the student) what will happen if the student does not address this problem effectively. Step 5 involves asking the student to suggest solutions for each identified hindrance to success, then engaging in detailed discussion of these suggestions in order to clarify their practicality, anticipate snags, and refine plans. Here, you need to be careful to elicit plans from the student rather than tell the student what to do. Once the student "owns" the goal of better grades, has recognized the connection between current study habits and future consequences, and has identified a specific and workable solution, there is no way to "unrecognize" these connections again. The student must accept personal responsibility for improving the grades.

The sixth step is a call for action (saying "OK, now what do you propose to do?" followed by questions about specifics). The seventh step is follow-up to assess whether the student has implemented the plan and eliminated the problem. Given the student's motivation to continue to underachieve, it is likely that the assessment will indicate either that the student continued to underachieve but simply dropped this one excuse and substituted another one, or else began to achieve in just the one area but not in others. This leads to a possibly lengthy Step 8, which involves repeating Steps 3 to 7 with a different excuse each time. Eventually, the student will run out of excuses and be forced to accept personal responsibility for academic performance.

When this occurs, there may be accompanying reactions such as panic, depression, anxiety, anger, regret, energy toward achievement, confusion, changes in social relationships, or intense introspection. At this point, your role shifts from taking away excuses and pressing for acceptance of responsibility to becoming a supportive, nonjudgmental listener and resource person who helps the student begin to express and struggle with questions such as "Why did I allow myself to get such poor grades?" and "What do I want my future to be?"

Other Strategies

Other sources of advice about coping with under-achievers describe strategies that range between the primarily confrontive approach represented by Mandel and Marcus and the primarily supportive approach that they rejected as ineffective. For example, Blanco and Bogacki culled the following recommendations from school psychologists: peer and cross-age tutoring; contracts that feature collaboration with the student in setting goals and with the parents in withholding or providing performance-contingent rewards; counseling sessions designed to allow underachievers to ventilate their concerns but also to pressure them to accept responsibility for their performance and commit themselves to realistic goals; and requiring the students to make up missed homework assignments during recess or after school.

McIntyre emphasized many of the same strategies, especially contracts and reward systems, collaborative learning with peers, improving performance gradually through successive approximations, and requiring the student to redo shoddy work and complete unfinished work. Other suggestions included:

- small-group cooperative learning methods in which each individual has a unique function to perform (thus creating peer pressure on underachieves to do their part);
- monitoring these students closely and checking back with them frequently to make sure that they stay on task during work times;
- teaching them study habits and self-regulation skills;
- making their work as interesting as possible and helping them to see its current or future application potential, but at the same time making it clear that they have the responsibility to apply themselves to accomplishing all curricular goals (boredom is not a valid excuse);
- letting them do extra credit work in areas of interest;
- discussing their occupational plans and then helping them to see that academic skills are required in those occupations;
- soliciting their suggestions about how you might be helpful to them and following through on those that are feasible.

Thompson and Rudolph developed a similar list and included the following strategies:

increase work production gradually through escalating contracts;

- avoid lecturing, nagging, or threatening;

- where feasible, have underachievers study or at least talk about study habits with a friend who models motivation to learn and conscientious work on assignments;
- reinforce and build on current accomplishments rather than emphasizing past faults and failures;
- structure the students' work by providing clear instructions and identifying specific goals.

References

Abbott, J. (1978). *Classroom strategies to aid the disabled learner*. Cambridge, MA: Educators Publishing Service.

Blanco, R., & Bogacki, D. (1988). *Prescriptions for children with learning and adjustment problems: A consultant's desk reference* (3rd ed.). Springfield, IL: Charles C. Thomas

Brophy, J. (Ed.). (1998). *Advances in research on teaching. Vol. 7: Expectations in the classroom.* Greenwich, CT: JAI Press.

Good, T., & Brophy, J. (2003). *Looking in classrooms* (9th ed.). Boston: Allyn & Bacon.

Levine, D. (1985). *Improving student achievement through mastery learning programs.* San Francisco: Jossey-Bass.

Wlodkowski, R. (1978). *Motivation and teaching: A practical guide.* Washington, DC: National Education Association.

6

Extrinsic Rewards and Motivation

Extrinsic motivation refers to motivation that comes from outside an individual. The motivating factors are external, or outside, rewards such as money or grades. These rewards provide satisfaction and pleasure that the task itself may not provide.

An extrinsically motivated person will work on a task even when they have little interest in it because of the anticipated satisfaction they will get from some reward. The rewards can be something as minor as a smiley face to something major like fame or fortune. For example, an extrinsically motivated person who dislikes math may work hard on a math equation because want the reward for completing it. In the case of a student, the reward would be a good grade on an assignment or in the class.

Extrinsic motivation does not mean, however, that a person will not get any pleasure from working on or completing a task. It just means that the pleasure they anticipate from some external reward will continue to be a motivator even when the task to be done holds little or no interest. An extrinsically motivated student, for example, may dislike an assignment, may find it boring, or may have no interest in the subject, but the possibility of a good grade will be enough to keep the student motivated in order for him or her to put forth the effort to do well on a task.

Grades and acquiring popularity are two sources of extrinsic motivation. Extrinsic motivation is motivation that is rooted in an external stimulus, something that is in the individual's environment. Extrinsic motivation provides the individual satisfaction in performing a task that even if the individual doesn't really like doing it, he or she continues to accomplish the work because of his or her anticipated reward.

Extrinsic motivation has been the fuel of many of man's activities – from education to the workplace. The various types of extrinsic motivation ranging from the more common ones such as money, fame and recognition, awards and prizes, status and privileges to the extreme ones like bribery, threats and punishments have been utilized by man of all ages and sizes, and in different circumstances.

Extrinsic motivation does induce an individual to perform a certain task even if there is no interest in it. But it doesn't mean that the person does not get pleasure from working or completing the task. It's just that the external reward lengthens the duration of the anticipated reward even if interest is long gone.

Value Aspects of Students' Motivation

The expectancy × value model implies the need to attend to the value aspects of students' motivation, not just the expectancy aspects. Otherwise, your students may be asking themselves, "I know I can do this, but where is my motivation?" To be motivated to do something, we need good reasons for doing it, not just confidence that we can do it if we try.

Eccles and Wigfield suggested that subjective task value has three major components: attainment value (the importance of attaining success on the task in order to affirm our self-concept or fulfill our needs for achievement, power, or prestige); intrinsic or interest value (the enjoyment that we get from engaging in the task); and utility value (the role that engaging in the task may play in advancing our career or helping to reach other larger goals). This is a useful classification scheme, but for applications to the classroom we would expand it to place more emphasis on the cognitive aspects of student motivation to learn academic content. A broadened version would include experiencing the satisfaction of achieving understanding or skill mastery under attainment value, aesthetic appreciation of the content or skill under intrinsic value, and awareness of the role of learning in improving the quality of one's life or making one a better person under utility value.

Until recently, research on motivation in education concentrated on its expectancy aspects. Attention to value aspects was needed not only to balance the expectancy × value equation but to broaden the purview from focus on achievement situations that feature relatively specific goals to consideration of the complete range of learning situations. Principles drawn from attribution theory, self-efficacy theory, and even goal theory apply most clearly to achievement situations that call for some particular performance that will be evaluated with reference to relatively specific success criteria. In contrast, theories dealing with the value aspects of motivation apply not only to these achievement situations but also to self-guided exploration and discovery learning, curricular enrichment activities, interest-driven reading done in or out of school, and other activities that offer opportunities for learning but do not necessarily involve striving to accomplish a particular goal.

The expectancy aspects of motivation feature beliefs about performance attainment (Can I succeed on this task? Why did I achieve the level of success that I did?). In contrast, the value aspects feature beliefs about the reasons for engaging in the task in the first place (Why should I care about this activity? What benefits will I obtain from engaging in it?). Traditionally, teachers have been advised to supply answers to the latter questions either by offering incentives for good performance (extrinsic motivation approach) or by teaching content and designing activities that students find enjoyable (intrinsic motivation approach).

Common Beliefs About Rewards

To begin thinking about the effects of extrinsic incentives, consider Students A and B: A and B are both fourth graders who enjoy and do well in school, although they approach school and relate to their teachers in different ways. For example, B did all this week's reading on the solar system knowing that completing assignments pleases the teacher. B made a couple of points during class discussion so the teacher would know B had done the reading. A also finished the reading because A got really interested in knowing all about the solar system. A continued to ask questions during the discussion, even after some of the other kids seemed tired of the topic. Since A knows grades don't always reflect work quality, A isn't that interested in grades and doesn't pay much attention to them, but B pays close attention to grades and uses them as a gauge by which to judge how B has been doing on recent work....

Given this information, how would you rate Students A and B in basic ability, degree of responsibility as students, or overall effort in school work? Which student would exert greater effort following failure? Which would show enhanced performance following success?

Barrett and Boggiano put these questions to groups of parents and college students. They found that the majority of both groups believed that extrinsically motivated Student B would exert more effort after failure, show enhanced performance following success, exert more overall effort in school work, and take more responsibility for completing work than intrinsically motivated Student A. However, they believed that B would have lower self-esteem than A. Only the last belief is supported by research comparing extrinsically and intrinsically motivated students.

This was one of a series of studies by Ann Boggiano and her colleagues on adults' beliefs about factors that motivate children. In other studies, they presented descriptions of students displaying either high or low intrinsic interest in various academic activities, then asked parents or college students to rate how effective they thought each of four social control techniques (rewards, reasoning, punishment, or noninterference) would be for maximizing the student's enjoyment or interest in the depicted activity. Both groups of adults rated rewards as more effective than the other three strategies, both short-term and long-term, regardless of the students' depicted levels of interest in the activity. They also believed that larger rewards would be more effective than smaller rewards. Studies in this series repeatedly confirmed that most adults believe that rewards are effective, not only as incentives for motivating students to put forth effort on academic activities, but also for stimulating their development of intrinsic interest in these activities.

Extrinsic Rewards in Education

In some respects, extrinsic motivation strategies are the simplest, most direct, and most adaptable of the methods for addressing the value aspects of motivation. These strategies do not attempt to increase the value that students place on the task itself. Instead, they link successful completion of the task to delivery of consequences that students already do value. By reminding students that successful completion is instrumental to accomplishment of some valued goal (where this contingency exists naturally) or by establishing an incentive system that offers extrinsic rewards contingent on successful completion, you can spur students to invest more effort in the task than they might invest otherwise. Rewards are one proven way to spur students to put forth effort.

However, from the standpoint of most motivational theorists, this is control of behavior, not motivation of learning. Some educators have always opposed extrinsic motivational methods on principle, viewing them as bribing students for doing what they should be doing anyway because it is the right thing to do or because it is in the best interests of themselves or of society.

Research findings that emerged during the 1970s and 1980s provided what appeared to be strong support for opponents of extrinsic rewards. These findings indicated that if you begin to reward people for doing what they already were doing for their own reasons, you may decrease their intrinsic motivation to continue that behavior in the future. Furthermore, to the extent that you focus their attention on the reward rather than on the task, their performance tends to deteriorate. They develop a minimax or piecework mentality, doing whatever will garner them the most rewards with the least effort, rather than trying to do the job as well as they can in order to create a high quality product. If allowed to choose, they select tasks that will maximize their access to rewards over tasks that offer more challenge or opportunities for them to develop their knowledge or skills (or over the longer run, choose "easy A" high school courses over more demanding courses so as to preserve high cumulative grade point averages).

For a time, it was thought that these undesirable outcomes were inherent in the use of rewards. Later work clarified that the effects of rewards depend on what rewards are used and especially on how they are presented. Decreases in performance quality and in intrinsic motivation are most likely when rewards have the following characteristics:

1. *High salience* (the rewards are very attractive or are presented in ways that call attention to them)
2. *Noncontingency* (the rewards are given for mere participation in the activity, rather than being contingent on achieving specific goals)
3. *Unnatural/unusual* (the rewards are artificially tied to behaviors as control devices, rather than being natural outcomes of the behaviors)

Attempts to use rewards to motivate students often violate these guidelines. For example, a well-known program that supplies free pizzas to students who read a certain number of books has all three of the aforementioned characteristics. Pizzas are very attractive rewards to most children, the program artificially makes reading a certain number of books instrumental to receiving the pizzas, and the pizzas are awarded merely for certifying that the required number of books have been read (not for reading them carefully, responding to them thoughtfully, or taking something meaningful away from the experience). This contingency could undermine students' intrinsic motivation to read because it implies that their behavior is controlled externally—that they are reading the books only because they must do so in order to earn pizzas. It might encourage them to select short, simple books, zip through them quickly, and move on to the next one.

Reinforcement and Behavior Modification

This is because these methods are conceived and implemented as behavioral control strategies rather than as motivation strategies. They work by making desired behavior (e.g., careful and persistent work on assignments) instrumental to attainment of contingent extrinsic rewards, usually by making this contingency explicit to students in advance. Heavy emphasis on these behavioral control techniques, and in particular, use of a token economy or some other earned-credits incentive system as one's basic approach to classroom management, is in many respects incompatible with the strategies that have emerged from research on motivation in education. As Reeve noted, motivation is not about principles of operant conditioning or behavior management; it is about how students' inner resources energize and direct their behavior.

You will need to make a fundamental choice between emphasizing a behavioral control system or a student motivational system as your basic approach to classroom management and motivational issues. The two general approaches are not completely incompatible, so if you choose one as your basic approach you can still supplement it with selected strategies drawn from the other. You cannot implement each approach fully, however, because there are too many contradictions. First, although it is more difficult to learn to implement consistently, the motivational approach is nevertheless more feasible for most teachers. In order to use reinforcement to shape students' behavior in ways that reflect consistent application of behavior modification principles, teachers have to be in position to supply reinforcement when and where it is needed. This is not possible in regular classrooms where teachers work with 20 or more students, although it may be possible in special classrooms with very low student-to-teacher ratios. Even here, though, it will require heavy reliance on programmed instructional materials, rather than tutoring or small-group instruction from the teacher, as the primary approach to curriculum and instruction (thus leaving the teacher free to circulate, monitor progress, and dispense rewards). A great deal of classroom research suggests that students need active instruction from their teachers, not solitary work with instructional materials, in order to make good achievement progress.

Second, the motivational approach seems clearly preferable to the behavioral control approach when students' long-run best interests are taken into account. Even when behavioral control methods work effectively, they accomplish only temporary, situational, and external control over students' behavior. Their behavior can and often does change drastically when the incentive system is terminated or when the students are in situations in which the system is not operative. In contrast, motivational approaches are designed not just to induce situational compliance in students but to develop attitudes, values, beliefs, and self-regulated learning strategies that they will use in appropriate learning situations in and out of school throughout their lives. To the extent that the motivational approach is successful in developing these self-regulation orientations and capacities in students, it yields desirable outcomes that generalize far beyond the immediate classroom situation.

Note, however, that it advocates using these strategies in ways that deemphasize their behavioral control aspects to make them compatible with more purely motivational strategies. In particular, the suggestions call for encouraging students to commit themselves to challenging yet realistic goals and helping students to appreciate their progress and accomplishments, while avoiding placing too much emphasis on reinforcement contingencies or salient rewards.

Undermining Intrinsic Motivation

Research on ways in which extrinsic considerations can undermine intrinsic motivation initially focused on rewards offered as incentives, and explanations for the undermining effect focused on people's attributional inferences. In fact, an early term for this undermining was the overjustification effect: To the extent that people become aware that they are being "bribed" to engage in a particular behavior, they are likely to infer that such bribing is considered necessary because they are not expected to engage in the behavior voluntarily. That is, the opportunity to engage in the behavior is not sufficient justification for doing so, and therefore extra incentives must be added. This line of reasoning leads to the conclusion that the overjustified behavior is aversive, or at least not worth performing in the absence of an extrinsic incentive to do so. This inference would undermine any intrinsic motivation for performing the behavior that might have been present originally.

As research findings accumulated, it became clear that this undermining effect can occur not only when people are offered rewards for engaging in a behavior, but whenever they become aware of any extrinsic factor that leads them to attribute their engaging in the behavior to external pressures rather than to their own intrinsic motivation. Other examples include awareness that the behavior is required (with expressed or at least implied threat of punishment if it is not performed), that one's performance is being monitored closely, that one's performance will be evaluated or compared to that of others, or that one is under pressure to meet a time deadline. Therefore, what undermines intrinsic motivation is not the use of rewards as such but offering rewards in advance as incentives and following through in ways that lead students to believe that they engaged in the rewarded behaviors only because they had to do so in order to earn the rewards, not because these behaviors have value in their own right or produce other outcomes that are in the students' best interests.

Pintrich, Marx, and Boyle noted that students often are in situations where multiple incentives or goals are operating. For example, students may have intrinsic interest in a topic or activity, may also value learning about it because such learning is important to their future career plans, and furthermore may be aware of the need to display their learning by meeting certain performance standards that will enable them to get acceptable grades. The important thing is to see that these and any other motivational influences that might be operating work in such a way as to encourage students to "think it through" rather than just to "get it done."

As the research accumulated, it became clear that attempts to address questions about the appropriate use of rewards requires attention to the nature of the rewards, the ways in which they are introduced and delivered, and the student outcomes under consideration. Rewards can be verbal or tangible, large or small, and salient or nonsalient. They can be given simply for participating in an activity (engagement-dependent), for completing the activity (completion-dependent), or for not only completing the activity but doing so in a way that fulfills some criterion for performance (performance-dependent). Effects of rewards might be considered with respect to immediate task effort or performance, changes in attitudes toward the task (e.g., finding it interesting), or changes in subsequent intrinsic motivation to perform the task voluntarily when future opportunities arise.

Using these kinds of distinctions, Eisenberger and Cameron performed a meta-analysis of existing research and concluded that verbal rewards have positive effects on motivation but tangible rewards sometimes have negative effects (when they are given merely for participation in the activity without attention to quality of engagement or level of performance, and even then, only when the students expected the rewards because they had been announced in advance). Eisenberger and Cameron claimed that the supposedly harmful effects of rewards had been overstated, and advised use of verbal rewards and performance-dependent tangible rewards.

The same authors subsequently published another meta-analysis and interpreted the results as showing that:

- Rewarding people for performing a task will increase their perceived self-determination, because the reward is a signal that the offerer does not control the person and thus the person is voluntarily accepting an invitation when agreeing to perform the task;
- the effects of reward on other aspects of intrinsic motivation are mostly positive or neutral;
- these effects depend mostly on the nature of the performance requirement.

Vague or minimal standards have negative effects because they indicate that the reward offerer doesn't care much about the task or considers it trivial, but specific and high standards have positive effects because they indicate that the offerer cares about the task or considers it important. They concluded that there is no reason for concern about using rewards with low-interest tasks, but that with high-interest tasks it is important to link delivery of rewards to accomplishment of specific (preferably challenging) performance criteria.

Eisenberger, Cameron, and their behaviorist colleagues represent one side of the argument, claiming that the concern about rewards undermining intrinsic motivation has been mostly a false alarm. The other side has been represented by Deci, Ryan, Lepper, and other investigators whose work has focused on intrinsic motivation. They criticize the meta-analyses just described, suggesting that they produced misleading conclusions because the authors were inappropriately selective in deciding which studies to include, they collapsed into the same categories several types of studies that should have been treated separately, they failed to distinguish between studies that used dull tasks and studies that used more interesting tasks, and they gave special attention to experimental studies that used artificial reward procedures that could not be applied in classrooms (e.g., telling participants that they would be rewarded only if their performance exceeded that of 80% of their peers, but in fact rewarding all of those who had been assigned to the "reward" group).

In support of their position, Deci, Koestner, and Ryan cited three previous meta-analyses all indicating that expected tangible rewards undermine intrinsic motivation for engaging in an interesting activity, regardless of whether these rewards are contingent upon doing, completing, or excelling at the activity. They also reported findings from the largest meta-analysis done to date, subsuming results from 128 studies. This analysis also indicated that expected tangible rewards undermine intrinsic motivation, whether those rewards are engagement-contingent, completion-contingent, or even performance-contingent. In fact, the most detrimental type of performance-contingent reward was the one in which the size of the reward is a direct function of the level of one's performance. This is the reward system most commonly used in applied settings, including school grading practices.

Rewards had strong negative effects on subsequent intrinsic motivation to engage in interesting tasks, but no significant effects on subsequent intrinsic motivation to engage in uninteresting tasks. Verbal rewards (positive feedback or praise) enhanced intrinsic motivation when they were primarily informational but decreased it when they were primarily controlling. The positive effects of verbal rewards were found primarily among college students, whereas the detrimental effects of tangible rewards were noticed primarily with children.

These authors concluded that although rewards can control behavior, they tend to forestall self-regulation because they undermine people's taking responsibility for motivating or regulating themselves. They suggested that verbal rewards can be used effectively if they are delivered in an informational rather than a controlling manner, and that tangible rewards might not be harmful if given occasionally and unexpectedly (rather than being announced in advance as reinforcers contingent upon attaining specified performance levels). Making rewards more informational requires minimizing authoritarian or pressuring language when presenting or delivering the rewards; acknowledging good performance but not using the rewards as re-inforcers to control behavior; providing opportunities for choice about how to do the tasks; and emphasizing the interesting or challenging aspects of tasks rather than treating them as work that must be completed.

Houlfort et al. introduced a further distinction that helps to understand why the two groups of researchers have generated seemingly conflicting findings. They noted that Deci and Ryan measured autonomy by asking people if they felt pressured in the situation, whereas Eisenberger and his colleagues measured autonomy by asking them if they felt free to choose to do something other than what the experimenter was asking them to do in exchange for a reward. In two new studies of the effects of performance-contingent rewards ($5 if performance met criteria), they measured both aspects of autonomy. They found that performance-contingent rewards increased people's perception of competence (because being given the reward indicated that they had done well on the task); had negative effects on the affective aspects of autonomy (feeling pressured); and had no effect on the decisional aspect of autonomy (feeling free to decline the offer and do something else instead). Thus, the results support Eisenberger and Cameron's claims that performance-contingent rewards enhance competence perceptions and support (or at least, do not undermine) autonomy perceptions in that they leave it up to the person whether or not to accept the invitation to pursue the reward. However, they also support Deci and Ryan's claim that such rewards undermine autonomy perceptions in that they make the person feel pressured to perform.

Ryan et al. extended this controversy from specific situations to general dispositions by studying relationships between the prominence of people's goals and their levels of life satisfaction. They reported that people in several countries tend to express greater overall satisfaction with their lives if their most prominent goals and aspirations are primarily intrinsic (relatedness, helpfulness to others, physical health, self-acceptance) rather than extrinsic (money, fame, social attractiveness to others). Ryan and Deci claimed that our culture has become strongly reward-oriented, leading away from our interests and desires for challenge, and toward a narrow instrumental focus. They added that over time, neglecting important needs in order to focus on pursuing rewards will be perceived as coercive and alienating, at cost to our well-being.

The Use of Rewards

This ongoing debate has been lively and the research connected with it has been informative. We now realize that the issues involved are much more complicated than they seemed at first. Both sides have put forth valid arguments, although unfortunately most of these concern the weaknesses in the other side's position rather than clear guidelines for using rewards in the classroom. Intrinsic motivation theorists are correct in raising concerns about overuse or inappropriate use of rewards, and in claiming that in classrooms it is difficult to reward students in ways that

(a) take into account their individual learning efforts and progress and

(b) avoid communicating the idea that they engage in academic activities merely to obtain the rewards rather than to learn what the activities are intended to teach.

However, behaviorists are correct in claiming that rewards can be used effectively in classrooms and in pointing out that the motivational problems facing teachers primarily involve getting students to put forth consistent learning efforts whether or not they find the learning tasks interesting or enjoyable, not just maintaining intrinsic motivation to engage in interesting tasks. That is, motivating students is mostly about fostering identified regulation, not preserving existing intrinsic motivation.

What about those corporate-sponsored programs that offer students coupons for pizzas or other rewards in exchange for reading a specified number of books? These programs have been excoriated by Kohn, and reading incentive programs in general have been criticized as violating important principles of motivation theory and literacy engagement. Because self-reported interest is one measure of intrinsic motivation, it appears that fears that this program would undermine intrinsic motivation for reading were unfounded. On the other hand, the data also indicated that the millions of dollars that the corporation spent implementing (and publicizing) this program did not yield positive results.

Such findings apparently are to be expected: McQuillan reviewed 10 studies of school and library reading encouragement programs that included incentives for reading, and found that five had at least some positive results and five did not. However, none of the positive effects could be attributed clearly to the incentives. McQuillan concluded that no clear causal relationship had yet been established between reading incentives and reading attitudes, achievement, or habits.

Classrooms are given 60 to 80 high-quality children's literature books (selected by the teacher), the students choose which 21 books they will read or listen to, and family members and older students participate by listening to the first graders read or by reading to them. Participants in the program showed increased reading motivation and activity relative to a control group.

We infer from this controversy that the key to rewarding effectively is to do so in ways that support students' motivation to learn and do not encourage them to conclude that they engage in academic activities only to earn rewards. For example, if students are offered rewards simply for participating in a reading incentive program or are offered significant prizes for reading 100 books, the students might well begin to view reading as drudgery and expect to be rewarded if they agree to do it. This approach is similar to other methods (e.g., science fairs where students demonstrate achievements to an interested audience) that allow students to enjoy public recognition for significant accomplishments.

In conclusion, extrinsic rewards do not necessarily undermine intrinsic motivation and even can be used in ways that support its development. One way is to provide unannounced rewards following task completion, so that the rewards are seen as expressions of appreciation or recognitions of accomplishment rather than as delivery of promised incentives. Other ways involve using rewards as informative feedback rather than as control mechanisms. It also helps to emphasize social rewards over material rewards and to deliver rewards in ways that encourage students to value the accomplishments being rewarded.

Strategies for Rewarding Students

Most teachers want to reward their students' praiseworthy efforts and accomplishments. They find it natural to do so in the process of building good relationships with students and encouraging and supporting their learning efforts. Types of rewards commonly used by teachers include material rewards (money, prizes, trinkets, consumables); activity rewards and special privileges (opportunities to play games, use special equipment, or engage in self-selected activities); grades, awards, and recognitions (honor rolls, displaying good papers); praise and social rewards; and teacher rewards (special attention, personalized interaction, opportunities to go places or do things with the teacher).

If you enjoy rewarding your students in one or more of these ways, you do not need to stop doing so for fear of undermining their intrinsic motivation. It is now clear that intrinsic motivation and extrinsic motivation are relatively independent, so that students in a given situation can be high in both or low in both, not just high in one and low in the other. It also is clear that rewards can be used in ways that support or at least do not undermine intrinsic motivation. However, it is important that you learn when and how to dispense rewards effectively, to ensure that your rewards have only positive and not mixed or even negative effects.

When to Reward

Rewards are more effective for increasing the intensity or duration of effort than for improving the quality of performance. They support learning more effectively when there is a clear goal and a clear strategy to follow than when goals are more ambiguous or when students must discover or invent new strategies rather than merely activate familiar ones. Therefore, rewards are better used with routine tasks than with novel ones, better with specific intentional learning tasks than with incidental learning or discovery tasks, and better with tasks where steady performance or quantity of output is of more concern than creativity, artistry, or craftsmanship.

It is better to offer rewards as incentives for meeting performance improvement standards on skills that require a great deal of drill and practice (arithmetic computation, musical scales, typing, spelling, free-throw shooting) than it is for work on a major research or demonstration project. With low-level tasks that demand rote learning, no other source of motivation may be operating, so rewards may be needed to motivate sustained effort (although a more basic strategy is to minimize students' encounters with such boring or aversive tasks).

It is not wise to offer rewards as primary incentives to motivate students to do things that you want them to continue to do on their own, such as watch educational television programs, read quality books, or participate in civic affairs or community improvement efforts. However, rewards may be helpful when initial level of interest in the activity is low or its value becomes apparent only through engaging in it for a long time or only after the learner has reached a critical level of mastery.

Rewards can act as motivators only for those students who believe that they have a chance to get the rewards if they put forth reasonable effort. Traditional grading systems and other commonly used school reward practices (e.g., multiple levels of honors) violate this principle routinely. Remember, if you wish to create incentives for the whole class and not just your high achievers, you will need to ensure that all students have equal (or at least reasonable) access to the rewards. This may require performance contracting or some less formal method of individualizing criteria for success.

For example, MacIver and Reuman described an incentives program in which students were rewarded either for maintaining high performance or for improving less satisfactory performance. Each week, students attempted to beat their current "base score" on the week's most important quiz, test, project, assignment, or performance task. They were rewarded according to the "improvement points" they earned.

Midgley and Urdan offered useful suggestions about the kinds of accomplishments that you might emphasize in providing students with recognitions or other symbolic rewards. First, recognize the quality of students' accomplishments rather than the quantity, and in particular, recognize students for taking on challenging work or stretching their abilities (even if they make mistakes). Also, recognize them for coming up with different or unusual ways to solve problems. These priorities give powerful messages about what is valued in your classroom.

Use multiple criteria that allow you to adapt your recognitions to individual differences, rather than using the same criteria for all students and thus ending up comparing them directly. However, make sure that your recognitions are for genuine accomplishments (given what is reasonable to expect from the student). Finally, although you may want to provide recognition to students in a variety of domains (athletics, good citizenship, etc.), make sure that every student has the opportunity to earn recognition in the academic domain.

How to Reward

Deliver rewards in ways that provide students with informative feedback and encourage them to appreciate their developing knowledge and skills, not just to think about the rewards. If you offer rewards in advance as incentives, emphasize your major instructional goals in setting criteria for judging performance and determining reward credits. Reward students for mastering key ideas and skills (or showing improvement in their mastery levels), not merely for participating in activities or turning in assignments. Include provisions for redoing work that does not meet minimum standards.

In explaining and following through on incentive systems, emphasize the importance of the learning and help students to appreciate and take pride in their accomplishments. Portray the rewards as verifications of significant and worthwhile achievements, not as the whole point of their efforts. This is less crucial with surprise rewards not announced in advance as incentives, but even when delivering surprise rewards it is wise to cast them as expressions of appreciation for your students' efforts and accomplishments, without making too much of the "big surprise."

These guidelines focus on praising students in ways that emphasize providing them with informative feedback rather than exercising control over their behavior. Most of what is said about praise also applies to other forms of rewards, and in particular, to what you might say to students in the process of delivering the rewards.

Praising your Students Effectively

Most teachers enjoy delivering praise and most students enjoy receiving it, at least when it is delivered as a spontaneous, genuine reaction to an accomplishment rather than as part of a calculated manipulation attempt. Praise is widely recommended as a way to reward students, although it does not always have this effect. Sometimes a teacher's praise is not even intended as a reward for a specific accomplishment, as when the praise is used in an attempt to build a social relationship with an alienated student ("I like your new shirt, John.").

Even when praise is intended as a reward, some students will not perceive it that way. For one thing, some students do not attach much value to teacher praise and thus do not feel particularly rewarded when they receive it. Also, many students appreciate praise that is communicated in private but are less enthused about being praised in front of their classmates.

Students may find it embarrassing to be singled out, humiliating to be praised for some minor accomplishment, or irritating to have classmates' attention called to their neatness, punctuality, or conformity behaviors rather than to more clearly noteworthy achievements. For example, a teacher's statement that "I like the way Susie is sitting up straight and ready to listen" is almost certain to embarrass Susie. It may even alienate her if she is sophisticated enough to realize that the statement is not really praise of her but an attempt to cue the behaviors of some of her classmates.

As related examples, consider the following expressions of teacher praise: "John, I really enjoyed your story, especially the machine that converts peanut butter into energy. I'd like you to read it to the class later today. Also, how about drawing a picture of what that machine might look like?... Mary, you did a fine job. I especially liked the way you wrote your story so neatly—centered headings, no smudges, writing carefully on the lines—keep up the good work!"

In these examples, the teacher's praise of John's work focuses on its substance and is likely to be appreciated because it identifies genuinely noteworthy accomplishments. By drawing attention to a particular detail of John's story, the teacher shows that she has paid attention to its content and appreciates its creativity. In contrast, her praise of Mary's work focuses on form and neatness rather than its substantive content or the creativity of her writing. She did not mention any of the particulars of Mary's story or even give any clear indication that she remembered any of it. Although well intended and apparently sincere, such praise is unlikely to be pleasing to Mary because it will cause her to suspect that the teacher did not like her story or does not think highly of her writing abilities.

Public praise can be problematic even when it is recognized as praise and appreciated as such both by the recipient and by classmates. Students who are eager for teacher attention may begin clamoring for it, and students who believe that they are just as deserving as classmates who have been praised may begin to feel slighted.

Praise should be informative and appreciative rather than controlling. Sometimes this is easier said than done. As Kohn observed, "... the most notable aspect of a positive judgment is not that it is positive but that it is a judgment ". Therefore, it is important to phrase praise statements as communication of informative feedback rather than as evaluation. Effective praise expresses appreciation for students' efforts or admiration for their accomplishments, in ways that call attention to the efforts or accomplishments themselves rather than to their role in pleasing the teacher. This helps students learn to attribute their efforts to their own intrinsic motivation rather than to external incentives supplied by the teacher, and to attribute their successes to their own abilities and efforts rather than to external supports. You might express such praise as part of a "celebration" of what has been learned or accomplished as you bring a unit or series of activities to closure.

Effective praise is genuine. Brophy and Evertson found that teachers were credible and spontaneous when praising students whom they liked, often smiling as they spoke and praising genuine accomplishments. These teachers praised students whom they disliked just as frequently, but usually without accompanying spontaneity and warmth and often with reference to appearance or conduct rather than accomplishments.

Some teachers praise poor responses as part of a well-intentioned attempt to encourage low achievers. This tactic often backfires, however, because it undermines the teacher's credibility and confuses or depresses the students (to the extent that they realize that they are being treated differently from their classmates). For example, students who notice they are frequently praised for minor accomplishments (e.g., answering a relatively routine question or completing an easy task) may infer that the teacher does not have much confidence in their abilities or potential. Students generally prefer private, quietly delivered praise to public, loudly delivered praise, and praise for their academic accomplishments to praise for their good conduct.

Even when praising significant achievements, it is better to focus on the effort and care that the student put into the work, on the gains in knowledge or skills that the achievement represents, or on the achievement's more noteworthy features than to portray the achievement as evidence of the student's intelligence or aptitude. The problem with the latter kind of praise is that it creates vulnerabilities for catastrophic reactions to failure in the future. Students who become accustomed to interpreting successes as evidence of high aptitude in a domain (e.g., mathematics) will also tend to interpret difficulties or failures as evidence of lack of aptitude. This makes them vulnerable to developing learned helplessness beliefs.

Students need informative feedback to support their learning efforts, but they do not need more intensive expressions of praise. Correlations between teachers' rates of praise and their students' achievement gains are low in magnitude and mixed in direction, suggesting that the most effective teachers are sparing rather than effusive in their praise. Keep this in mind when deciding when and how to praise students.

1. Praise simply and directly, in a natural voice, without gushing or dramatizing.
2. Praise in straightforward, declarative sentences ("I never thought of that before") instead of gushy exclamations ("Wow!") or rhetorical questions ("Isn't that terrific!"). The latter are condescending and more likely to embarrass than reward.
3. Specify the particular accomplishment being praised and recognize any noteworthy effort, care, or perseverance ("Good! You figured it out all by yourself. I like the way you stuck with it without giving up" instead of "Good work"). Call attention to new skills or evidence of progress ("I notice you've learned to use different kinds of metaphors in your compositions. They're more interesting to read now.").
4. Use a variety of phrases for praising students. Overused stock phrases soon begin to sound insincere and give the impression that you have not paid much attention to the accomplishments you are praising.
5. Combine verbal praise with nonverbal communication of approval. "Good job!" is much more rewarding when delivered with a smile and a tone that communicates appreciation or warmth.
6. Avoid ambiguous statements that students may take as praise for compliance rather than for learning (e.g., "You were really good today"). Instead, be specific in praising their accomplishments ("I'm very pleased with your reading this morning, especially the way you read with so much expression. You made the conversation between Billy and Mr. Taylor sound very real.").
7. *Ordinarily, students should be praised privately.* This underscores that the praise is genuine and avoids the problem of sounding as though you are holding the student up as an example to the rest of the class.

Wlodkowski summarized many of these same principles in his "3S–3P" guidelines: Praise (or other rewards) should be Sincere, Specific, Sufficient (adapted to the accomplishment), and Properly attributed for genuinely Praiseworthy accomplishments, in a manner Preferred by the learner.

Henderlong and Lepper completed a meta-analysis of the research on praise and verified many of the principles suggested by Brophy. In particular, they concluded that praise enhances intrinsic motivation and increases perseverance when it is perceived as sincere, encourages adaptive performance attributions, promotes perceived autonomy, provides information about competence without relying heavily on social comparisons, and conveys standards and expectations that are realistic for the student.

Capitalizing on Existing Extrinsic Rewards

Often it is possible to make students aware of naturally existing extrinsic incentives for mastering academic content or skills instead of offering them artificial rewards for doing so. A good curriculum is constructed as a means rather than an end in itself, so that all of its components are intended as vehicles for moving students toward outcomes that will enrich their lives and equip them to function successfully in our society. At least in theory, it is in a student's best interest to engage in any academic activity seriously and complete it successfully, so as to obtain the benefits that it was designed to yield. However, school activities differ in the degree to which their life application potential is immediate and obvious to students. Some knowledge and skills taught in school can be applied in the students' current lives or obviously will be needed as "life skills" later. These natural consequences of task mastery can be powerful incentives for motivating learning efforts. Therefore, whenever you see the opportunity to do so, help your students to appreciate that the knowledge or skills developed by an activity are useful in enabling them to meet their own current needs, providing them with a "ticket" to social advancement, or preparing them for occupational or other success in life. In the process, cite examples by relating your own personal experiences or telling anecdotes about individuals with whom your students can identify (such as famous people that they look up to or former students from your school).

The strategy of calling students' attention to the life application value of what they are learning is not used as often as it could be, and when it is, it is often used in self-defeating ways. Rather than stress the present or future application value of what is being learned in positive terms, many teachers only mention negative outcomes that may result from failure to learn it. These include personal embarrassment ("You don't want people to think you are ignorant") or future educational or occupational disasters ("You'll never get through the sixth grade"; "How are you going to get a job if you can't do basic math?"). Other teachers use variations that cast the student in a more positive light but portray society as a hostile environment (urging students to learn to count so that merchants don't shortchange them or to learn to read so that they don't get cheated when signing contracts).

Rather than distract your students with such worries, be more positive as you help them appreciate the potential applications of what they are learning. Basic language arts and mathematics skills are used daily when shopping, banking, driving, reading instructions for using some product, paying bills, carrying on business correspondence, and planning home maintenance projects or family vacations. Scientific knowledge is useful for everything from coping effectively with minor everyday challenges to making good decisions in emergency situations. Knowledge of history and related social studies topics provides a basis for making personal, social, and civic decisions. In general, a good working knowledge of the information, principles, and skills taught in school prepares people to make well-informed decisions that can save time, trouble, expense, or even lives. It also empowers people by preparing them to appreciate and take advantage of the opportunities that society offers.

Help your students to recognize such connections between classroom learning and life outside of school, so that they come to see academic activities as enabling opportunities to be valued rather than as unwelcome impositions. More generally, help your students to appreciate that schools are established by society for their benefit. In this regard, you might note that the educational opportunities that we take for granted in our country are avail-able only to the privileged few in many countries. Do not preach to your students or make them feel guilty, but do heighten their awareness of education as opportunity and underscore the idea that conscientious learning efforts are in their own best interests, not just duties that they must perform in order to please you or their parents.

Competition

The opportunity to compete can add excitement to classroom activities, whether the competition is for prizes or merely for the satisfaction of winning. Competition may be either individual (students compete in pairs or as individuals working against everyone else) or group (students are divided into teams that compete with one another or the class competes with other classes). Traditionally, competitions have been structured around test scores or other performance measures, but it also is possible to build competitive elements into ordinary instruction by including activities such as argumentative essays, debates, or simulation games that involve competition. In fact, debates or other activities that encourage students to develop conflicting positions rather than seek concurrences can have both motivation and learning benefits, although it is important to make sure that the discourse remains constructive and focused on the topic.

Despite its popularity among many teachers and its considerable motivational potential, most motivational theorists oppose the use of competition or place heavy qualifications on its applicability as a motivational strategy. There are several good reasons for this.

First, participating in classroom activities already involves risking public failure and a great deal of competition is already built into the grading system. Therefore, it may be counterproductive to introduce additional competitive elements.

Second, competition is even more salient and distracting than rewards for most students. For example, Ames and Ames found that students working on their own tended to evaluate their progress with reference to their prior performance, noting and appreciating developments in knowledge and skill. In contrast, students working in competitive structures were so focused on comparisons and winning/losing that they paid little attention to what they were supposed to be learning.

Third, involvement in competitions is more coercive than motivational when participation is mandatory. This is all the more true when the games and rules are imposed by authority figures and high stakes are attached to the outcomes.

Fourth, the qualifications that apply to the use of rewards as incentives also apply to competition. In particular, competition is more appropriate for use with routine practice tasks than with tasks calling for discovery or creativity, and it can be effective only if everyone has a good (or at least an equal) chance of winning. To ensure this, it may be necessary to use team competition in which the teams are balanced by ability profiles or to use individual competition in which a handicapping system enables each student to compete with his or her own previous performance rather than with classmates.

Finally, a root problem with competition is that it creates losers as well as winners (and usually many more losers than winners). Even when there is no rational reason for it, a loser's psychology tends to develop whenever individuals or teams lose competitions. Individuals may suffer at least temporary embarrassment, and those who lose consistently may suffer more permanent losses in confidence, self-esteem, and enjoyment of school. Members of losing teams may devalue one another and scapegoat those whom they hold responsible for the team's loss.

In combination, these considerations should give you pause about introducing competition as a motivational strategy. If you are thinking about doing so, plan to minimize its risks by making sure that all students have an equal chance to win, that winning is determined primarily by degree of effort (and perhaps a degree of luck) rather than by level ability, that attention is focused more on the task than on who wins and who loses, and that reactions to the outcome emphasize the positive (winners are congratulated but losers are not criticized or ridiculed; the accomplishments of the class as a whole, not just of the winners, are acknowledged).

There are ways to depersonalize competition. For example, you might divide the class into several teams and ask each team to develop a campaign speech based on specified criteria. Next, the class would use these criteria to critique the speeches. Then, each team would take the best features from all of the initial versions and produce an improved speech that represents the class's best thinking. This series of activities involves competitive elements, but it focuses on the content rather than the competition.

Student Team Learning Methods

One way to exploit the motivational potential of competition while avoiding most of its undesirable effects is to use student team learning methods in which students cooperate in addition to competing. These methods feature both a handicapping system to supply individual criteria for scoring each student's work and an incentive system that offers group rewards to teams whose combined individual scores enable them to win competitions against other teams.

Teams–Games–Tournament (TGT)

The original student team learning method was called Teams–Games–Tournament (TGT). In TGT, students work together in four- or five-member heterogeneously composed teams to help one another master content and prepare for competitions against other teams. The teacher first presents the material to be learned, then team members work together filling out worksheets. They discuss the material, tutor one another, and quiz one another to assess mastery. These forms of cooperative learning continue throughout the week in preparation for tournaments held on Fridays.

For the tournaments, students are assigned to three-person tables composed of students from different teams who are similar in achievement level. The three students compete at academic games covering the content taught that week and practiced during team meetings. Most of these games are simply numbered questions on a handout. A student draws a number card and attempts to answer the corresponding question. Students can earn points by responding to questions correctly or by successfully challenging and correcting the answers of the other two students at the table. These points are later summed to determine each team's score, and the teacher prepares a newsletter that recognizes successful teams and unusually high scores attained by individuals. The newsletter may also contain cumulative team scores if tournaments last longer than one week.

Prior to the next tournament, the teacher may assign certain students to different tournament tables in order to keep the competition at each table as even as possible. This ensures that even though the teams are heterogeneous in composition and team membership remains the same, all students begin each tournament with an equal chance to earn points for their teams because they are competing against peers whose achievement levels are similar to theirs. This incentive structure motivates students not only to master the material on their own but also to help their teammates master it.

Student Teams-Achievement Divisions (STAD)

Student Teams-Achievement Divisions (STAD) is a simplification of TGT. STAD follows the same heterogeneous grouping and cooperative learning procedures as TGT but replaces the games and tournaments with a quiz. Quiz scores are translated into team competition points based on how much students have improved their performance over past averages.

Both TGT and STAD combine cooperative learning with team competition and use group rewards for cumulative individual performance. However, STAD depersonalizes the competition. Rather than compete face-to-face against classmates at tournament tables, students in STAD classrooms try to do their best on quizzes taken individually. STAD is generally consid-ered an improvement on TGT because it is easier to implement and it reduces the salience of the competition.

Jigsaw II

Jigsaw II is an adaptation of the original Jigsaw, a cooperative learning method that ensures that students interact with and learn from one another because each team member possesses unique information that must be communicated to the others. Jigsaw II combines competitive elements with these cooperative elements. Students begin by reading a narrative to provide them with a common base of information. Then, to develop the material, each member of a team is given a separate topic on which to become an expert. Students from different teams who have been assigned to the same topic meet in "expert groups" to discuss their topics. Then they return to their teams to teach what they have learned to their teammates.

Except for the topic on which they have become expert, students must depend on their classmates to provide them with information that is not included in the base narrative. Furthermore, as team members, students have responsibilities not only to master the material themselves but to teach it effectively to teammates so that all team members can be successful in the competition. At the end of the week, students take a quiz, their individual scores are summed to compute team scores, and team accomplishments are recognized through the class newsletter. Despite their potential motivational benefits, many educators are skeptical of Jigsaw methods because they fear that students will learn an incomplete or distorted version of the content because their peers will not teach it as effectively as the teacher would and because they will not have texts to support their efforts to learn on their own.

Team-Assisted Individualization (TAI)

Team-Assisted Individualization (TAI) is an adaptation of individualized mathematics instruction that introduces cooperative learning methods and team competition with group reward, as in STAD. TAI combines direct instruction by the teacher (to small, homogeneously formed groups), follow-up practice using programmed instructional materials, and a student team learning approach to seatwork management.

Student team learning methods consistently show positive effects on achievement. These achievement benefits are related to the use of group rewards based on team scores computed by adding the team members' individual performance scores. Methods that ensure the accountability of individual group members to their groupmates produce higher achievement than methods that allow one or two students to do the work while the others take more passive roles. The highest achievement outcomes result from methods that combine group goals with individual accountability.

Note that the achievement advantages of student team learning methods reside in their group reward and individual accountability features, not their competitive features. There is no evidence that group competition offers advantages over other cooperative learning methods so long as arrangements are made to provide group rewards based on the cumulative performance of individual group members. Besides using direct competitions (as in TGT and STAD), good results have been obtained by giving teams certificates for meeting preset standards (independently of the performance of other teams) and by using task specialization to motivate students to encourage their teammates. Thus, although the effects of student team learning on achievement appear to be primarily motivational, the key is not motivation to win competitions against other teams but motivation to assist one's teammates to meet their individual goals and thus ensure that the team will do well. Like other forms of cooperative learning, student team learning methods have produced positive effects on outcomes other than achievement. These methods promote friendships and prosocial interaction among groupmates as well as positive outcomes on individual affective variables such as self-esteem, academic self-confidence, and liking for the class and for classmates.

Extrinsic motivational strategies can be effective in certain circumstances, but you should not rely on them too heavily. If your students become preoccupied with rewards or competition, they may not pay enough attention to what they are supposed to be learning or develop much appreciation for its value. The quality of task engagement and of ultimate achievement tends to be higher when students perceive themselves to be engaged in activities for their own reasons rather than in order to please an authority figure, obtain a reward, or escape punishment.

Your students are unlikely to become preoccupied with extrinsic rewards or pressures if you confine your extrinsic motivational strategies to noting the instrumental value of what is being learned or offering after-the-fact praise or rewards to show appreciation for their learning efforts and achievements. There is danger of such preoccupation, however, whenever you announce your intentions to implement an incentive system, so that students know beforehand that they will be trying to earn a reward or win a competition as they engage in classroom activities.

What can happen was shown in a study by Meece and Holt, who interviewed students about their goals and correlated this information with other measures of motivation and achievement. They found that students who emphasized only mastery goals showed better achievement and more desirable patterns on other motivational measures than students who mentioned both mastery goals and ego/social goals (demonstrate high ability, please the teacher). This is another reminder that "more" motivation doesn't necessarily translate into better or optimal motivation, especially if it leads to the use of effort-minimizing strategies instead of more active learning strategies.

Under some circumstances, however, performance goals can supplement learning goals, especially if they translate into hard work to get good grades rather than into a preoccupation with self-worth protection. For example, Bouffard, Boisvert, Venzeau, and Larouche reported that college students, especially males, who were highly invested in both learning and performance goals showed higher academic achievement than peers who were highly invested in only one type of goal. In turn, the latter students outperformed peers who were not highly invested in either type of goal. Even this study suggested that learning goals were preferable to performance goals, however, because they were associated with better scores on other measures of motivation and on measures of the students' use of cognitive and metacognitive strategies for regulating their learning.

References

Berndt, T., & Miller, K. (1990). Expectancies, values, and achievement in junior high school. *Journal of Educational Psychology*, 82, 319–326.

Heckhausen, H. (1991). *Motivation and action* (2nd ed.). New York: Springer-Verlag.

Johnson, D., & Johnson, R. (1999). *Learning together and alone: Cooperative, competitive, and indi-vidualistic learning* (5th ed.). Boston: Allyn & Bacon.

Sansone, C., & Harackiewicz, J. (2000). *Intrinsic and extrinsic motivation: The search for optimal motivation and performance.* San Diego: Academic Press.

Stipek, D. (2002). Motivation to learn: *Integrating theory and practice* (4th ed.). Boston: Allyn & Bacon.

7

Intrinsic Motivation

Intrinsic motivation is striving inwardly to be competent at something and to reward yourself inwardly. There exists a basic question of whether or not extrinsic motivations (rewards provided by outward sources) undermine intrinsic motivation (self-motivation). Research shows that having extrinsic rewards for something that would naturally be intrinsically motivated, decreases intrinsic motivation.

An intrinsically motivated person will work on a math equation, for example, because it is enjoyable. Or an intrinsically motivated person will work on a solution to a problem because the challenge of finding a solution is provides a sense of pleasure. In neither case does the person work on the task because there is some reward involved, such as a prize, a payment, or in the case of students, a grade.

Intrinsic motivation does not mean, however, that a person will not seek rewards. It just means that such external rewards are not enough to keep a person motivated. An intrinsically motivated student, for example, may want to get a good grade on an assignment, but if the assignment does not interest that student, the possibility of a good grade is not enough to maintain that student's motivation to put any effort into the project.

Some treatments of intrinsic motivation emphasize the affective quality of students' engagement in an activity—the degree to which they enjoy or derive pleasure from the experience. This kind of intrinsic motivation is more typical of play or recreational activities than learning activities. Other treatments of intrinsic motivation place more emphasis on its cognitive aspects— the degree to which students find participation in the activity to be self-actualizing, competence-enhancing, or otherwise meaningful and worthwhile.

Most intrinsic motivation theorists do not directly address distinctions between its affective/fun aspects and its cognitive/learning aspects. Instead, they focus on the issue of control, emphasizing that actions must be experienced as self-determined if intrinsic motivation is to develop.

Until recently, intrinsic motivation theorists tended to depict intrinsic motivation and extrinsic motivation as incompatible opposites, and to caution teachers against using extrinsic incentives lest they erode their students' intrinsic motivation to learn. This tendency to portray a simple dichotomy has receded in favor of the idea that relative autonomy increases by degrees as one moves from purely extrinsic motivation (externally controlled) through mixed forms to purely intrinsic motivation (autonomous). Most intrinsic motivation theorists now concede that extrinsic incentives can be used in ways that complement other motivational strategies and do not undermine students' intrinsic motivation. Even so, these theorists still argue that intrinsic motivational approaches to teaching are preferable to extrinsic approaches. Deci and Ryan reviewed several studies indicating that self-determined learning tends to be of higher quality than ex-trinsically motivated learning. Teachers tend to agree.

The concept of intrinsic motivation began as a reaction to drive-reduction or need theories. Its emergence was part of the attempt to balance the notion that people are driven to respond to felt needs with the notion that we often engage in activities because we want to rather than because we feel a need to.

Abraham Maslow spoke of self-actualization needs that we begin to express when our lower needs are satisfied. These include needs for creative self-expression, satisfaction of curiosity, and other exploratory or skill-enhancing activities that appear to be intrinsically motivated.

Robert White suggested that we often act out of competence motivation: We want to deal effectively with the environment and master and control the things around us. This energizes activities such as exploration, attention, thought, and play. It also causes to seek new challenges rather than wait for events to happen, and to experience such challenges as intrinsically motivating.

Recently, leading intrinsic motivation theorists, notably Edward Deci and Richard Ryan, have begun to define intrinsic motivation in terms of the presence of subjective perceptions of self-determination rather than in terms of the absence of extrinsic incentives or pressures. That is, if we feel self-determined, then for practical purposes we are self-determined, even if extrinsic incentives are in effect or if our behavior is constrained in various ways. As an extreme example, consider a murderer sentenced to life in prison without possibility of parole. Although incarcerated for life and regulated by enforced prison routines, this man has the opportunity to exercise autonomy in making decisions about how to manage those aspects of his life over which he still has control. Rather than descend into chronic rage or depression, for example, he can decide to make the best of the situation by keeping fit, cultivating friendships, and engaging in a variety of educational and recreational activities (and feel self-determined in making and following through on these decisions).

Other conceptions of intrinsic motivation also emphasize our subjective experiences during task engagement. In discussing flow, for example, Csikszentmihalyi emphasized the experience of becoming absorbed in a task. He noted that this can occur with any task that offers challenges that are well matched to our current knowledge and skills.

Eckblad defined extrinsically motivated activity as activity where there is a clear differentiation in awareness between means and ends. In contrast, intrinsically motivated activity is not experienced as a means undertaken to achieve some goal. In a pure state of intrinsic motivation, there is no awareness of means–end separation, of the self, or of striving to achieve some goal separate from the ongoing activity.

Self-determination Theory

Most of these themes are included in the self-determination theory put forth by Edward Deci and Richard Ryan. Along with goal theory, self-determination theory has been the inspiration for much of the research on motivation in education done in recent decades, especially research on its value aspects. Deci and Ryan believe that a full understanding of goal-directed behavior, and of psychological development and well-being generally, requires addressing the needs that give goals their psychological potency and influence people's self-regulated activities. They have identified three psychological needs—for autonomy, competence, and related-ness—

as universal, fundamental, and broad ranging in their influences on goal-oriented pursuits. If those needs are fulfilled, people's motivation will be autonomous and their pursuits will be well aligned with their sense of self and will reflect what they view as interesting or important. If not, their motivation will be more controlled and their pursuits will be less self-determined.

Satisfaction of the three basic needs provides the necessary conditions that allow people the freedom to engage in self-determined activity. Instead of intrinsically motivated pursuits, they are likely to focus on getting their needs met, or if that cannot be done easily, on developing defenses or need substitutes (such as pursuing wealth, fame, or popularity). If sustained over time, this will have negative consequences for their vitality, integrity, and health.

Deci and Ryan define intrinsically motivated actions as performed out of interest and requiring no external prods, promises, or threats. These actions are experienced as wholly self-determined, as representative of and emanating from our sense of self. We pursue them out of interest when we are free from external pressures. In contrast, extrinsically motivated actions are performed instrumentally to attain some separate consequence. These actions usually would not occur spontaneously and therefore must be prompted by incentives or other external pressures.

Extrinsic Regulation

Deci and Ryan have elaborated their original version of self-determination theory to include a developmental analysis of extrinsic motivation. This analysis differentiates subtypes of extrinsic motivation and explains how extrinsically motivated actions can become self-determined through the developmental processes of internalization and integration. Internalization refers to the transformation of an externally prescribed regulation or value into an internally adopted one. Integration is the process through which internalized regulations and values become integrated into the self.

By enabling to assimilate external values and reconstitute them into personally endorsed values and self-regulations, the internalization process allows to feel self-determined when enacting them. When the process functions optimally, we identify with the importance of social regulations, assimilate them into our integrated sense of self, and thus fully accept them as our own. However, the internalization process can become forestalled, so that some values and regulations remain external or become internalized only partially. Deci and Ryan identified four types of extrinsic regulation that can be ordered along a continuum from external control to autonomous self-regulation.

External regulation occurs when our actions are regulated by external rewards, pressures, or constraints. In the classroom, students are externally regulated when they attend to lessons or work on assignments solely because they will be rewarded if they do or punished if they do not.

1. *Introjected regulation* occurs when we act as we do because we think we should or would feel guilty if we did not. Such regulation is internalized to the extent that we have learned to produce the expected behavior and no longer require external prodding to do so. However, we are responding to felt pressure that is still external to our sense of self. In the classroom, introjected regulation is seen in students who attend to lessons or work on assignments primarily because they know that they will get bad grades and disappoint their parents if they do not.
2. *Identified regulation* occurs when the regulation or value is adopted by the self as personally important and valuable. In the classroom, identified regulation is seen in students who attend to lessons and work on assignments because they view these activities as important for their self-selected goal of attending college or entering a particular occupation.
3. *Integrated regulation* is the most self-determined form of extrinsic motivation. It results from the integration of identified values and regulations into one's coherent sense of self. Any conflicts between different values and associated action tendencies (e.g., the desire to be both a good student and a rock musician) are eliminated by making whatever adjustments might be needed to achieve harmonious coexistence.

Actions that are higher on the continuum from external regulation to integrated regulation are increasingly self-determined and thus more like intrinsically motivated actions. We do them because we view them as important. They are still extrinsically motivated, however, because they are performed as means to attain separate goals. In contrast, intrinsically motivated actions are done "for their own sake." We do them because we view them as interesting or enjoyable.

These distinctions are illustrated in representative items from a scale developed by Pelletier et al. to measure sport motivation. Besides incorporating Deci and Ryan's levels of external regulation, these authors distinguished among three subtypes of intrinsic motivation. As adopted by Standage, Duda, and Ntoumanis, the scale asks for students to rate the degree to which the items correspond to their reasons for participating in physical education (PE) activities:

- Intrinsic motivation to know ("For the fun of discovering new skills/ techniques")
- Intrinsic motivation toward accomplishments ("For the satisfaction I experience while I am perfecting my abilities")
- Intrinsic motivation to experience stimulation ("For the excitement I feel when I am really involved in the activity")
- Identified regulation ("Because it is one of the best ways I have chosen to develop other aspects of myself")
- Introjected regulation ("Because I must do PE to feel good about my self")
- External regulation ("To show others that I am good at PE")
- Amotivation ("I used to have good reasons for doing PE, but now I am asking myself why I have to")

According to Deci and Ryan, the degree to which people are able to synthesize cultural values and regulations and incorporate them into the self depends on the degree to which fulfillment of their basic psychological needs is supported as they engage in relevant activities. People tend naturally to internalize the values and regulations of their social groups, but the process is facilitated by feelings of relatedness to the socializers and perceptions of competence to perform the expected behaviors. This includes understanding the meaning or rationale behind a regulation as well as the ability to enact it. Support for relatedness and competence needs may promote partial internalization of a regulation or value, but support for autonomy needs is also needed to enable internalization to progress to the level of integration. Excessive external pressures, controls, or evaluations are likely to forestall this process.

Autonomy, Competence, and Relatedness

Deci and Ryan believe that social settings promote intrinsic motivation when they satisfy people's needs for autonomy, competence, and relatedness. That is, people are inherently motivated to feel connected to others within the setting, to function effectively in it, and to feel a sense of personal initiative while doing so. When teachers and classroom climates support satisfaction of these needs, students will feel self-determined and intrinsically motivated; when they do not, students will feel controlled and extrinsically motivated.

At first glance, there appears to be a contradiction between the need for autonomy and the need for relatedness. That is, to the extent that a teacher requires students to do things that they would not choose to do spontaneously, the students' desire to please the teacher (which is part of their need for relatedness) would motivate them to adopt the teacher's agenda rather than pursue their own. However, keep in mind that the key feature of intrinsic motivation is the students' subjective sense of self-determination, not the degree to which extrinsic incentives or pressures may be present. Hodgins, Koestner, and Duncan have shown that when the need for autonomy is expressed as a tendency to experience self-determination of one's behavior (rather than as a tendency to prefer acting independently without any influence from others), it actually promotes connectedness with others and positive perceptions of social experiences.

Deci and Ryan's suggestions to teachers emphasize socializing and instructing students in ways that encourage self-determined learning initiatives and thus result in intrinsically motivated learning. They identified three factors that promote self-determination in classrooms:

1. providing students with meaningful rationales that will enable them to understand the purpose and personal importance of each learning activity;
2. acknowledging students' feelings when it is necessary to require them to do something that they don't want to do (by letting them know that you are aware of their feelings and taking time to explain why the requirement is needed); and
3. managing the classroom and instructing students using a style that emphasizes choice rather than control.

To the extent that the goal of intrinsic motivation is not fully attained and extrinsic motivation enters the picture, they favor socializing and teaching students in ways that produce higher level rather than lower level forms of extrinsic regulation. Their ideas, presented in the following sections, overlap consider-ably with the principles involved in orienting students toward learning goals rather than performance goals.

Responding to Students' Autonomy Needs

Despite recent advances in their theorizing and broadening of their purview on motivation, most of the advice to teachers offered by Deci, Ryan, and their colleagues continues to focus on supporting students' sense of self-determination in the classroom by offering them opportunities for autonomy and choice and by avoiding overtly controlling behaviors.

Encourage Students to Function as Autonomous Learners

Research based on self-determination theory indicates that autonomous forms of student motivation are associated with a broad pattern of desirable correlates, whereas controlled forms are associated with a broad pattern of undesirable correlates. For example, Ryan and Connell asked children to choose among external, introjected, identified, and intrinsic reasons as explanations for their engagement in school activities. They found that externally regulated students showed less interest, value, and effort at school and tended to disown responsibility for failures by blaming the teacher or the school. Introjected students reported more effort, but also more anxiety and self-blame. They reacted to failure by amplifying anxiety and self-criticism. Identified students showed higher levels of effort, interest, enjoyment of school, and positive coping than the introjected or externally regulated students. Finally, students who were intrinsically motivated showed the highest levels of interest, enjoyment, confidence, and effort.

Subsequent research done at several grade levels and in several countries has yielded similar findings. Some studies have extended these findings to other measures such as grades or test scores or staying in versus dropping out of school. However, some also have suggested that the benefits of intrinsic motivation or perceptions of autonomy are limited to the affective aspects of task engagement and do not result in better achievement.

Deci, Ryan, and their colleagues have emphasized the importance of supporting autonomous rather than controlled forms of motivation in classrooms, and have investigated what is involved in autonomy-supportive teaching. Deci, Schwartz, Sheinman, and Ryan asked teachers to rate the appropriateness of various responses to problems that students might display (e.g., not turning in homework, misbehaving). Autonomy-supportive teachers tended to endorse responses that involved investigating and working from the child's perspective, whereas controlling teachers tended to endorse responses that involved rewards and punishments, social comparisons, or application of external praise, pressure, or contingencies. Later in the school year, the researchers assessed these teachers' students' motivation. They found that students of autonomy-supportive teachers showed more curiosity, desire for challenge, and other evidence of mastery motivation, whereas the students of controlling teachers showed less of this mastery motivation and expressed lower confidence in their academic abilities and lower self-worth perceptions. Other investigators also have reported more positive patterns of motivation among students of autonomy-supportive teachers compared with students of controlling teachers.

Grolnick and Ryan suggested that autonomy-supportive teachers believe that it is important for their students to learn to solve their own problems. These teachers see their role as facilitating independent thought and decision making. They try to involve students in the process of learning by giving them choices. They support students' problem-solving attempts by using discussion and other autonomy promoting techniques rather than by imposing their own solutions on the students. In contrast, control-oriented teachers overmanage their students using detailed directions backed by rewards, grades, and threats. These techniques lead students to experience their learning in school as instrumental (i.e., as means to good grades) rather than as self-determined.

Valas and Sovik painted a similar picture of autonomy-supporting teachers. These teachers provide their students with choices, minimize extrinsic performance pressures (grades and normative comparisons, competition, continuous close monitoring), encourage students to solve problems in their own ways rather than insisting on a single method, and invite students to ask questions and suggest ideas for individual learning projects.

Reeve, Bolt, and Cai found that autonomy-supportive teachers listened more to their students, encouraged more student initiative with instructional materials, asked questions about the students' wants, replied to the students' questions, and offered empathic perspective-taking statements more frequently. In contrast, controlling teachers more frequently talked instead of listening, communicated "should" statements, used praise or criticism, asked controlling questions, stated deadlines, and generally created a pressuring atmosphere.

In summary, autonomy-supportive teachers promote intrinsic motivation by understanding students' perspectives, supporting their initiatives, creating opportunities for choice, being encouraging rather than demanding or directive, and allowing students to work in their own way. They also promote internalization by encouraging questions and allowing expression of negative feelings, providing rationales that help students understand the purpose and value of activities, stimulating interest, and supporting confidence. Fundamentally, autonomy support is more about how expectations are communicated than about the number or extent of these expectations.

Allow Students to Make Choices

Offer your students choices of alternative tasks or opportunities to exercise autonomy in pursuing alternative ways to meet requirements. If they are likely to make undesirable choices if left completely on their own, provide them with a menu of choices to select from or help them to make choices that are well-suited to their interests and reading levels. Take students' interests into account when considering choice options.

Many instructional goals involve developing skills and strategies rather than learning informational content. In these situations, many different information sources and instructional materials or media may be useful as means for accomplishing the learning goals. In addition, if you invite them to do so, your students might suggest additional means that you had not considered but would be willing to approve as equivalent alternatives. By offering such choices, you provide students with opportunities to assume responsibility for regulating their own learning and to experience a sense of self-determination as they do so.

Offer autonomy and choice opportunities to all students, not just higher achievers. Some teachers provide frequent autonomy and choice opportunities for their higher achievers but micromanage the learning efforts of their lower achievers. Lower achievers often need more explicit directions and more structuring and scaffolding of their learning efforts, but they also need opportunities to experience self-determination and self-regulation of their learning.

One way to build in choice opportunities for all students is to set up learning centers where students can work individually or in collaboration with peers on a variety of projects. Some of the projects may be required because they are essential to accomplishment of your unit goals in one or more subject areas, but others might be optional—viewed as enrichment activities and included at least in part because most students find them interesting or enjoyable.

For example, a language arts or social studies center might include children's literature selections relating to the topic of the current social studies unit. The collection would include a variety of genres of children's literature written at a range of reading levels, although it would be limited to books considered suitable as content sources for enriching students' knowledge about the unit topic (e.g., pioneer life or the Civil War). Students might be required to read and write their reactions to one or more of these books, but they would be allowed to decide which books to read. They also might be allowed at least some autonomy (along with any needed guidance) concerning the content and organization of their reports.

Reynolds and Symons engaged third graders in an activity calling for them to locate information in books. Some were allowed to choose which of three books they would use, but others were assigned to the books randomly. These authors found that students allowed to choose their books used more efficient search strategies and were faster at locating information than students not given this choice.

Morrow developed a writing and reading appreciation program that included significant provisions for student autonomy and choice in working on language arts projects. Students worked on these activities several times each week when they were assigned to the literacy center in a corner of the classroom. At any given time, the center contained 5 to 8 books per child, including picture story books, poetry, informational books, magazines, biographies, and other fictional and nonfictional sources. Selections were changed periodically, especially to create collections relating to topics being taught concurrently in science or social studies.

The center also included six types of manipulative materials that students might use with their projects:

- felt board stories (characters from a book made of oaktag or construction paper that could be used when retelling the story by displayingthem on a felt board)

- taped stories that children could listen to through headsets as they followed along in the accompanying book
- roll movies (illustrated stories that could be advanced scene by scene by scrolling them through a viewing apparatus)
- prop stories (collections of materials for use in retelling a story, such as three stuffed bears, three bowls, and a yellow-haired doll for telling the story of *Goldilocks*)
- puppet stories (various types of puppets to use in retelling stories)
- chalk talks (materials for drawing a story on a chalkboard or sheet of paper while the story is being read or told).

While in the literacy center, students could use these or other materials to: read a book, magazine, or newspaper; read to a friend; listen to someone read to them; listen to a taped story and follow the words in the book; use the felt board with a storybook and felt characters; use the roll movie with its storybook; write a story; draw a picture about a story they had read; write a story and then make it into a book; make a felt story or a tape for a book they had read or a story they had written; write and perform a puppet show; record activities in the log; check out books to take home and read; or follow directions on a task card for some other selected activity.

The teacher demonstrated how to use these materials and carry out activity choices, then moved students toward independent and collaborative functioning. Students chose whether they wanted to work alone or with peers. If they chose to work with peers, the group decided who would act as leader and what tasks they would pursue. The students operated mostly independently of the teacher in deciding what tasks to work on and how to complete them. However, they were encouraged to select activities that included both reading and writing, to try activities they had not tried before and work with classmates they had not worked with before, and to take on significant projects and follow them through to completion rather than flit from one thing to another (unfinished projects could be stored for resumption when the students next returned to the literacy center).

Students involved in this program expressed more interest in reading and writing than students in classes restricted to more traditional activities. They also performed better on tests of reading comprehension and oral and written literacy. Note that this approach not only responded to students' autonomy needs but also responded to their relatedness needs by allowing them to work together with classmates of their own choosing. A variation that might be used with any subject matter is to divide students into self-selected interest groups and allow them to do worthwhile content-related research projects.

Students' Competence Needs

Intrinsic motivation theorists have pointed out that people tend to enjoy and become absorbed in activities that are well matched to their current levels of knowledge and skill and thus provide optimal challenges that allow them to develop their competence. This principle has several potential applications in classrooms.

First, as a prerequisite, make sure that learning activities are in fact well matched to your students' levels of knowledge and skill. If activities are ill-matched to your students' levels, and especially if they are too difficult for them, there will be no potential for intrinsic motivation.

Within the range of activities that are optimally challenging, some are especially enjoyable or absorbing because they offer good opportunities for students to satisfy their competence needs. Examples include activities that allow students to make active responses and get immediate feedback, incorporate game-like features that most students find enjoyable, and incorporate features that are associated with job satisfaction in the work place.

Active Responses

Students tend to prefer activities that allow them to respond actively—to interact with you or with one another, manipulate materials, or do something else other than just listen or read. Routine recitation, boardwork, or seatwork activities provide only limited potential for active response. Students should get frequent opportunities to go beyond simple question–answer formats in order to do projects, experiments, discussions, role play, simulations, computerized learning activities, educational games, or creative applications.

Even within traditional lesson formats, you can create opportunities for more active student involvement by going beyond factual questions to stimulate students to discuss or debate issues, offer opinions about cause-and-effect relationships, speculate about hypothetical situations, or think creatively about problems. Students need to master basic facts, concepts, and definitions, but they also need frequent opportunities to address higher level objectives by applying, analyzing, synthesizing, or evaluating what they have learned at the knowledge or comprehension level.

Also, avoid overemphasis on convergent questions that admit to only a single correct answer. Questions asked during everyday lessons should include frequent opportunities for students to state opinions, make predictions, suggest sources of action, formulate solutions to problems, or engage in other forms of divergent thinking.

Language arts instruction should include dramatic readings and prose and poetry composition; mathematics instruction should include problem-solving exercises and realistic application opportunities; science instruction should include experiments and other laboratory work; social studies instruction should include debates, research projects, and simulation exercises; and art, music, and physical education instruction should include opportunities to use developing skills in authentic application activities, not just to practice the skills in isolation. Such activities allow students to feel that school learning involves doing something.

Research on students' attitudes toward academic activities consistently shows that they prefer active over passive forms of learning. For example, 11- and 12-year old students interviewed by Cooper and McIntyre associated effective teaching with methods that produced high levels of imaginative and practical involvement in lesson activity. Examples included storytelling by the teacher (which the students found engaging even though it is primarily a listening activity), drama and role-play exercises, use of visual stimuli (photographs, drawings, diagrams, videos), whole-class and small-group discussion, and opportunities to collaborate in pairs and groups in brainstorming, problem solving, or developing some group product.

Immediate Feedback

Activities that offer the greatest potential for student enjoyment and for flow experiences are those that allow students not only to respond actively but also to get immediate feedback that they can use to guide subsequent responses. This feedback feature is an important reason for the popularity of computer games and other pastimes featured in arcades. Automatic feedback features are also built into many educational games and computerized learning systems.

You can provide such feedback yourself when leading the class or a small group through a lesson or when circulating to supervise progress during independent work times. When you are less available for immediate response (such as when you are teaching a small group), you can still arrange for students who are working independently to get feedback by consulting answer keys; following instructions about how to check their work; consulting with an aide, adult volunteer, or appointed student helper; or discussing their work in pairs or small groups.

Although it is not always necessary for learning purposes, immediate feedback enhances the psychological impact of an activity. Most students are eager to receive and respond to immediate feedback when learning something for the first time, but much less enthused about the prospect of going back to try to relearn something that "we did already."

Incorporating Game-like Features into Learning Activities

Many learning and application activities can be structured to include features typically associated with games or recreational pastimes. With a bit of imagination, ordinary seatwork assignments can be transformed into "test yourself" challenges, puzzles, or brain teasers that allow students to satisfy their competence needs. Some such activities involve clear goals but require students to solve problems, avoid traps, or overcome obstacles in order to reach the goals. For example, students might be asked to suggest possible solutions to a science or engineering problem or to find a shortcut for a tedious mathematical procedure. Other such activities challenge students to "find the problem" by identifying the goal itself and then developing a method for reaching it. Many "explore and discover" activities follow this model.

For example, McKenzie described three ways to introduce mystery to inquiry or problem solving in social studies or science. First, as a way to engage students in inquiry leading to discovery of a concept or generalization, provide students with different examples or illustrations of phenomena that seem to be unrelated at first. Then inform the students that all of the cases are alike in some way and challenge them to discover the similarity or pattern. The resultant discovery will be a definition of a concept or a statement of a generalization. For example, pictures of pioneers on the frontier, the Wright brothers with their plane, African-American students integrating a segregated school, and an astronaut might be presented along with the challenge, "All of these people are pioneers. Can you figure out what pioneers have in common?"

A variation on this method is to provide a set of clues, such as artifacts, divergent historical accounts of an event, or other data arranged to tell some story, then to ask students to reconstruct the event by acting as a detective (or an archaeologist or historian). A third technique is to present some situation that seems familiar and ask students what they think will happen. After they make predictions, demonstrate that in fact something unexpected happens. Then challenge the class to try to explain why the unexpected event occurred. You might use this technique to introduce the concept of gravity, for example, by dropping pairs of objects together to illustrate that a smaller, lighter object such as a coin will reach the floor just as quickly as a larger, heavier object such as a baseball (contrary to most students' expectations).

Some game-like activities involve elements of suspense or hidden information that emerges as the activity is completed (puzzles that convey some message or provide the answer to some question once they are filled in). Still other game-like activities involve a degree of randomness or uncertainty about the outcome of one's performance on any given trial (knowledge games that cover a variety of topics at several difficulty levels and assign questions according to card draws or dice rolls—Trivial Pursuit is an example).

Covington described games and simulations that engage students in cooperative learning and higher order thinking as they work to develop explanations for puzzling phenomena (e.g., how birds can migrate for thousands of miles and yet keep returning to the same place each year) or solutions to technical problems (e.g., how to use x-rays to destroy a cancerous tumor without harming the surrounding healthy tissue). When designed as opportunities to apply principles developed through instruction in school subjects, these game-like activities can have powerful motivational as well as instructional value.

Note that most of these game-like features involve presenting intellectual challenges to individuals working alone or to groups working cooperatively. This illustrates that game-like features has a much broader meaning than games, a term that most teachers associate specifically with competitions. The game-like features described here are less distracting from learning objectives and more effective in promoting student motivation to learn than are games, especially competitive games that emphasize speed in supplying memorized facts rather than thoughtful integration or application of learning.

Ideas From Research on Job Characteristics

Industrial psychologists have studied workplace conditions and job characteristics that affect workers' job satisfaction and work motivation. Their findings concerning leadership and workplace conditions overlap considerably with classroom findings concerning teacher leadership style and classroom climate. However, the job characteristics literature also points to certain features of work that have not yet received much attention in educational research: skill variety, task identity, and task significance. All three have implications for designing school activities that respond to students' competence needs.

Skill Variety

Skill variety refers to the range of different activities needed to carry out a task, as well as the range of skills that these activities entail. Workers tend to enjoy jobs that include a variety of activities and provide them with opportunities to use a variety of skills. In contrast, most workers find jobs that involve constant repetition of the same task to be boring and aversive. Students show the same preferences.

Alleman and Brophy (1993–1994) interviewed college students about learning activities that they remembered from K–12 social studies. Their responses were coded for what they said about the cognitive and affective outcomes of the activities. Desirable affective outcomes were coded when the students reported that an activity had produced interesting learning or enabled them to empathize with the people being studied and see things from their point of view. Negative assessments were coded when the students disparaged activities as pointless (e.g., learning about state birds) or as boring and repetitive.

Analyses indicated that the students frequently mentioned desirable affective outcomes, and never expressed negative assessments, when describing thematic units (such as on pioneer life or a foreign country) that included a variety of information and activities; field trips; class discussion and debate activities; or pageant or role-enactment activities. They expressed less enthusiastic, but still generally positive, reactions to simula-tion activities, research projects, construction projects, and lecture/presentation activities. In contrast, seatwork was in a class by itself because it yielded practically no descriptions of desirable affective outcomes but frequent negative assessments (especially complaints about boring, repetitive seatwork that had to be done individually and silently).

Task Identity

Task identity refers to the opportunity to do a complete job from beginning to end. Workers tend to enjoy jobs that allow them to create a product that they can point to and identify with more than jobs that do not yield such tangible evidence of the fruits of their labor. Students probably respond similarly to academic tasks. That is, they are likely to prefer tasks that have meaning or integrity in their own right over tasks that are mere subparts of some larger entity, and are likely to experience a satisfying sense of accomplishment when they finish such tasks. Ideally, task completion will yield a finished product that students can use or display.

Many writers concerned with motivation in education have pointed out that knowledge is decontextualized in school. Abstract principles and skills that have wide application are taught in circumstances far removed from those in which they will be used. Also, much school knowledge is modularized—broken into component parts taught separately. One result of this decontextualization and modularization is to remove much of the intrinsic motivation potential from school learning. You can recapture some of this potential by creating classroom activities that resemble the situated learning that occurs in out-of-school settings.

Scholars who have studied learning in home and job settings believe that it is a mistake to separate knowing from doing, or what is learned from how it is learned and used. They believe that learning is situated; that is, that knowledge is adapted to the settings, purposes, and tasks to which it is applied (and for which it was constructed in the first place). Consequently, they argue, if we want students to learn and retain knowledge in a form that makes it usable for application, we need to make it possible for them to develop that knowledge in the natural setting, using methods and tasks suited to that setting. In this view, the ideal model for schooling is on-the-job training that occurs as experienced mentors work with novices or apprentices.

Obviously, there are limits to the degree to which in-school learning can be shifted to out-of-school settings. However, the notion of situated learning has implications for the design of in-school instruction as well. In particular, it implies that we need to be conscious of potential applications when we select and plan our teaching of curricular content, and we should emphasize those applications in presenting the content to students.

Also, as much as possible, we should allow students to learn through engagement in authentic tasks. Authentic tasks require using what is being learned for accomplishing the very sorts of life applications that justify the inclusion of this learning in the curriculum in the first place. If it is not possible to engage students in the actual life applications that the curriculum is supposed to prepare them for, then at least engage them in realistic simulations of these applications.

Theory and research on task identity as a job characteristic and on situated learning and authentic tasks in education lead to similar ideas about the kinds of learning activities that students are likely to find intrinsically motivating. In particular, they underscore the value of engaging students in authentic life applications of the knowledge and skills they are learning in school, especially applications that yield some conclusion or product that students can appreciate as a significant accomplishment.

Task Significance

Task significance refers to the degree of impact that the job has on the lives of other people, both immediately within the workplace and potentially in other contexts. This concept also connects with educators' notions of task authenticity and with the principle of teaching school subjects with an eye toward applications to life outside of school. You can enhance your students' perceptions of the significance of everyday activities by structuring them as opportunities to develop and apply big ideas. In addition, you can occasionally incorporate activities of special significance such as service learning projects, student-led assessment conferences (in which students present their work portfolios to their families), or science or social studies projects that culminate in some service to the community or lobbying of local authorities to adopt some policy or take some action.

Students' Relatedness Needs

Be a supportive teacher who cares about your students as persons and helps them succeed as learners. In addition, teach your students to act as members of a learning community by listening carefully and responding thoughtfully during lessons and discussions and by supporting one another's learning when working in pairs or small groups.

In this kind of collaborative classroom climate, students will be able to please both you and their classmates (and thus meet their relatedness needs) simply by acting in accordance with learning community values. A prevailing norm of "We're all in this together, learning and helping one another learn" creates alignment among the actions needed to satisfy needs for autonomy, competence, and relatedness. Therefore, students can meet all of these needs simultaneously by asking and answering questions, working collabor-atively on assignments, and engaging in other everyday learning activities. Such alignment does not exist in competitive or hostile climates, where students may be unable to meet their relatedness needs or able to meet them only at cost to their sense of autonomy, their self-concept, or other components of their motivational systems.

Provide Opportunities for Students to Collaborate with Peers

In classrooms that feature a positive interpersonal climate and norms of collaboration, students are likely to experience enhanced intrinsic motivation when they participate in learning activities that allow them to interact with their classmates. You can build interaction opportunities into whole-class activities such as discussion, debate, role-play, or simulation. In addition, you can shift many of the practice and application components of your curriculum from solitary seatwork to collaborative activities that allow students to work together in pairs or small groups to tutor one another, discuss issues, develop solutions to problems, or work as a team to produce a report, display, or some other group product. Such cooperative learning activities offer potential motivational benefits because they respond directly to students' relatedness needs, as well as potential learning benefits because they engage students in the social construction of knowledge.

Emphasize Purely Cooperative Learning Formats

Consequently, they are primarily extrinsic approaches to motivation. However, there are other approaches to paired or small-group learning that are purely cooperative and thus likely to enhance students' intrinsic motivation. Three of the best known of these methods are Learning Together, Group Investigation, and Jigsaw.

Learning Together

The learning together model was developed by David and Roger Johnson. In this model, students work on assignments in four- or five-member groups, ultimately turning in a single product that represents the group's effort. The Learning Together model incorporates four key features:

1. *Positive interdependence.* Students are interdependent with other members of their group in achieving a successful group product. Positive interdependence can be structured through mutual goals (goal interdependence); division of labor (task interdependence); dividing materials, resources, or information among group members (resource interdependence); assigning students unique roles (role interdependence); or giving group rewards (reward interdependence).
2. *Face-to-face interaction among students.* Activities that call for significant interaction among group members are preferred over activities that can be accomplished by having group members work on their own.
3. *Individual accountability.* Mechanisms are needed to ensure that each group member has clear objectives for which he or she will be held accountable and receives any needed assessment, feedback, or instructional assistance.
4. *Instructing students in appropriate interpersonal or small-group skills.* Students cannot merely be placed together and told to cooperate. They need instruction in skills such as asking and answering questions, ensuring that everyone participates actively and is treated with respect, and assigning tasks and organizing cooperative efforts.

Group Investigation

Group Investigation methods were developed by Shlomo Sharan and his colleagues in Israel. In this model, students form their own two- to six-member groups to work together using cooperative inquiry, group discussion, and planning and carrying out of projects. Each group chooses a topic from a unit studied by the whole class, breaks this topic into individual tasks, and carries out the activities needed to prepare a group report. Eventually, the group makes a presentation or display to communicate its findings to the class and is evaluated based on the quality of this report.

Jigsaw

Developed by Elliot Aronson and his colleagues, the Jigsaw approach ensures active individual participation and group cooperation by arranging tasks so that each group member possesses unique information and has a special role to play. The group product cannot be completed unless each member does his or her part, just as a jigsaw puzzle cannot be completed unless each piece is included. For example, information needed to compose a biography might be broken into early life, first accomplishments, major setbacks, later life, and world events occurring during the person's lifetime. One member of each group would be given access to the relevant information and assigned responsibility for one of the five sections of the biography, and other group members would be assigned to other sections. Then they would return to their regular groups and take turns teaching their group mates about their sections. Because the only way that students can learn about sections other than their own is to listen carefully to their groupmates, they are motivated to support and show interest in one another's work. The students then prepare biographies or take quizzes on the material individually.

A variation entitled Jigsaw II was developed by Robert Slavin. One feature of Jigsaw II is that the teacher does not need to provide each student with unique materials. Instead, all students begin by reading a common narrative and then each group member is given a separate topic on which to become an expert. This adaptation also can be used with the original Jigsaw. If it is adopted without also incorporating the team competition features of Jigsaw II, it will simplify Jigsaw but still preserve its purely cooperative format.

Another way to differentiate roles within groups is to assign group members specific responsibilities for ensuring that the group functions effectively. For example, one member might monitor turn taking and participation, a second might record whatever needs to be written down, a third might identify points of agreement and disagreement, and a fourth might press for arguments and evidence to support stated opinions.

Research on small-group cooperative learning methods indicates that they do indeed respond to students' relatedness needs. These methods have been shown to promote friendships and prosocial interaction among students who differ in achievement, gender, race, ethnicity, and handicapping conditions. In addition, they tend to have positive effects on outcomes such as self-esteem, academic self-confidence, liking for the class, liking and feeling liked by classmates, and dispositions toward empathy and social cooperation.

Certain qualifications on the use of cooperative learning methods should be noted, however. First, although most students prefer to collaborate with peers, some prefer to work alone. You may have good reasons for requiring the latter students to work together with peers under some circumstances, but whenever you are using cooperative learning purely for intrinsic motivation reasons, you should allow students who want to work alone to do so. Second, even if all of the students in a group enjoy working in the cooperative format, they may become distracted from learning goals if they begin to socialize, have difficulty negotiating roles, or begin to become concerned that some members of the group are not fulfilling their responsibilities. Third, bear in mind that the intrinsic motivational benefits of cooperative formats do not guarantee accomplishment of your instructional goals. To ensure that cooperative approaches yield acceptable learning outcomes, you will need to make sure that the tasks you assign are suited to the cooperative learning format that you want your students to follow, to prepare the students to collaborate effectively, and to monitor group interactions and intervene if necessary.

Pairs/Partners

Although most research attention has focused on cooperative learning in small-group formats, some formats call for pairs of students to work together as partners. Many language arts programs, for example, include components calling for pairs of students to listen to each other read or spell and provide corrective feedback or to read and respond to each other's written compositions. Also, many teachers assign pairs of students to act as study partners who correct and provide feedback concerning each other's work on mathematics assignments, to act as laboratory partners in carrying out science experiments, or to collaborate in "study buddy" relationships in working on homework assignments. Less formally, they may invite students to seek help from seatmates or friends in the classroom (within certain guidelines, such as that helpers should not merely give answers but provide helpees with whatever clues or explanations they may need in order to move forward on their own and eventually accomplish the learning goal).

Techniques have been developed to create interdependence between partners and encourage them to collaborate fruitfully. One such technique is scripted cooperation. As applied to a text study assignment, for example, the scripted cooperation method begins with breaking down of the text into sections. The other partner plays the role of "listener-detector" by listening carefully and attempting to detect errors or omissions in the recall. Both partners then share ideas about how to elaborate the information to make it more memorable. They proceed in this manner, switching roles each time they start a new section, until they complete the material to be studied. Research indicates that pairs of students using the scripted cooperation method tend to learn more than students who study alone or pairs of students who are asked to study together but not instructed to use the scripted cooperation techniques of alternation of roles, overt rehearsal, active listening, and collaborative elaboration on the content.

Slavin emphasized that group goals combined with individual accountability are usually needed to ensure that students in pairs or small groups consistently help their partners or teammates to meet their individual goals and thus ensure their team will do well. However, he noted that these features may not be needed when students form voluntary study groups (indicating that they already are motivated to help one another), when they are enacting cooperative learning models that call for them to carry out specific roles (thus ensuring that help is provided), or when the activity calls for higher-order thinking and negotiation of multiple or conflicting opinions rather than following a clear path to resolution of a problem or controversy.

New Directions of Self-determination Theory

Self-determination theory has been highly successful as both an inspiration and an organizer for much recent research about the value aspects of motivation, particularly intrinsic motivation. In its early stages it appeared to have limited potential for classroom application, because it was focused on comparisons of intrinsic with extrinsic motivation without considering mixed forms of motivation that lie between these extremes. However, this deficiency was remedied with the addition of the continuum of extrinsic regulation that ranges from external regulation through introjected regulation and identified regulation to integrated regulation. This addition to the theory explicitly recognizes that students might willingly engage in academic activities and pursue their learning goals because they realize that they are important, even though they may not find them intrinsically interesting or enjoyable. It also opens the way more clearly for investigations of ways that socializers might affect students' motivation, especially by helping them to appreciate the value or importance of social regulations and expectations that apply to them (including expectations that they learn the school's curriculum). In a related shift, Deci and Ryan have begun to emphasize that the key to understanding motivational dynamics is not an intrinsic vs. extrinsic motivation dichotomy, but the degree to which the person perceives rewards or other extrinsic features of the situation as informational versus controlling.

Basic Needs

Self-determination theory still has its critics, however. Some of the objections focus on Deci and Ryan's identification of autonomy, competence, and relatedness as three basic needs. Critics have suggested that this list ought to be expanded to include such possibilities as self-preservation needs, safety needs, self-esteem needs, or self-actualization needs. Deci and Ryan have responded by clarifying that their theory focuses on psychological needs (so it assumes people's physical well-being while investigating factors affecting their psychological well-being), and that needs for self-esteem and self-actualization are implied in their treatment of the need for competence (especially when it is considered in tandem with the needs for autonomy and relatedness). Also, given the logical circularity that previous need theories encountered when they began proliferating the numbers of needs included, they are hesitant to extend their list without compelling evidence of a need to do so.

Their hesitancy is understandable. So far, a great deal of research has accumulated supporting the notion that autonomy, competence, and relatedness are basic needs that must be satisfied to allow people to enjoy a sense of psychological well-being and position them to engage in intrinsically motivated pursuits. Additional support for these assumptions has been generated by Sheldon, Elliot, Kim, and Kasser in a study entitled "What is satisfying about satisfying events?" These authors asked samples of American and Korean college students to think about the single most personally satisfying event that had occurred in their lives recently and rate their feelings during this event, using descriptors reflecting satisfaction of 10 potential needs: self-esteem, relatedness, autonomy, competence, pleasure-stimulation, physical thriving, self-actualization-meaning, security, popularity-influence, and money-luxury. The ordering of those needs reflects the relative prominence with which they appeared in the American students' responses. These students were especially likely to indicate that highly satisfying experiences were related to satisfaction of needs for self-esteem, relatedness, autonomy, or competence. The South Korean students' responses were similar, except that relatedness needs replaced self-esteem needs at the top of the list.

These data were supportive of Maslow's list of basic needs and even more supportive of Deci and Ryan's identification of autonomy, competence, and relatedness as universal fundamental needs. However, they also suggested that self-esteem might be worth treating as a separate basic need, not just as an extension of the need for competence.

Additional support for the basic nature of Deci and Ryan's three primary needs can be seen in related work done on people's sense of well-being. Reis et al. asked college students to keep diaries for two weeks, reporting on their social activities and related moods and need satisfactions. They found that daily fluctuations in the students' emotional well-being were closely related to the degree to which their autonomy, competence, and relatedness needs were being satisfied. Also, Sheldon and Elliot asked college students about personal goals that they would seek to attain in the coming weeks (e.g., get more exercise, get at least a B in chemistry), then contacted them again later to find out their degree of effort expended and success attained in pursuing these goals. The results indicated that autonomous motivation (intrinsic or identified) predicted goal attainment but controlled motivation (externally regulated or introjected) did not. The students had focused on things that they personally viewed as interesting, important, or enjoyable, but were less invested in pursuits that they had listed as goals primarily because someone (parents, instructors) or something else ("ought" feelings associated with potential shame, guilt, or anxiety) was compelling them to do so. Koestner, Lekes, Powers, and Chicoine found similar results in another study.

Value of Choices

Several recent studies indicate the need to qualify Deci and Ryan's claims about the value of providing students with choices. First, several studies have indicated that although providing students with opportunities to choose a reading selection or other learning task can enhance their reported enjoyment of the task or their sense of confidence or control as they engage in it, these affective benefits usually are not accompanied by cognitive benefits—the students do not do better on learning measures than students who are not given the opportunity to choose. More generally, a review of relevant studies indicated that although choice is related positively to affective aspects of engagement such as intrinsic motivation, feelings of satisfaction, and reduced anxiety, it has less of an influence, and often none at all, on cognitive aspects such as strategy use, recall of main ideas, or generating inferences. Sometimes choice does not even affect intrinsic motivation, especially if the available choices are all similar to one another or if none of them is especially appealing.

A second qualification on the value of offering choices is that the choice set should feature options that will allow students to engage in activities with autonomous (intrinsic or identified) motivation. Assor, Kaplan, and Roth found that students in Grades 3 to 8 in Israel could differentiate among three types of autonomy-enhancing teacher behaviors (fostering relevance, allowing criticism, and providing choice), as well as three types of autonomy-suppressing behaviors (suppressing criticism, intruding, and forcing unmeaningful acts). Of these teacher behaviors, the two that had the most important effects on students' feelings toward learning and cognitive engagement in the classroom were fostering relevance and suppressing criticism. Offering choices of learning activities frequently was ineffec- tive because the students did not perceive a connection between any of the choices and their personal goals and interests. The authors emphasized the importance of both making sure that the choices do in fact have value (i.e., are authentic activities) and helping students to perceive that value and thus appreciate the importance of the activities. As they put it in the title of their article, "Choice is good, but relevance is excellent."

A third qualification on providing students with choices is that the number and variety of choices available needs to be calibrated to the students' current readiness to choose sensibly. Schwartz argued that opportunities for autonomy, self-determination, and choice can become excessive to the point that they are experienced as a kind of tyranny. This implies that an optimal number of choices is best in a given situation, rather than that "more is better." Iyengar and Lepper generated intriguing data supporting this conclusion in three studies in which people were presented with an extensive array of choices (24 or 30) or a more limited array (6). In each case, the people presented with an extensive array of choices expressed more initial satisfaction than the people presented with a limited array, but follow-up data indicated more positive results for the limited-choice condition.

Two of the studies involved opportunities to sample and purchase specialty foods (jams or chocolates). In each case, people were more likely to actually purchase the foods if they were shown only six choices, and also more likely to express satisfaction with their choices later. The third study was done in a college classroom. Students were given the opportunity to write a two-page essay as an extra-credit assignment, selecting from either 6 or 30 potential essay topics. The data indicated that students given 6 options were more likely to complete the assignment than students given 30 options, and their essays were of higher quality. The authors concluded that "too many" choices may be initially appealing but nevertheless undermine choosers' subsequent satisfaction and motivation.

A fourth qualification is cultural. Iyegar and Lepper have shown that motivation (and performance) are optimized for people with independent selves (e.g., most Americans) when they are allowed to make personal choices, but optimized for people with interdependent selves (e.g., most Asians) where the choices are made for them by valued in-group members.

Other Issues

There are other critiques of self-determination theory as well. For example, Carver and Scheier noted that many forms of intrinsically rewarding activity do not involve a competence dimension at all, and furthermore that it is possible for people to find certain activities intrinsically rewarding even though they are unskilled at them (e.g., people who are not good at particular sports but participate in them regularly because they enjoy doing so). Similarly, many intrinsically motivated activities are pursued when one is by oneself, so they do not involve a relatedness dimension, and some students are low in interpersonal orientation and do not especially value opportunities to interact with peers as they work on school assignments.

Also, some critics believe that needs for autonomy and for relatedness will inevitably clash in some situations. Deci and Ryan's response has been to clarify that motivation refers to subjective experience and that satisfying the need for autonomy involves experiencing perceptions of self-determination rather than necessarily acting independently of outside influences. This is an elegant solution to the problem at the theoretical level, but it introduces other problems at the practical level. It moves motivational theory and research away from issues of greatest concern to educational policymakers and the general public (which focus on questions about how to get students to study hard and ultimately do well on tests). Although it is important not to confuse motivation with performance, it also is important to take into account learning (not just motivation) in designing research and developing implications for teachers.

Students in a motivation class taught by the have identified a related concern: the distinction that many motivational theorists (especially intrinsic motivation theorists) want to make between motivating and controlling students' behavior can be confusing and can constrict people's perceptions of the apparent relevance or power of motivational principles. For example, people juggling multiple agendas will tend to give first priority to things they must do because of extrinsic pressure reasons, and only secondary priority to things they are intrinsically motivated to do but do not have to do. Several Asian students, for example, have suggested that students from their countries were so controlled by extrinsic pressures (at least prior to taking the high-stakes tests that determined their future opportunities) that the term "motivation" would have limited applicability to attempts to explain or change their behavior. Even if they began to develop intrinsic motivation to pursue certain topics, they wouldn't have the time to do so.

Norwich collected data on students' reported reasons for putting forth effort in schoolwork and found that the students' identified reasons were closely related to their intrinsic reasons, whereas both of those were contrasted with their introjected reasons. This suggests that identified regulation has more in common with intrinsic motivation than it does with introjected regulation (at least in students' thinking), despite Deci and Ryan's theorizing that identified regulation is extrinsic motivation and thus should have more in common with other forms of extrinsic motivation (such as introjected regulation) than it does with intrinsic motivation.

Theory and Research on Interest

Interest implies focused attention to a lesson, text passage, or learning activity that occurs because the learner values or has positive affective responses to its content or processes. Some authors treat interest as a form of intrinsic motivation, but others distinguish it by virtue of the fact that interest is focused on particular content or activities. Interesting activities provide learners with forms of input or opportunities for response that they find rewarding and want to pursue.

Possible sources of intrinsic interest in activities include the following:

- genetically based temperament or predispositions (e.g., high-arousal people are more likely to prefer active pursuits, whereas low-arousal people are more likely to prefer quieter ones)
- fun, enjoyment
- relevance/utility to one's agendas
- self-actualization potential (allows one to feel empowered, creative)
- meaningful, satisfying (allows one to experience new understandings, take satisfaction in achieving new insights or syntheses of knowledge)
- identification/self-projection (allows one to project oneself into a situation, such as by identifying with a central character in a story, simulation, or historical text)
- identification/assimilation to self (experience with an activity or exposure to modeling or information about it makes one want to engage in it,to learn more about it, etc.).

Most authors distinguish between individual interest and situational interest. Individual interest (also known as personal interest or topic interest) refers to an enduring disposition to engage with particular content or activities whenever opportunities arise. Situational interest is triggered in the moment, emerging in response to something in the situation that catches our attention and motivates to focus on it and explore it further. Situa-tional interest may dissipate quickly (as when we investigate an unexpected sound and discover that it was just the wind blowing something over), or it can become the basis for more sustained investigation and learning (as when an encounter with an interesting anecdote about Albert Einstein motivates a reading of his biography, which in turn motivates a more sustained individual interest in nuclear physics).

Individual Interest

Research on relationships between interest and achievement provides some support for the frequently recommended strategy of capitalizing on students' existing motivation by adapting the curriculum to students' individual interests. One way is to offer activity choices that allow them to pursue those interests. Another way is to use stable individual interests (e.g., in sports) to provide contexts for mathematical problems, writing assignments, or other skill-development activities. When reading in areas of individual interest, students display heightened attention, concentration, positive affect, immediate comprehension of the material, and subsequent test performance.

Students usually have larger and better organized networks of prior knowledge available in their areas of individual interest than in other content domains, which makes it easier for them to assimilate new information in their high-interest areas. However, such interest will not necessarily translate into attainment of curricular goals. This individual interest should serve him well during literacy activities that call for comprehending stories and relating personal reactions to them. However, it may not provide much motivation for activities that call for analyzing stories with respect to formal construction or genre characteristics. For these aspects of literacy instruction, Sam is likely to need assistance in forming appropriate learning goals and maintaining attention to his learning strategies.

Situational Interest

Other motivational strategies call for manipulating learning content or activities so as to stimulate situational interest. These strategies are especially promising because situational interest is more controllable by teachers than individual interest and because research has shown that stimulated situational interest promotes learning and often leads to development of individual interest.

Texts

Manipulations of learning content have focused on three aspects of texts: coherence, vividness, and seductive details.

1. *Coherence* refers to factors that affect readers' ability to recognize and organize the text's main ideas. Many investigators have reported that students not only learn more from easy-to-follow texts, but rate them as more interesting than less coherent tests.
2. *Vividness* refers to text segments that stand out because they are surprising, create suspense, or are otherwise engaging. Vivid text segments tend to be rated as more interesting and remembered better than less vivid segments.
3. *Seductive details* are segments that are unimportant to the text's main themes but memorable because they deal with controversial or sensational topics such as sex, death, or romantic intrigue. Seductive details also are rated as highly interesting and likely to be

remembered—so much so, unfortunately, that they interfere with attention to and memory for main themes or other important text content. The implication here is that any details added to "spice up" a presentation should be included because they support, or at least do not interfere with, attainment of the learning goals.

Besides coherence, vividness, and seductive details, other aspects of texts that stimulate interest include, imagery characters with whom readers can identify, emotionally charged or provocative content, content that is familiar but not overly familiar, and relevance to the readers' personal goals.

Wade, Buxton, and Kelly asked college students to read expository texts and then interviewed them about what they found interesting and uninteresting. Texts characteristics associated with interest included information that was important, new, and valued; information that was unexpected; connections that the readers made between the text and their prior knowledge or experience; imagery and descriptive language; and connections made by the authors using comparisons and analogies. The major factor associated with low interest was low coherence or difficult vocabulary that made the text hard to follow. These findings once again indicate that the overall value and coherence of a text is more closely related to interest than isolated "grabbers" occasionally inserted into individual segments. The authors concluded that there is no need to spice up texts with seductive details, but it is important to present students with coherent renderings of new information that they value as important.

Activities

Independent of their potential interest in its content, learners might be interested in an activity's processes. If such interest is not already present, teachers may be able to stimulate it by encouraging students to expand their goals and task-engagement strategies so as to make the task more interesting for them. For example, students might make the task of copying letters from a template more interesting by: competing against themselves or a friend, competing against time, trying to increase the artfulness of their tracings, varying their procedure, or sorting and categorizing different problems. These or other interest-enhancing task transformations might be encouraged so long as they support progress toward learning goals.

Chen, Darst, and Pangrazi examined the activity aspects of situa-tional interest in a physical education context. They asked students to rate activities with respect to the degree to which they: were new to them (novelty), were experienced as enjoyable (instant enjoyment), stimulated curiosity or interest in exploring the activity (exploration intention), required focused attention (attention demand), and were complex and difficult (challenge). They found that overall interest in the activities was associated primarily with instant enjoyment and secondarily with novelty and exploration intention. Attention demand was less clearly related and challenge was unrelated, leading the authors to suggest that students are unlikely to perceive activities as enjoyable and interesting if they also perceive them as overly challenging.

Pfaffman asked high school students to think about their favorite class and rate the relative importance of five clusters of reasons that might explain why they enjoyed the class so much. He found that reasons related to learning (learning strategies and methods, reading about the subject, learning about dates, places, people, or things), creation (seeing the fruits of their labor, expressing themselves, creating something new or rare), or flow (overcoming new challenges, having clear goals and feedback, doing something as an end in itself) tended to be rated highly, whereas social (to be liked, to belong to a group, to share conversation) and extrinsic (to gain social stature, to win competitions, or to be better than others) reasons were rated much lower. In short, students' favorite classes were those they found intrinsically rewarding. Covington reported similar patterns in college students' reports about what aspects of their classes they most valued.

Askell-Williams and Lawson asked middle-school students to identify the features of interesting lessons. Along with features related to meeting their needs for autonomy, competence, and relatedness, the students frequently mentioned hands-on activities, experiments, work that relates to the outside world, and activities that allow them to design or make things and use their imaginations or be creative, or to do a variety of different things.

Adapting Activities to Students' Interests

To the extent that doing so will support your instructional goals, you can select expository reading assignments and design your classroom presentations to feature elements that enhance their interest value for students. For example, Hidi and Baird found that students' interest was enhanced when the main ideas in an expository text were elaborated through insertions that featured one of the following motivational principles:

character identification (information about people with whom the students could identify, such as those whose inventions or discoveries led to the knowledge under study); novelty (content that was interesting to the students because it was new or unusual); life theme (applications or other connections to things that were important to the students in their lives outside of school); and activity level (content that included reference to intense activities or strong emotions).

Means, Jonassen, and Dwyer increased students' interest in and learning from texts by addressing material that brought out connections between the text content and the students' lives. Others have shown that students' perceptions of the relevance of text content can be increased by asking them to adopt a particular perspective as they read or to read with a particular purpose in mind.

Whenever instructional goals can be accomplished using a variety of examples or activities, incorporate content that students find interesting or activities that they find enjoyable. People, fads, or events that are currently prominent in the news or the youth culture can be worked into everyday lessons as applications of the concepts being learned. For example, a history teacher pointed out that the Ark of the Covenant mentioned in the ancient history text was the same ark featured in the movie Raiders of the Lost Ark. Similarly, a geography teacher sparked interest in studying the coordinates (latitude and longitude) by noting that the sunken remains of the Titanic can be located easily, even though they lie on the ocean floor hundreds of miles out to sea, because the discoverers fixed the location precisely using the coordinates.

Another way to incorporate interests into activities is to encourage students to ask questions and make comments about the topic. Relevant questions and comments create "teachable moments" that you can pursue by temporarily suspending the planned sequence of events in order to address issues raised by students. Such questions or comments indicate interest on the part of students who make them, and chances are good that other students will share this interest.

It also is helpful, both from instructional and from motivational points of view, to plan lessons and assignments that include divergent questions and opportunities for students to express opinions, make evaluations, or in other ways respond personally to the content. For example, after reviewing information about the Christians and the lions, the gladiators, and other excesses of the Roman circuses, a history teacher asked his students why they thought such practices had developed in Roman society and how otherwise cultured people could take pleasure in such cruelty. This led to a productive discussion in which students made contributions and developed insights about issues such as violence in sports and in contemporary society generally, the role of peer pressure in escalating aggression once conflict flares up, and the difference between enjoyment of pleasures and indulgence in excesses. This same teacher, after describing life in Athens and Sparta, asked students which city they would rather live in and why. Again, this led to a lively discussion that included parallels among modern nations that focus on building military strength (at a cost in quality of civilian life) versus maintaining more balanced priorities.

Adapting Traditional Learning Activities

Mark Lepper and Thomas Malone developed theory and research on ways in which conventional school learning activities might be altered or embellished to increase their intrinsic motivation potential. In particular, they suggested making adjustments to enhance one or more of the following four sources of intrinsic motivation: challenge (adjust difficulty levels so that tasks are optimally challenging); curiosity (include elements that will stimulate curiosity); control (offer choices or in other ways encourage students to experience a sense of autonomy or self-determination when they engage in the activities); and fantasy (embellish activities in ways that encourage students to engage in them with a playful set, an identification with fictional characters, or an involvement in a world of fantasy).

Induce Curiosity or Suspense

Student curiosity is the driving force that underlies many theorists' suggestions for motivating students. Successful use of these strategies involves stimulating curiosity in ways that foster development of continuing interest in broad topics or knowledge networks, especially interest in the key ideas around which these networks are structured. Otherwise, students may focus their curiosity on seductive but trivial details or may lose interest in the topic once their initial curiosity is satisfied.

Covington and Teel suggested two strategies for stimulating curiosity: question asking, and discovering mysteries, puzzles, and oddities. Question asking can be used to stimulate curiosity about an upcoming topic ("As we begin our study of France, what are some questions that you have about that country?"), as well as to stimulate renewed enthusiasm following initial development of the topic ("What would you like to know about France that wasn't addressed in the textbook?"). The strategy of discovering mysteries, puzzles, and oddities involves asking students to take note of and bring up for discussion anything in their readings that seems incongruous or surprising.

Some teachers have not only developed techniques for stimulating students' curiosity or whetting their anticipation but also incorporated these techniques within frequently used routines. For example, a mathematics teacher began most classes with an intriguing problem which was written on the board but covered by a rolled down map. His students quickly learned to notice when the map was pulled down and anticipate the moment when he would roll it up with a flourish and "allow" them to see the problem. When he did, he usually had their full attention. Another teacher achieved a similar effect by concealing props within a large that she placed on her desk for use on days when she was going to do some interesting demonstration. Again, all eyes were on her when she opened that box.

Karmos and Karmos described a mathematics teacher who periodically started a lesson by saying "Last night, I went down to my basement and I found..." The first time, he told of finding a tree that doubled its number of branches each hour on the hour, and then used this "discovery" as the basis for posing interesting mathematics problems. Things "found in his basement" on other occasions included alligators and a diesel train. It wasn't long before whenever this teacher said "Last night, I went down to my basement...," his students knew that they could anticipate some preposterous claim followed by some interesting problems.

A topic or activity need not be new in order to generate curiosity. In fact, we often develop curiosity about aspects of topics with which we are familiar and knowledgeable. Such curiosity usually develops when we experience doubt or confusion because we have become aware that our existing ideas appear to be contradictory or incomplete (unable to account for some phenomenon). This motivates to want to sort things out or acquire more information that will allow to resolve the gaps or discrepancies in our thinking.

You can stimulate curiosity or suspense by posing questions or doing "set ups" that make students feel the need to resolve some ambiguity or obtain more information about a topic. To prepare students to read material about Russia, for example, you could ask them if they know how many time zones there are in Russia or how the United States acquired Alaska. Such questions help make new information food for thought and convert "just another reading assignment" into an interesting learning experience. It is mind-boggling for most students to discover that one country encompasses 11 time zones or that the United States purchased Alaska from Russia. These are just two basic facts found in most treatments of the history or geography of Russia.

Whether students find such facts interesting and think about them rather than merely attempt to memorize them depends largely on the degree to which their teachers stimulate curiosity about them and provide contexts for thinking about their associations with prior knowledge or beliefs. This example further illustrates two important points made earlier: Interest resides in people rather than in topics or activities, and the motivation that develops in particular situations does so as a result of interactions among persons, tasks, and the larger social context.

You can stimulate your students' curiosity about a topic and encourage them to generate interest in it by (a) asking them to speculate or make predictions about what they will be learning; (b) raising questions that successful completion of the activity will enable them to answer; and (c) where relevant, showing them that their existing knowledge is not sufficient to enable them to accomplish some valued objective, is internally inconsistent, is inconsistent with new information, or is currently scattered but can be organized around certain general principles or powerful ideas.

Keller noted that one general way to stimulate curiosity is to put students into an active information-processing or problem-solving mode as you introduce learning activities. You can do this by posing interesting questions or problems that students will address as they engage in the activity. For example, the scientific concept of condensation might be introduced by calling students' attention to the water that begins to appear on the outside of a glass of ice water and asking them to explain this phenomenon. If necessary, you could prompt their thinking by suggesting seemingly plausible possibilities ("Is the water seeping through the glass?")

Reeve suggested five strategies for stimulating curiosity: suspense, guessing and feedback, playing to students' sense of knowing, controversy, and contradiction.

Suspense strategies focus students' attention on competing hypotheses or problems with uncertain conclusions. By inviting students to consider competing answers to questions such as what caused the Civil War or why the dinosaurs became extinct, you can create within them a sense of mental struggle that Reeve compared to the struggles experienced by heroes in dramatic plots. Students, especially those prone to say "just tell the answer," can learn to value the process of seeking answers to challenging intellectual questions, as well as to experience the satisfactions of doing so.

The strategy of guessing and feedback involves introducing a topic by giving students a pretest or leading them through a prior knowledge assessment activity that requires them to answer specific questions about the topic. The questions should be usefully connected to key ideas but also likely to produce a variety of responses, so that most students will find they have answered some of them incorrectly (Which is the northernmost state: Colorado, Kansas, or Nebraska?). Reeve argued that the knowledge that one has guessed incorrectly piques one's curiosity to learn more about the topic.

Playing to students' sense of knowing is a related strategy that applies when students already possess considerable prior knowledge about the topic. For example, by the time they reach junior high school, most students have had a great deal of exposure to U.S. maps and geography. If they have begun to respond to these topics with boredom or complacency, a question such as "Name the eight states that border one of the Great Lakes" might restimulate their curiosity and interest, because most of them will be able to identify many but not all of these states correctly.

Controversy strategies involve eliciting divergent opinions on an issue and then inviting students to resolve these discrepancies through sustained discussion. In the process, students may recognize the need to con-sult textbooks or reference materials or conduct other research to obtain needed information.

The contradiction strategy is used after students have assimilated a body of information that has led them to formulate a conclusion. At this point, you introduce additional information that contradicts this conclusion, forces students to recognize that the issue is more complicated than they thought, and stimulates them to develop more complete understandings. Or, having established that humans "sit atop the evolutionary developmental ladder," you might point out that there are more insects than any other species and that their combined weight exceeds that of all animals.

Embellish Learning Activities With Appealing Fantasy Elements

Research on embellishing learning activities with fantasy elements has been done by Mark Lepper and his colleagues. This research has been done in computerized learning situations, but its implications should apply to more conventional learning activities as well. One study was done with a mathematics program designed to teach students about Cartesian coordinates. In the unembellished version, students were asked to find a "hidden dot" lying beneath one of the intersections of an 11 × 11 Cartesian grid, with axes labeled from -5 to +5. Students were to find the dot by guessing its location. After each incorrect guess, they were provided with written and visual feedback (in the form of an arrow) indicating the direction in which the hidden dot lay relative to the point guessed. When they eventually guessed correctly, they were given congratulatory feedback.

In the embellished version, the same problems were presented within a fantasy context designed to heighten interest. Students were invited to help a fantasy character hunt for hidden treasures buried on a desert island. When correct guesses were made, small icons representing a treasure (e.g., an ivory comb, a silver goblet, or a rusty hook) appeared on the screen, accompanied by sound effects.

In another study, students learned to work with a computerized graphics program by completing activities calling for them to draw lines connecting objects on the screen, negotiate passage through a series of mazes, and construct a series of geometric shapes. The unembellished versions of these activities simply called for the students to construct the necessary lines or geometric shapes. The embellished versions involved constructing the same lines or shapes, but presented these tasks within one of three fan-tasy contexts: a pirate in search of buried treasure, a detective hunting down criminals, or an astronaut seeking out new planets in space.

Cordova and Lepper and Iyengar and Lepper demonstrated the value of personalizing the fantasy elements of learning activities. They allowed elementary students to make choices concerning instructionally irrelevant and seemingly trivial aspects of the activities (e.g., the "astronaut" would be allowed to choose the name of the spaceship and include several personal friends as fellow crew members). They found that the students both learned more and showed greater subsequent intrinsic interest in such activities when given these personalization options.

Schank and Cleary developed even more elaborately embellished computerized learning opportunities that incorporated simulation-based learning by doing, incidental learning, learning by reflection, case-based teaching, or learning by exploring. For example, a program for teaching foreign languages leads students through scenarios that require them to use the language they are learning in realistic situations (e.g., arriving in the country by plane and going through customs, finding transportation, and checking in at a hotel). At each step, students interact with simulated people who appear in video clips and respond to what they say. When these communications are successful, the students move on to the next scenario. When communication breaks down, the program offers them options for getting help and then returning to the situation.

An incidental learning program teaches U.S. geography and map skills by allowing students to take simulated car trips around the United States. They begin with a map of the country, zoom in on a particular state by clicking on that state, then see a state map that allows them to zoom in further by clicking on a city. Students then can travel from city to city along the interstate highway system. When they reach a chosen destination, they can watch video clips that feature sports highlights, movie clips, music videos, amusement parks, or historical footage associated with the location. In the process, they familiarize themselves with U.S. states and cities and learn to plan travel using maps.

A case-based approach to teaching biological principles invites students to create their own animal by taking an existing animal and changing it in some way. They begin by selecting possibilities from lists of animals and potential changes, then explore the ramifications of the "created" animal by answering questions. If they select a fish that has wings, for example, the program might ask them to reflect on why the ability to fly would be useful to a fish, when this ability might be used, or what might be some limitations on its use. In the process, they view videos relating to these questions.

An elaborate simulation activity called Broadcast News allows groups of high school social studies students to produce their own news shows on current events, working with real news sources from a day in the recent past. Students follow actual television news procedures and use video equipment to research, write, and edit stories; prioritize and sequence the stories for inclusion in the newscast; then put it all together under "live taping" conditions.

Research on embellishments of conventional learning activities has shown that students prefer the embellished versions and usually show improved learning outcomes as well. Furthermore, these effects are not restricted to children. Moreno and Mayer engaged college students in multimedia science lessons presented either in neutral, third-person language or in more personalized, first- and second-person language. For example, the introduction to the neutral version read, "This program is about what type of plants survive in different planets. For each planet, a plant will be designed. The goal is to learn what type of roots, stem, and leaves allow plants to survive in each environment. Some hints are provided throughout the program." The parallel personalized version read, "You are about to start a journey where you will be visiting different planets. For each planet, you will need to design a plant. Your mission is to learn what type of roots, stem, and leaves will allow your plant to survive in each environment.

Another successful use of the personalization strategy was reported by deSousa and Oakhill. They asked 8- and 9-year-old children to study text passages and attempt to detect problems such as prior knowledge violations, internal inconsistencies, and nonsense words. Some of the children were simply asked to edit the passage, whereas the others were asked to pretend to be detectives while looking for the problems. The children asked to act as detectives found the task more interesting and were more successful in detecting the problems.

Fantasy elements add interest value to activities because they allow students to identify with fantasy characters, feel emotional reactions, and vicariously experience situations that may not be open to them in real life. Fantasy environments can evoke mental images of physical or social situations that are not actually present and thus produce the cognitive advantages that accrue from linking the known to the unfamiliar. Especially useful are fantasy elements that provide helpful metaphors for learning new skills (the family metaphor for mathematical set concepts) or provide real-world contexts within which the skills can be used (simulating running a lemonade stand).

However, Lepper and Cordova cautioned that motivational embellishment strategies do not always have such beneficial effects. The best results can be expected when the embellishments draw students' attention to the key ideas or processes that the activity is designed to teach, and when students must learn these key ideas or processes in order to complete the activity successfully and thus accomplish its fantasy goal. Where fantasy elements do not support learning in this fashion, they may function merely as "bells and whistles" that enhance the affective aspects of intrinsic motivation but do not engage the cognitive aspects that produce desired learning outcomes. Students may learn no more, or even less, from these embellished versions than they would from conventional versions of the same activities.

For example, Reynolds and Symons asked third-grade children to search for information in a text and then record their answers. Half of the children were asked to record answers by writing them on a conventional worksheet, but the other half were allowed to use markers to record their answers and then display them by pasting them to attractive theme boards. The latter children apparently enjoyed these task embellishments, but they did not complete the task any more successfully or show any more interest in the topic than the children who used worksheets.

Fantasy embellishments do not need to be as elaborate as the ones already described. For example, Anand and Ross showed that both motivational and learning benefits resulted when problems on division of fractions were personalized by incorporating references to the students or to people or things with whom they identified (the teacher, their friends, or their favorite foods). You can introduce fantasy or imagination elements into your everyday instruction that will engage your students' emotions or allow them to experience events vicariously. In studying poems or stories, for example, you can encourage students to debate the authors' motives in writing the works or to learn about formative experiences in the authors' lives. In studying scientific or mathematical principles and methods, you can help students to appreciate the practical problems that needed to be solved or the personal motives of the discoverers that led to development of the knowledge or skills being taught.

Alternatively, you can set up role-play or simulation activities that allow students to identify with real or fictional characters or to deal with academic content in direct, personalized ways. Rather than just assign students to read history, for example, you can make it come alive by arranging for them to role play Columbus and his crew debating what to do after 30 days at sea (or at the secondary level, by arranging for them to take the roles of the American, British, and Russian leaders meeting at Yalta).

To dramatize the importance of a genuinely secret ballot, you might have students act out an election scene in a totalitarian state where one must get a pencil from the election supervisors (i.e., officials of the ruling party) if one wishes to write in names instead of voting for the single slate of candidates. To demonstrate the efficiency of assembly lines, you might organize some of your students into an assembly line in which each participant performs one step in the process of making sandwiches or collating information packets.

Elaborate simulations have been developed for teaching many social studies topics, particularly economics. For example, Kourilsky designed the Mini-Society program to teach 7 to 12 year-olds primarily about economics and secondarily about government, career, consumer, and value issues through participation in economic activities followed by debriefing of what was learned. The learning experiences involve participation in a market economy couched within a democratic society. Students learn that scarcity is the problem posed when limited resources are balanced against relatively unlimited wants, and they study the advantages and disadvantages inherent in various economic systems. Then they create within their classroom a minisociety based on market mechanisms. The society includes a name, a flag, a currency system, civil servants, and some initial mechanisms through which citizens can earn money by meeting criteria of good citizenship or accomplishment (as a way to introduce money into circulation). The main activities of the minisociety, however, involve setting up and running businesses that offer goods or services in exchange for minisociety money. In the process, students collaborate with partners to plan and run businesses; vote on taxes, government services, and other policy issues; and engage in a great deal of analysis and decision making on issues in economics and government.

A popular economics simulation for secondary students acquaints them with investing principles by inviting them to establish a simulated investment portfolio. They allocate a given sum to an initial set of investments of their own choosing, then "manage" the portfolio throughout the rest of the term by making any desired changes and updating the associated bookkeeping. The simulated investments are tracked and discussed periodically so that students can understand what would have happened if they had been investing real money and try to determine why some investment decisions worked out better than others. Other economics-based experiential learning activities go beyond simulation by engaging students in developing and running actual businesses, with participation in profits or losses.

Simulation activities are not confined to full-scale drama, role play, simulation games, and other "major productions." More modest simulation exercises can be incorporated into everyday instruction. You can invite students to briefly project themselves into fictional or nonfictional situations under study by asking them "If you were (the story's hero, the president of the United States, a homeless person, etc.), what would you think or feel when that happened? What actions might you take?" In teaching a mathematical procedure, you might ask students to identify problems in everyday living that the proce-dure might be used to solve (and then list these on the board). Material on totalitarian societies might be "brought home" by asking students to imagine and talk about what it would be like to seek housing in a country where the government owned all of the property or to get accurate information about world events in a country where the government controlled all of the media. Reports on states, nations, or cultures might be written as travel brochures or newspaper articles, with students asked to keep their chosen purpose and audience in mind when deciding what to include and how to present it. Such fantasy or simulation exercises do not take much time or require special preparations, but they can stimulate students to relate to the content more personally and to take greater interest in it.

Incorporating Motivational Principles in Instruction

Several broad educational philosophies incorporate principles for connecting with students' existing intrinsic motivation or for supporting its development by engaging them in learning activities designed to be intrinsically motivating (progressive education, discovery learning, open education, Foxfire, whole language). These principles also are emphasized in certain more focused models for incorporating motivational principles in curriculum and instruction.

Motivated Literacy

Julianne Turner described what she called the motivated literacy approach to beginning literacy instruction, defining it as an emphasis on open tasks over closed tasks. Teachers who emphasized closed tasks taught a literacy curriculum focused heavily on teacher-directed skills lessons followed by seatwork assignments on which students worked individually, attempting to provide correct answers to closed-ended questions. In contrast, teachers who favored a motivated literacy approach emphasized more open and authentic tasks. Open tasks included interactive-constructive tasks, in which students could manipulate materials to reach an outcome, such as in a game, or arrange words to reconstruct a nursery rhyme; partner reading, in which two students shared the oral reading of a story; composition, in which students wrote on self-selected topics; and trade-book reading, in which they read self-selected books.

Open tasks allow students to decide what information to use and how they want to use it to solve some larger problem. These tasks feature characteristics emphasized by Lepper and Hodell as associated with intrinsic motivation: challenge and self-improvement, student autonomy, the pursuit of individual interests, and social collaboration. Emphasis on such open tasks promoted significantly greater student engagement in literacy activities, as indicated by increased reading strategy use, persistence, and following through to task completion and accomplishment of learning goals.

Several teachers reproduced texts from stories or nursery rhymes on oaktag, cutting the sentences into individual words. Then they invited their students to reconstruct the sentences in meaningful ways. This was a challenging activity for even the best readers, yet still accessible to readers at lower levels. It required students to use a sophisticated array of strategies including designing a plan, rehearsing, decoding, monitoring for upper- and lowercase letters and punctuation, sequencing, and backtracking for comprehension. Errors prompted them to try other word sequences. Frequently they tried many arrangements, rereading each time to determine if they were satisfied with their construction.

Other teachers designed multiple activities that supported their instructional goals and then allowed students to select from among them. For example, one classroom featured a week-long celebration of Clifford's Birthday Party which embedded activity options including writing about the party described in the book, writing about a parallel party held in their classroom, writing party invitations, making a list of party supplies, drawing and labeling Clifford's gifts, and reading other Clifford books. In carrying out these activities, the students produced products that showed care, planning, and originality and sparked task-oriented conversations. Turner attributed this in part to the students' opportunities to select activities that they found most interesting.

Several teachers allowed their students to work with selected partners to choose learning tasks and then sequence their learning activities. These teachers helped each pair of partners to think through their choices, make decisions about how to plan and monitor their work, evaluate their completed products, and note things to keep in mind for the future.

Some teachers connected with students' interests by allowing them to select books to read. The added incentive of choosing an intriguing book supported students' engagement during oral reading times and encouraged them to persist in reading difficult texts. Similarly, frequent composition opportunities allowed students to explore topics of importance to them. In one class, for example, all students wrote on the theme of butterflies, but responses ranged from discussions of the life cycle to pretend fantasies.

Students in motivated literacy classrooms often worked in pairs or small groups, which allowed them to pique one another's curiosity, share interests, and model expertise that classmates could emulate. This reflected the fact that open tasks are more flexible and conducive to student collaboration than closed tasks that allow for only one approach or answer.

Miller and Meece, in a study of third graders, also found a preference for open and challenging tasks over closed and less challenging tasks. Students reported feeling creative, experiencing positive emotions, and taking satisfaction in working hard at high-challenge tasks, but feeling bored and not engaged in productive thinking when working on low-challenge tasks.

Anderman described a motivating approach to writing instruction. In this study, third and fourth graders were asked to spend time each day writing in journals about any topic they wished to address. They also participated in weekly feedback sessions in which they read their writings to the teacher and other students. Over time, these students not only developed their writing abilities but acquired a continuing desire to engage in journal writing. Their writing became more communicative, consisting of letters and stories rather than lists. It also revealed a broader understanding of the uses of writing, greater persistence at writing tasks, and increased creativity.

Project-Based Learning

Phyllis Blumenfeld and her colleagues described project-based learning, a comprehensive approach to classroom teaching and learning that incorporates several principles for capitalizing on students' intrinsic motivation. It calls for engaging students in projects: relatively long-term, problem-focused, and meaningful units of instruction that integrate concepts from a number of disciplines or fields of study. Within the framework, students pursue solutions to authentic problems by asking and refining questions, debating ideas, making predictions, designing plans or experiments, collecting and analyzing data, drawing conclusions, communicating their ideas and findings to others, asking new questions, and creating products.

There are two essential components to projects: They require a question or problem that organizes and drives activities, and the activities result in a series of products that culminate in a final product that addresses the driving question. The final products represent the students' problem solutions, organized and presented in a form (e.g., a model, report, videotape, or computer program) that can be shared with others and critiqued. Feedback from others permits students to reflect on and extend their emergent knowledge and to revise their products if necessary. Project-based learning incorporates the following motivational features: Tasks are varied and include novel elements, problems are authentic and challenging, students exercise choice in deciding what to do and how to do it, they collaborate with peers in carrying out the work, and the work leads to closure in the form of production of the final product.

These motivational features of project work do not guarantee that students will acquire needed information, generate and test solutions, and evaluate their findings carefully. Teachers using project-based learning need to make sure that students possess whatever subject-matter knowledge and research skills are required to complete their projects successfully, learn key ideas and skills in the process of carrying them out, view the projects as authentic, and value the products they create.

Howard Gardner proposed a radical restructuring of K–12 schooling in which students would spend most of their time engaged in project-based learning, in and out of classroom settings. Projects can be developed for any subject, although they are especially well suited to science and social studies. Blumenfeld et al. suggested ways in which projects can be designed to maximize their motivational impact. Some of these involve using emerging technology that enables students to work with computerized data bases in conducting their research or to use computerized design, video technology, and other innovations in developing their products. Singer, Marx, Krajcik, and Chambers drew on experiences using project-based learning in middle schools to identify principles for designing projects and for scaffolding students' work on them to ensure that they engage in desired forms of collaborative inquiry.

Teachers' Experience-based Motivational Strategies

For example, all of the 36 teachers interviewed by Flowerday and Schraw endorsed offering choices as an effective motivational strategy, although the nature and extent of the choices they offered their students varied considerably. The teachers believed that increased student choice leads to increased interest, engagement, and learning, across Grades K–12, especially for students who do not show much motivation for school activities. They felt that choice gives students a greater sense of responsibility that increases their ownership in the activity and thus their motivation to learn. Noting that students may choose unproductively if left on their own, the teachers suggested two strategies for dealing with this problem. The first involved requiring students to choose from a menu of provided selections. In developing these menus, the teachers would make sure that all of the selections were suited to the instructional goals but also likely to be attractive options to students. The second strategy involved scaffolding students' choice-making by helping them take into account relevant criteria such as whether they were likely to find the task engaging, to be able to complete it successfully, and to gain the intended learning benefits from it.

Nolen and Nicholls investigated teachers' beliefs about the relative effectiveness of different motivational strategies. They found that the teachers emphasized encouraging cooperative learning, offering stimulating tasks, giving choices, and attributing thought and interest over strategies such as praising, publicizing superior performance, or using task-extrinsic rewards.

Hootstein interviewed eighth-grade teachers about the strategies they used to motivate students to learn U.S. history. The 10 most frequently mentioned strategies were: having students role-play characters in historical simulations (mentioned by 83% of the teachers), organizing projects that result in the creation of products (60%), playing games with students as a way to review material for tests (44%), relating history to current events or to students' lives (44%), assigning students to read historical novels (44%), asking thought-provoking questions (33%), inviting guest speakers from the community (33%), showing historical videos and films (28%), organizing cooperative learning activities (28%), and providing small-scale hands-on experiences (28%).

Hootstein also gathered responses from the eighth graders taught by these teachers. He showed them the strategies mentioned by their teachers and asked them to identify the single strategy that would most motivate them to want to learn U.S. history. Role playing historical characters was the strategy mentioned most often, followed by participating in group discussions of the textbook or other material. The students also mentioned teacher attempts to make the subject interesting to them, to relate it to current events or their own interests, or to inject humor through jokes, stories, or anecdotes. Here is additional evidence that students do not necessarily need technology, games, or various "bells and whistles" to enjoy learning, and that they even enjoy relatively passive forms of learning if the teacher makes the material interesting to them.

Zahorik asked 30 elementary and 35 secondary teachers enrolled in a graduate course to write papers on what makes for a good learning experience; a very interesting activity they had used; how they created interest; and subject-matter facts and concepts they had found to be interesting to students. The teachers' papers once again emphasized the intrinsic motivational strategies, although in ways that underscored their limitations as well as their strengths.

The actions that teachers reported taking for generating interest in learning were concentrated in eight categories. The most popular category, mentioned by 100% of the teachers, was hands-on activities. Examples included manipulatives such as pattern blocks in mathematics; playing games of all kinds; simulations, role play, and drama; projects such as growing seedlings in science or making television commercials in Spanish; and solving problems or puzzles such as determining the sugar content of chewing gum.

Personalized content was mentioned by 65% of the teachers. These responses took three forms: tying content to students' prior knowledge, experiences, or interests (beginning a unit on weather by having students discuss their experiences with tornadoes); allowing students to generate the content to be studied, often through teacher-student planning; selecting from the required curriculum that content which is likely to interest students (appealing novels; rules for how married names are composed in Spanish). Also mentioned by 65% of the teachers were student trust techniques that show respect for students' intelligence, integrity, and pride. They permit students to share their ideas and experiences through dialogue, reporting, debating, and displaying work; to make decisions for themselves and use their creativity; or to develop ownership of classroom events through involvement in planning units and choosing tasks.

Group tasks were mentioned by 55% of the teachers. These were activities that students carried out cooperatively in small groups, such as performing a group science demonstration on water evaporation and condensation.

The remaining categories included using a variety of materials (29%), teacher enthusiasm (28%), practical tasks that involve students in activities that have utility outside of school or produce a useful product (17%), and using a variety of activities (11%). In speaking of variety, the teachers especially mentioned materials, resources, or activities that were atypical in some way, such as field trips, guest speakers, artifacts, or animals. Examples of teacher enthusiasm included being humorous and emphasizing fun, describing personal experiences to students, participating in tasks as an equal group member, showing excitement, and communicating a sense of purpose, direction, or organization to students. One teacher, for example, dressed up as a story character. Another told her students about her recent trip to Spain. Practical activities included artwork that could be used as gifts, producing a book for others to read, learning how to read a menu, planning a trip to a national park, and discussing contraception.

Among activities that they avoided for motivational reasons, teachers mentioned sedentary activities (explaining, giving directions, reviewing, testing, reading textbooks, doing workbooks, taking notes); unsuitable tasks (too difficult or extensive, or too easy or redundant); artificial tasks that have no perceived practical utility or application outside of school; student distrust (unilateral actions taken by the teacher in areas where student choice could have been provided); and teacher insipidity (the teacher displaying lack of enthusiasm, caring, fun, or involvement).

The teachers had disappointingly little to say about putting students into contact with inherently interesting content. Their content-related responses focused more on topics than ideas, and usually involved adding interesting elements to the content rather than helping students to develop interest in or appreciation for the content base itself. The teachers reported that their students were interested in the following categories of topics: human (anything that has to do with people or culture, such as the skeleton, food, family, diseases, pets, weapons, holidays, sex, death, violence, or money); now (topics of current importance in the students' lives such as television, drugs, fashion, music, gangs, shopping malls, and slang); nature (topics relating to the physical and biological world such as dinosaurs, giraffes, the sea, ecology, wolves, and weather); and functional (any topic that could be shown to be practical or useful, such as safety, consumerism, map reading, the stock market, or computers).

When the teachers did mention ideas embedded in the content that could provide a basis for capturing students' interest, many of their responses referred to very limited ideas or specific facts (such as that Van Gogh cut off his own ear). However, some teachers, especially secondary teachers, did mention more broadly applicable ideas (no country exists that does not need another country for something; plants and animals exist in symbiotic relationships; the passive voice is used in Spanish to shift blame away from persons).

In discussing these findings, Zahorik expressed concern that many of the teachers seemed to treat hands-on activities more as ends than as means. At least a third of their reported hands-on activities seemed gratuitous—likely to generate interest but not to lead to important learning. For example, a fifth-grade social studies unit on the 1950s included activities calling for singing Elvis Presley songs, impersonating Elvis, writing essays speculating on whether Elvis was still alive, and critiquing Elvis's movies. Like others who have commented on this point, Zahorik cautioned that hands-on activities will not produce important learning unless they include minds-on features that engage students in thinking about powerful ideas.

Among activities that they avoided for motivational reasons, teachers mentioned sedentary activities (explaining, giving directions, reviewing, testing, reading textbooks, doing workbooks, taking notes); unsuitable tasks (too difficult or extensive, or too easy or redundant); artificial tasks that have no perceived practical utility or application outside of school; student distrust (unilateral actions taken by thc teacher in areas where student choice could have been provided); and teacher insipidity (the teacher displaying lack of enthusiasm, caring, fun, or involvement).

The teachers had disappointingly little to say about putting students into contact with inherently interesting content. Their content-related responses focused more on topics than ideas, and usually involved adding interesting elements to the content rather than helping students to develop interest in or appreciation for the content base itself. The teachers reported that their students were interested in the following categories of topics: human (anything that has to do with people or culture, such as the skeleton, food, family, diseases, pets, weapons, holidays, sex, death, violence, or money); now (topics of current importance in the students' lives such as television, drugs, fashion, music, gangs, shopping malls, and slang); nature (topics relating to the physical and biological world such as dinosaurs, giraffes, the sea, ecology, wolves, and weather); and functional (any topic that could be shown to be practical or useful, such as safety, consumerism, map reading, the stock market, or computers).When the teachers did mention ideas embedded in the content that could provide a basis for capturing students' interest, many of their responses referred to very limited ideas or specific facts (such as that Van Gogh cut off his own ear). However, some teachers, especially secondary teachers, did mention more broadly applicable ideas (no country exists that does not need another country for something; plants and animals exist in symbiotic relationships; the passive voice is used in Spanish to shift blame away from persons).

In discussing these findings, Zahorik expressed concern that many of the teachers seemed to treat hands-on activities more as ends than as means. At least a third of their reported hands-on activities seemed gratuitous—likely to generate interest but not to lead to important learning. For example, a fifth-grade social studies unit on the 1950s included activities calling for singing Elvis Presley songs, impersonating Elvis, writing essays speculating on whether Elvis was still alive, and critiquing Elvis's movies. Like others who have commented on this point, Zahorik cautioned that hands-on activities will not produce important learning unless they include minds-on features that engage students in thinking about powerful ideas.

Zahorik concluded by suggesting that the key to the minds-on aspect of learning activities is getting students in touch with the powerful ideas that an-chor content structures, reflect major instructional goals, and provide the basis for authentic applications. This is another way of saying that in order to support significant learning, intrinsic motivation needs to include the cognitive/learning aspects associated with motivation to learn, not just the affective/fun aspects associated with interest or enjoyment. Middleton studied the motivational beliefs of teachers and students in middle-school mathematics classes. He found that both groups emphasized both expectancy and value issues when discussing motivation, although high-achieving students placed more emphasis on value (they wanted tasks to be interesting) and low-achieving students placed more emphasis on control (they wanted tasks that they could handle without difficulty).

Teachers' beliefs about what makes mathematics intrinsically motivating to students were associated not only with the teachers' motivational practices but also with their students' motivational ideas. For example, one teacher believed that involving his students in applications to real-life problems was the key to motivation in mathematics. His students were especially likely to report that application activities were more fun than other mathematics activities. In contrast, another teacher believed that her students were most motivated when they found the work easy, and in fact this is what her students reported. A third teacher placed relatively equal emphasis on task difficulty and challenge, learning with understanding, and hands-on activities, and her students showed a similar variety and balance in talking about what makes mathematical activities fun. These findings underscore the fact that teachers can shape their students' motivational orientations, not just react to them.

This same point was emphasized by Mitchell, who followed up on an idea originally suggested by John Dewey in distinguishing between catching students' interest and holding their interest. Mitchell's research in secondary mathematics classrooms suggested that motivational techniques such as presenting students with brain teasers or puzzles, allowing them to work on computers, or allowing them to work in groups were effective in catching initial interest in mathematical learning activities but not in holding that interest in ways that led to accomplishment of significant learning goals. Instead, the latter outcome was associated with content emphases that reflected the principle of meaningfulness and instructional methods that reflected the principle of involvement. A subsequent study at the college level also found that "hold" factors were better predictors of continuing interest in the subject than "catch" factors.

REFERENCES

Aronson, E., Blaney, N., Stephan, C., Sikes, J., & Snapp, M. (1978). *The Jigsaw classroom.* Beverly Hills, CA: Sage.

Csikszentmihalyi, M. (1993). *The evolving self: A psychology for the third millennium.* New York: HarperCollins

Eckblad, G. (1981). *Scheme theory: A conceptual framework for cognitive-motivational processes.* New York: Academic Press.

Rogoff, B., Turkanis, C., & Bartlett, L. (2001). *Learning together: Children and adults in a school community.* New York: Oxford University Press.

Sansone, C., & Morgan, C. (1992). Intrinsic motivation and education: Competence in context. *Motivation and Emotion,* 16, 249–270.

8

Motivation to Learn

Infants and young children appear to be propelled by curiosity, driven by an intense need to explore, interact with, and make sense of their environment. Rarely does one hear parents complain that their pre-schooler is unmotivated. Unfortunately, as children grow, their passion for learning frequently seems to shrink. Learning often becomes associated with drudgery instead of delight. A large number of students—more than one in four—leave school before graduating. Many more are physically present in the classroom but largely mentally absent; they fail to invest themselves fully in the experience of learning. Awareness of how students' attitudes and beliefs about learning develop and what facilitates learning for its own sake can assist educators in reducing student apathy.

Student motivation naturally has to do with students' desire to participate in the learning process. But it also concerns the reasons or goals that underlie their involvement or noninvolvement in academic activities. Although students may be equally motivated to perform a task, the sources of their motivation may differ. A student who is intrinsically motivated undertakes an activity for its own sake, for the enjoyment it provides, the learning it permits, or the feelings of accomplishment it evokes. An extrinsically motivated student performs in order to obtain some reward or avoid some punishment external to the activity itself, such as grades, stickers, or teacher approval.

The term *Motivation to Learn* has a slightly different meaning. It is defined by one author as the meaningfulness, value, and benefits of academic tasks to the learner—regardless of whether or not they are intrinsically interesting. Another notes that motivation to learn is characterized by long-term, quality involvement in learning and commitment to the process of learning.

According to Jere Brophy, motivation to learn is a competence acquired through general experience but stimulated most directly through modeling, communication of expectations, and direct instruction or socialization by significant others (especially parents and teachers).

Children's home environment shapes the initial constellation of attitudes they develop toward learning. When parents nurture their children's natural curiosity about the world by welcoming their questions, encouraging exploration, and familiarizing them with resources that can enlarge their world, they are giving their children the message that learning is worthwhile and frequently fun and satisfying.

When children are raised in a home that nurtures a sense of self-worth, competence, autonomy, and self-efficacy, they will be more apt to accept the risks inherent in learning. Conversely, when children do not view themselves as basically competent and able, their freedom to engage in academically challenging pursuits and capacity to tolerate and cope with failure are greatly diminished.

Once children start school, they begin forming beliefs about their school-related successes and failures. The sources to which children attribute their successes (commonly effort, ability, luck, or level of task difficulty) and failures (often lack of ability or lack of effort) have important implications for how they approach and cope with learning situations.

The beliefs teachers themselves have about teaching and learning and the nature of the expectations they hold for students also exert a powerful influence (Raffini). As Deborah Stipek notes, "To a very large degree, students expect to learn if their teachers expect them to learn."

Schoolwide goals, policies, and procedures also interact with classroom climate and practices to affirm or alter students' increasingly complex learning-related attitudes and beliefs.

And developmental changes comprise one more strand of the motivational web. For example, although young children tend to maintain high expectations for success even in the face of repeated failure, older students do not. And although younger children tend to see effort as uniformly positive, older children view it as a "double-edged sword". To them, failure following high effort appears to carry more negative implications—especially for their self-concept of ability—than failure that results from minimal or no effort.

In this chapter by *motivation to learn*, we mean a student's tendency to find academic activities meaningful and worthwhile and to try to get the intended learning benefits from them. In contrast to intrinsic motivation, which is primarily an affective response to an activity, motivation to learn is primarily a cognitive response involving attempts to make sense of the activity, understand the knowledge it develops, and master the skills that it promotes. Interest leading to play or casual exploration is not the same as motivated and focused learning. If students construe a situation as play rather than learning, they usually will not activate relevant learning schemas so as to systematically extract the gist of the experience and "organize and file" it for later application. Students may be motivated to learn from an activity whether or not they find its content interesting or its processes enjoyable. They may not get to choose the activity, but they can choose to make the most of the learning opportunities it presents. In essence, motivation to learn is adoption of learning goals and related strategies; it is not linked directly to either extrinsic motivation or intrinsic motivation.

Motivational Concepts

It is a broader concept, however, meant to apply not only to achievement situations that involve specific goals but also to other situations in or out of school that offer the potential for learning. This learning may be incidental rather than intentional—discovered in the process of task engagement rather than acquired systematically through goal-directed behavior.

This definition of motivation to learn harks back to the distinction between learning and performance: Learning refers to the information processing, sensemaking, and advances in comprehension or mastery that occur while one is acquiring knowledge or skill; performance refers to the demonstration of such knowledge or skill after it has been acquired. Strategies for stimulating students' motivation to learn apply not only to their performance (work on tests or assignments) but also to their information-processing during learning (attending to lessons, reading for understanding, comprehending explanations, putting things into their own words). Stimulating motivation to learn involves encouraging students to use thoughtful information-processing and skill-building strategies when they are learning. This is quite different from merely offering them incentives for good performance later.

The learning taught in schools is mostly cognitive—abstract concepts and verbally coded information. To make good progress, students need to develop and use generative learning strategies. That is, they need to process information actively, relate it to their existing knowledge, make sure that they understand it, and so on. Therefore, motivating students to learn means not only stimulating them to take an interest in and the value of what they are learning, but also providing them with guidance about how to go about learning it.

Teachers frame lessons and assignments in terms of what students will learn from them and emphasize the importance of thinking and understanding over supplying "right answers" and completing worksheets. Students come to themselves as learners and problem solvers who are expanding their understandings with guidance from their teachers. Hermine Marshall contrasted these learning orientation classes with classes that featured a work orientation. Here, students tended to view assignments as tasks to be completed so that they could receive a reward or go out to recess. They frequently did not understand the purposes of activities, and they engaged in them using surface-level rather than deeper-level information processing and retention strategies. Their teachers made frequent references to "work" and the need to get "work" finished, and their curricula emphasized dittos and workbooks. In contrast, the learning oriented classrooms featured many more open-ended and authentic tasks.

Penny Oldfather described the continuing impulse to learn as an ongoing engagement with learning that is propelled and focused by the thoughts and feelings that emerge when students construct meaning. It is characterized by intense involvement, curiosity, and a search for understanding. The continuing impulse to learn goes well beyond situational interest in a topic or activity. Developing it requires creating classroom cultures in which students discover what they care about, create their own learning agendas, and most importantly, connect who they are to what they do in school. In a study of high school literacy teachers recognized as successful at motivating their students to learn what was taught in their courses, Oldfather and Thomas found that these teachers used a variety of techniques but all shared two core beliefs: It is essential for teachers to build personal relationships with their students, and teaching needs to integrate what occurs in the classroom with the world out of school.

Authors writing about curiosity or interest sometimes describe subtypes that resemble motivation to learn. For example, Kintsch distinguished between emotional interest and cognitive interest in a text. Emotional interest refers to the arousal of feelings in response to text features that initially catch attention, whereas cognitive interest is a more intellectual response to the meaning and relevance of the text's content. Alexander reviewed research suggesting that cognitive interest and related learning goals can be stimulated by encouraging students to define learning goals for themselves, pursue their individual interests in meaningful ways, and experience self-determination or choice as they do so. She argued that students primed to become more knowledgeable about a topic are likely to display cognitive interest in expository texts, even if they lack the more naturally engaging features of narrative text.

Phyllis Blumenfeld and her colleagues also developed a concept of student motivation to learn that combines motivation and cognitive engagement, based on studies of fifth-and sixth-grade science classes. In classes in which students reported lower motivation to learn, the teachers focused on recitation, quizzes, and grades. In classes in which students reported higher motivation to learn, teachers stressed ideas rather than facts, highlighted the value of science through stories about scientists or about how science connects to everyday events, and expressed their own enthusiasm for the subject by relating stories of their personal scientific experiences. They made conceptual material more concrete and interesting by providing examples and connecting the material to their students' experiences or to current events. They also assigned more varied tasks and encouraged students to cooperate in small groups.

Four factors characterized the classes in which students reported higher levels of motivation to learn:

1. *Opportunities to learn.* The teachers (a) focused lessons around mid-level concepts that were substantive but not overwhelming to students; (b) made the main ideas evident in presentations, demonstrations, discussions, and assignments; (c) developed concepts by presenting concrete illustrations of scientific principles and relating unfamiliar information to their students' personal knowledge; (d) made explicit

connections between new information and things that students had learned previously and pointed out relationships among new ideas by stressing similarities and differences; (e) elaborated extensively on textbook readings rather than allowing the book to "carry the lesson"; (f) guided students' thinking when posing high-level questions; and (g) asked students to summarize, make comparisons between related concepts, and apply the information they were learning. In combination, these methods provided students with frequent opportunities to learn, and where necessary, with assistance in helping them do so.

2. *Press.* The teachers pressed for thinking through their expectations for lesson participation, their questions to students, and their follow-up to the students' responses. They (a) required students to explain and justify their answers; (b) prompted, reframed the question, or broke it into smaller parts when students were unsure, and probed students when their understanding was unclear; (c) monitored for comprehension rather than procedural correctness during activities; (d) encouraged responses from all students through such techniques as asking students to vote or to compare their responses and debate the merits of different ideas (rather than allowing a small subgroup to dominate the lessons); and (e) supplemented the "short answer" assignments in the commercial workbooks by adding questions that required explanations of results or alternative representations of information in the form of diagrams or charts. They required their students to actively think about what they were hearing or reading, instead of just monitoring it passively or trying to memorize it.

3. *Support.* These teachers supported their students' attempts to understand through modeling and scaffolding. They (a) modeled thinking, suggested strategies, and worked with students to solve problems when the students had difficulty (instead of just providing answers); (b) reduced the procedural complex-ity of manipulative tasks by demonstrating procedures, highlighting problems, providing examples, or allowing for planning time; and (c) encouraged collaborative efforts by requiring all students to make contributions to the group. Thus, besides exerting a consistent press for thinking and learning through the demands they made on their students, these teachers gave the students whatever help they needed to enable them to meet those demands.

3. *Evaluation.* These teachers' evaluation and accountability systems emphasized understanding and learning rather than work completion, performance, peer comparisons, or right answers. They used mistakes as ways to help students check their thinking, and they explicitly encouraged students to take risks. Finally, they allowed students who had done poorly to redo assignments or retake quizzes.

All four of these factors need to be present and working together in order to develop motivation to learn that includes high levels of cognitive engagement in the content and learning activities. For example, one teacher's students reported high levels of motivation but low levels of cognitive engagement. He typically began each lesson by trying to pique students' interest using humor, dramatic visual aids, connections to students' experiences, or his own enthusiasm. However, he did not follow up by using teaching techniques that encourage high cognitive engagement. His questions tended to be low level, generally requiring only recall. He rarely checked to make sure that students understood main ideas before moving on. He did not call on many students to respond and usually provided elaboration himself rather than eliciting it from students. Nor did he ask students to make and justify predictions, to relate points under discussion to prior knowledge, or to summarize or extend their learning. Instead, he relied heavily on information presentation, often reading from the textbook or calling on students to read aloud, then asking questions that required only repetition or simple paraphrasing of the reading. He sometimes inserted comments or asked questions designed to sustain students' interest in the material, but he did not provide them with opportunities to synthesize or apply what they were learning.

In summarizing their findings, Blumenfeld et al. stated that teachers need to do two things in order to motivate their students to learn and to think carefully about what they are learning: Bring the lesson to the students by providing opportunities for them to learn and stimulating them to take interest or value in the learning, and bring the students to the lesson by requiring them to think about and use the material and supporting their efforts to do so. The teacher just described did a good job of enhancing the interest value of his lessons, but he did not consistently provide students with quality opportunities to learn. He did not "bring them to the lesson" by requiring them to think about the material and supporting their learning efforts.

Middleton and Midgley provided additional support for the importance of bringing students to the lesson in a study of students' perceptions of press for understanding in middle-school math classes. They found that students had higher self-efficacy perceptions, engaged in more self-regulated learning, and were more willing to seek help in classes that they perceived as high in press for understanding than in classes they perceived as low in press for understanding. They emphasized that productive press focuses on understanding (challenging students to think deeply about the content, rather than merely demanding good performance on assignments and tests).

Socializing Appreciation for School Activities

Students do not need to enjoy school activities in order to be motivated to learn from them, but they do need to perceive these activities as meaningful and worthwhile. To develop such perceptions in your students, you will need to make sure that your curriculum content and learning activities are in fact meaningful and worthwhile, and develop this content and scaffold your students' engagement in learning activities in ways that enable them to and appreciate their value.

To ground your efforts to socialize students to value school activities, you will need to focus your curriculum on content that is at least potentially relevant to students and applicable to their lives outside of school. If your instructional planning is guided by appropriate purposes and goals phrased in terms of student outcomes, your curriculum should feature content that students can appreciate as worthwhile and activities that they can appreciate as authentic. This will put you in position to help students learn with awareness of each lesson or activity's purposes and goals.

These powerful ideas will be developed in sufficient depth to promote deep understanding of their meanings and connections, appreciation of their significance, and exploration of their applications to life outside of school. As much as possible, this learning will occur through engagement in authentic activities that require using what is being learned for accomplishing the very sorts of life applications that justify inclusion of this content in the curriculum in the first place.

Assuming that your curriculum content and associated learning activities are potentially meaningful and worthwhile for your students, how can you help your students to appreciate their value and become motivated to want to learn from them? Despite the obvious importance of this question, only a small portion of the motivational theory and research developed to date can be applied to it, because most of the available theory and research addresses the expectancy or milieu aspects of motivation but not its value aspects. To illustrate this, consider the following examples:

1. Two seemingly similar students in the same classroom have the same exposure to the same potential learning experience (hearing or reading a selection from a story book or history text; watching a video that dramatizes a story or depicts a historical event). As a result of this experience, one of the students gets "turned on" to that literary genre or historical era, but the other does not. Why?
2. A teacher wants to teach *King Lear* (or the U.S. Constitution, or photosynthesis) in ways that motivate students not only to remember key ideas but to appreciate Shakespeare (or civics, or biology), value it, and seek to learn more about it on their own.

What motivational concepts or principles might help to explain Example 1 or formulate good advice to the teacher in Example 2? The current knowledge base doesn't take very far in addressing these questions beyond identifying parameters within which value may be nurtured: that is, motivation is unlikely to thrive when the task is too difficult, when learners feel pressured or threatened, and so on. Once these boundary conditions are met, the question becomes: Given situational conditions that create a supportive social context and optimize the expectancy aspects of motivation, what features of the learning domain or activity affect the value aspects, and how might these features be configured or adjusted to help students appreciate the value of what they are learning?

Optimal Matching

Models of cognitive development and learning typically include an optimal match principle: The best learning activities are optionally challenging, being neither too easy nor too difficult for the learner. Sociocultural models extend this idea to include the role of the teacher in optimizing the match, because mediation (via modeling, coaching, and scaffolding) can transform a task that is too difficult for self-guided learning into a task that lies within the zone of proximal development for mentor-guided learning.

Similar concepts are needed in the motivational sphere. First, we need a motivational optimal match principle which postulates that the features of a learning domain or activity must line up with the learner's prior knowledge and experiences in such a way as to stimulate interest in pursuing the learning. This would occur when the domain or activity is familiar enough to be recognizable as a learning opportunity, and attractive enough to interest the learner in pursuing it. It would not occur if the activity were overly familiar to the point that the learner had become satiated with it (at least temporarily), if it were so unfamiliar that the learner could not understand or appreciate its potential value, or if the learner's prior experiences with it had been unrewarding.

We also need a motivational analog of the "zone of proximal development" concept to incorporate the idea that teachers or other mentors can help learners begin to see the value in potential learning opportunities that they have not yet come to appreciate (and might never come to appreciate) on their own. Motivationally effective teachers make school learning experiences meaningful for students not only in the cognitive sense (enabling the students to learn the content with understanding), but also in the motivational sense (enabling them to appreciate its value, particularly its potential applications in their lives outside of school).

In summary, the classroom learning situation is optimal from a motivational standpoint when it features curricular content and learning activities that are well matched to the learner's current characteristics because they are either (a) already familiar to the learners and valued as learning opportunities worth pursuing or (b) less familiar to or valued by the learners but nevertheless within their motivational zones of proximal development, so that they can begin to value them if the teacher mediates their learning experiences effectively.

Identification/Self-Relevance Perceptions

To explain group and individual differences in the initiation and development of sustained interests and appreciations, we also need concepts that describe the "task attraction" or "rewarding experience" elements of the optimal match described earlier. At minimum, learners must perceive some relevance of the potential learning opportunity to their personal agendas. Better yet, they should respond to the potential learning situation in a more personal or intense fashion—in effect, saying to themselves "I am that," "I want to do that," "This is for me," and so on.

The concept of identification is useful here—construed to include not only identification with a person or model, but also identification with an interest area or genre of knowledge or skill (hereafter called a learning domain). Lawrence Kohlberg used the latter identification concept in his gender-role identification theory: As toddlers and young children become aware that they are either boys or girls, they become motivated to explore what this means and to identify with anything (e.g., types of clothing, toys, developmental tasks, or recreation activities) that they come to perceive as linked to their own gender. That is, boys tend to develop preferences for and motivation to pursue "male" interests, and girls "female" interests.

Also potentially useful here are various self-concepts, including ideal selves or possible selves. As children develop, their self-concepts become more salient and better articulated, and these begin to spawn self-relevance perceptions that may apply to any aspect of life.

In summary, location of a learning opportunity within or below the learners' motivational zones of proximal development makes it possible for them to come to appreciate the value of the learning. The development of such appreciation becomes much more likely, however, to the extent that the learners perceive the learning as relevant to their personal agendas.

Ideally, they will respond to the learning opportunity in a personal or intense fashion—in effect saying to themselves, "I am that," "I want to do that," "This is for me," and so on. If they do not identify with the learning so intensely, they should at least perceive it as self-relevant. If self-relevance is not already obvious to them, their teacher will need to mediate the learning in such a way that desired self-relevance perceptions are developed.

Building Motivated Learning Schemas

Creating motivationally optimized learning situations requires attention to both curriculum and instruction. A goal-oriented curriculum is crucial because unless there are good reasons for learning something and authentic activities to use as vehicles for developing this learning, there is no basis for appreciating the learning. Instruction is crucial as well, however, because optimally mediated learning experiences raise students' consciousness of the purposes and goals of each activity and help them to build schemas that will enable them to learn with understanding, appreciation, and life applications (and thus to derive the motivational benefits as well as the knowledge and skill benefits that the learning activities are designed to develop).

Much of what we teach in school, especially in the humanities and social sciences, is primarily cognitive rather than perceptual or sensorimotor, and often is relatively abstract and complex. Consequently, so are the aesthetic and other forms of satisfaction that may be experienced in learning this content, as well as the processes involved in applying it to life outside of school. Given these complexities, few students are likely to experience the satisfactions and acquire the application potentials that school learning opportunities offer unless we do a better job of building these outcomes into our instructional goals.

We include the term appreciation to connote that students should not merely understand what they are learning but value it because they realize that there are good reasons for learning it. These reasons include not only practical applications but ways that the learning might enrich students' repertoires of insights and recognitions or otherwise enhance the quality of their inner lives. We include the term life application as a reminder that students should experience authentic activities that will enable them to apply what they are learning to their lives outside of school. Many so-called "application exercises" do not qualify as authentic activities because they are too artificial to be very useful as preparation for genuine applications, and many so-called "authentic activities" are so far removed from everyday life that they have application potential only for specialists in the disciplines. Most students' life applications of school subjects involve acting as consumers/appliers of discipline-based knowledge, not as disciplinary practitioners engaged in producing such knowledge.

The notion of learning with understanding, appreciation, and attention to life applications implies much more than mere interest in a topic, and it includes cognitive strategies and metacognitive control components along with affective components. We find it helpful to view this kind of motivated learning as a schema (or, if you prefer, a family of related schemas)—a network of connected insights, skills, values, and dispositions that enable students to understand what it means to engage in academic activities with the intention of accomplishing their learning goals and with awareness of the strategies they use in attempting to do so. The total schema cannot be taught directly, although some of its cognitive and skills components can. In addition, its value and dispositional components can be stimulated and supported through modeling and communication of attitudes, beliefs, values, expectations, and related dispositions to action.

Like other schemas, motivated learning schemas differ on dimensions such as generic versus situation-specific or sketchy and uncertain versus well developed, elaborated, and coordinated. The schemas that are most instantly accessible and usable for guiding information processing and problem solving tend to be domain- or situation-specific. They form part of a pattern of expertise based on a rich accumulation of prior knowledge and experience. Such schemas enable experts who know their way around a domain to immediately begin systematic exploration of new exposures to it by activating well-developed and integrated schemas, whereas novices must grope for clues as to what the domain is all about, what cues are significant, and how to proceed.

These principles apply as much to the motivational aspects of learning as to the information-processing aspects. Students who are ignorant (or misled) about a learning domain (e.g., studying dramatic plays in language arts) cannot generate much appreciation for the domain because they are unable to see its potential. Lacking concepts (e.g., foreshadowing, Achilles Heel) and strategies (analyzing plot developments and making predictions based on them, noting clues to characters' personal strengths and flaws) to guide their information processing, students without much prior knowledge or development of schemas for studying dramatic plays are not yet able to experience many of the insights and satisfactions that such study offers. Even those who appreciate the play as a story (rather than merely as "stuff" to be memorized for a test) may not find much personal relevance in it unless they have learned, for example, to identify with dramatic characters and think about how they (the students) might act in parallel situations.

The point here is that learners may need to develop relatively elaborated schemas that include motivational as well as cognitive components before they can engage in learning activities with appreciation (not just learning) goals and can experience some of the satisfaction or other intrinsic reward potential that they offer. Students do not need much motivational scaffolding to induce them to begin motivated learning of primarily physical skills such as certain sports and recreation activities. Relatively brief observation of models playing kickball, ping pong, pinball, or simple computer games may be enough to convey a basic sense of the nature of the activity, how to engage in it, and what kinds of rewards or satisfactions to expect. However, much more extensive scaffolding may be required to bring students even to such initial levels of readiness to appreciate certain academic content and learning activities, especially as the curriculum moves away from basic skills. In the case of relatively advanced content in the humanities and social studies, such motivated learning may not become possible for most students unless teachers provide sufficient scaffolding to enable these students to begin to appreciate the potential value in the domain and begin to explore it in ways that enable them to experience its satisfactions.

In summary, to explain the mediated acquisition of new values or interests in domain-specific activities, we need a concept of scaffolded appreciation. This concept assumes that motivated functioning in a domain is schema-driven. Mere exposure may be sufficient to stimulate rapid development of needed schemas when novices can observe what is involved in carrying out the activity and can "see the point to it" immediately. For other activities, however, especially in cognitive domains like those taught in school, a mentor needs to scaffold novices' exposures so as to provide a "take" or entry point that will allow them to experience activities in the domain as meaningful and satisfy-ing. Both in selecting activities in which to engage learners and in scaffolding their subsequent engagement, the mentor's work should be guided by motivational goals as well as learning goals.

These ideas about how teachers might scaffold students' appreciation of what they are learning might seem novel at first, but they are based on well-established principles of socialization or sociocultural learning. Young people acquire most of their self-referenced attitudes, beliefs, expectations, and dispositions to action through exposure to socializing influences. Parents, teachers, peers, social institutions, and the media convey expectations not only about how people (in general and in various categories such as male/ female, child/ teenager/adult, etc.) should act, but also about how they should think and feel. This includes attitudes and beliefs about the nature of learning in particular content domains—whom these learning experiences are meant for, whether they are enjoyable or worth pursuing, and if so, what one will get out of them.

Depending on the extent and nature of their prior experiences, particular learners (e.g., high school students) might view a potential learning experience (e.g., upcoming study of King Lear) with counterproductive attitudes and beliefs (Shakespeare is boring, difficult, and "not for me"), with productive attitudes and beliefs (Shakespeare is well worth study for his gripping plots, rich characterizations, and deep insights into the human condition, and King Lear is considered one of his masterpieces), or with no strongly formed attitudes and only vague beliefs. The latter students will develop clearer attitudes and beliefs through their experiences during the unit, including both the input they receive from their teacher and classmates and their own emergent responses as they read and discuss the play.

Many different concepts and related bodies of theory could be brought to bear in identifying instructional methods that might help students to appreciate what they are learning and to develop motivated learning schemas. However, given that we have construed these appreciations and schemas as acquired primarily through sociocultural learning and talked about nurturing them within a motivational zone of proximal development, we will stick with sociocultural terms and speak of the teacher as a mentor mediating the motivated learning of student novices through modeling, coaching, and scaffolding processes. These processes usually are defined in ways that focus on the cognitive aspects of teaching and learning, but their definitions are easily extended to address the motivational aspects.

Modeling

Teachers and other mentors can nurture motivation to learn by socializing as they instruct. One powerful socializing mechanism is modeling, particularly cognitive modeling that includes overt verbalization of the thinking that guides one's behavior when engaged in an activity. Appreciation-oriented modeling of engagement in a learning activity (e.g., reading King Lear) would communicate not just the strategies used to accomplish whatever tasks need to be accomplished (e.g., becoming able to answer questions about the plot, characterization, etc.), but also the thoughts and feelings involved in savoring the experience and enjoying the aesthetic satisfactions that it offers (e.g., making connections between characterization and plot elements depicted in the play and parallel elements in one's own life or experiences, putting oneself in the place of Lear and thinking about how one might handle the dilemmas he faced, etc.). For example, a teacher described by Blank and White introduced Hamlet by posing the following question to his class: "Imagine you've been away from home for several years. When you come back, you find that your father has died and your mother, a few weeks after your father's death, has married your father's brother. Then you start uncovering clues that lead you to think that your uncle may have been responsible for your father's death. What do you think you would do under the circumstances?"

Other forms of socialization (besides modeling) are also helpful, notably direct instruction and other verbal comments designed to induce positive attitudes, beliefs, and expectations about the learning domain. However, these methods merely tell students that worthwhile experiences await them if they pursue the domain. Cognitive modeling, in contrast, shows them what these experiences look and feel like. Good cognitive modeling should convey not only the strategies needed to meet the demands of the task, but also the aesthetic experiences, personal satisfactions, celebrations of new insights, pleasures taken in familiar recognitions, and other manifestations of what it looks and feels like to engage in the activity with appreciation and motivation to learn.

Coaching

Similar extensions would apply to our thinking about coaching. Preparatory instruction, hints, and cues given to guide students' task responses, as well as feedback given following such responses, communicate information about what to do or avoid doing. However, such coaching can also convey enthusiasm for the activity, help students to experience the satisfactions that it offers, and stimulate appreciation of the nature and progress of their learning. Appreciation-oriented coaching would help students to take satisfactions in, develop connections among, or draw implications from their insights as they learn (e.g., by cueing them to think about key aspects of the personalities or motives of the characters in the play, complimenting them on the insights they have developed about these characters, or inviting them to speculate about what these insights portend about the outcome of the drama or tell about what Shakespeare was saying about the human condition).

Scaffolding

Mentors also scaffold novices' development of expertise in a domain, gradually transferring responsibility for guiding learning to the novices as their expertise develops. So far, theory and research about scaffolding has focused on its role in helping learners acquire skills. However, scaffolding also can be construed to include developing learners' capacities for valuing and deriving satisfactions from the learning domain or activity (gradually transferring responsibility for managing these motivational aspects of task engagement to the learners as they acquire the capacities for doing so).

Appreciation-oriented scaffolding would begin with (a) selecting appropriate learning activities in which to engage students in the first place, then following through by (b) introducing them in ways that inform students about the activities' purposes and about what students can expect to get out of them, (c) providing coaching that includes making statements or asking questions that draw students' attention to aspects of the learning experience from which they can take satisfactions (i.e., helping the students to appreciate the activity's "affordances"), and (d) providing feedback that stimulates students not only to recognize but also to appreciate their developing expertise. Such appreciation-oriented feedback provides not just knowledge of results but also commentary on noteworthy qualitative features of the learners' responses or accomplishments, especially features that suggest developing interests or talents that might be pursued further. Where appropriate, this might be followed up with questions to learners about why they chose the general approach that they chose or how they might improve or elaborate on what they have accomplished so far.

These and related forms of scaffolding help communicate in subtle ways the notion that the learner not only is doing something worthwhile, but is doing it in ways that represent seriousness of purpose, growth in knowledge or craftsmanship, aesthetic qualities that reflect his or her individuality, and so on.

Dewey and Transformative Experiences

The writings of John Dewey have inspired recent theory and research on ways in which teachers can mediate students' encounters with powerful ideas so as to foster transformative experiences. Transformative experiences occur when we learn something that does not merely add to our fund of knowledge but enables to see some aspect of the world in a new way, such that we find new meaning in it and value the experience. For example, if an encounter with Monet's paintings becomes a transformative experience, the person may acquire a richer perception of the world—taking more notice of light, shadows, and colors, and in general, seeing the world through Monet's eyes. Motivational theorists have noted that encounters with powerful ideas also have this potential, and have begun doing research on ways to bring it about.

Pugh developed and tested an application of these ideas to teaching science in high school. Modeling and scaffolding were prominent features of his approach. He began a zoology unit on adaptation and evolution by inviting students to talk about their favorite animals, then telling them about some of his own. He then shared some unique encounters he had had with wild animals and showed some home video footage of encounters with a moose and a grizzly bear. Next he expressed his fascination with animals and told the students that the purpose of the upcoming unit would be to learn to appreciate animals better, explaining

What we want to do this week is learn more about how every animal is truly an amazing design. Because every animal... is designed to survive and thrive in a particular environment. And when you learn how to see animals in terms of how they're adapted to their environment, every animal becomes an amazing creation.

To awaken students' anticipation about how the concept of adaptation could enable them to see animals in exciting, new ways, he foreshadowed by telling them that they would learn to see the polar bear as a walking greenhouse and the common cat as a marvel of nature. He added that every animal has a historical record hidden within it and that evolution is the lens that allows to read that record.

Pugh frequently modeled examples of ways that he noted adaptation in everyday observations of animals, as well as adaptation-related questions that he generated (e.g., seeing a flock of Canadian geese and wondering whether their combination of a black head with white neck has an adaptive purpose). He also scaffolded students' initial attempts to see and discuss animals in terms of adaptations, by using their shoes as a metaphor for the relationship between form, function, and environment and then guiding the students as they examined photos or videos of animals to identify aspects of their appearance or physical features that suggest adaptation (such as features that might make them more successful predators or make it harder for predators to see or catch them). He also encouraged students to notice and record signs of adaptation that they encountered outside of class. Analyses indicated that, compared to a parallel class taught using a case approach, the class taught with emphasis on transformative experiences learned the key ideas (adaptation and evolution) more thoroughly, discussed them more frequently with their friends or families outside of class, noticed applications of the concepts outside of class, and reported related transformative experiences. The students also reported that they found these key concepts both interesting and valuable.

Socializing Motivation to Learn

Each person has a unique motivational system, developed in response to experiences and to socialization from significant others in his or her life. In the case of students developing motivation to learn academic knowledge and skills, teachers are important "significant others." Therefore, rather than just accommodate classroom activities to students' existing motivational patterns, teachers can shape those patterns through socialization designed to develop students' motivation to learn.

It begins with three general strategies for establishing a learning environment that creates a favorable context in which to socialize students' motivation to learn. These strategies involve helping students come to understand that classrooms are primarily places for learning and that acquiring knowledge and skills contributes to their quality of life.

Model your own Motivation to Learn

Model interest in learning throughout all of your interactions with your students. This modeling will encourage students to value learning as a rewarding, self-actualizing activity that produces personal satisfaction and enriches their lives. Besides teaching what is in the textbooks, share your interests in current events and items of general knowledge (especially as they relate to the subjects you teach). Call attention to current books, articles, television programs, or movies on these subjects and to examples or applications in everyday living, in the local environment, or in current events.

Modeling means more than just calling your students' attention to examples or applications of concepts taught in school. It means acting as a model by sharing your thinking about such examples or applications—showing your students how educated people use information and concepts learned in school to understand and respond to everyday experiences in their lives and to news about events occurring elsewhere.

Without being preachy about it, you can relate personal experiences illustrating how you use language arts knowledge to communicate or express yourself effectively in important life situations, how you use mathematical or scientific knowledge to solve everyday household-engineering or repair problems, or how you use social studies knowledge to help you appreciate things that you see in your travels or to understand the significance of events in the news. Through such modeling, help your students come to see how it is both stimulating and satisfying to understand (or even just to think, wonder, or make predictions about) what is happening in the world around us.

Much of your modeling will occur in the process of carrying out everyday instruction. Such modeling may be subtle or indirect, but if it is displayed consistently it will have cumulative effects on your students' attitudes and beliefs. One important place to model curiosity and interest in learning is when responding to students' questions, especially questions that are not covered in the textbook. Questions usually indicate that students are interested in the topic and thinking actively about it rather than just listening passively. Consequently, be prepared to respond in ways that show that you value such questions. First, acknowledge or praise the question itself: "That's a good question, Latonya. It does seem strange that the people of Boston would throw the tea into the water, doesn't it?" Then, answer the question or refer it to the class: "How about it, class? Why would they throw the tea into the water instead of taking it home with them?"

You also can model curiosity in responding to questions for which you do not have ready answers: "I never thought about that before. Why didn't they take the tea home with them? They must have decided not to steal it but to throw it into the water instead. How come?" At this point, you could continue to think aloud in this vein or else invite suggestions from the class. If no one is prepared to answer the question, suggest some strategy to address it. You might promise to get the answer for the student, or better yet, invite the student to go to the library, the Internet, or another resource to find the answer and then report back to the class.

Other occasions for modeling curiosity and interest in learning arise when you convey information to students about your life outside of school. If you read a book, magazine article, or newspaper item of interest, mention it so that students can read it for themselves if they wish (better yet, make the item available for loan). Also, announce television programs, museum exhibits, or other special events of educational or cultural value.

You can also model your own curiosity and interest in learning through comments made in passing during class. Without belaboring the point, you can communicate that you regularly read the newspaper ("I read in the paper that..."), watch the news ("Last night on the news they showed..."), and participate in various educational and cultural pursuits. Your students should be aware that you think carefully about and participate in elections, keep abreast of current events, and otherwise show evidence of an active, inquiring mind.

For example, a junior high school teacher used modeling effectively in connection with an assignment involving reading about current events in the newspaper. He went on to discuss the newspaper's position and his own position on a forthcoming summit meeting, noting that he was initially pessimistic about the likely outcome of this meeting but that he had become more interested and optimistic about it as he became better informed by reading the paper and watching news programs. This led to a stimulating discussion that clarified for the students, and provoked many questions about, the positions of the United States and other countries on issues to be discussed at the meeting. The teacher went on to provoke further interest and curiosity by noting that, although he was sharing his own position on the issues discussed that day, he usually withheld his positions on issues discussed in class to encourage students to think for themselves and avoid inhibiting those who might disagree with him. This teacher probably increased his students' interest in newspaper articles and television programs about current events, as well as giving them a model to follow in responding to those news sources in active, thoughtful ways.

Communicate Desirable Expectations and Attributions

In your everyday teaching, routinely project attitudes, beliefs, expectations, and attributions (statements about the reasons for your students' behavior) implying that students share your enthusiasm for learning. To the extent that you treat students as if they already are eager learners, they will be more likely to become eager learners. Let them know that they are expected to be curious, to want to learn with understanding, and to want to apply what they are learning to their everyday lives.

Minimally, this means avoiding suggestions that students will dislike academic activities or work on them only to get good grades. More directly, it means treating students as active, motivated learners who care about their learning and are trying to learn with understanding.

For example, an elementary teacher communicated positive expectations by announcing at the beginning of the year that she intended to make her students into "social scientists." She referred to this idea frequently throughout the year in comments such as, "Since you are social scientists, you will recognize that the description of this area as a tropical rain forest has implications about what kinds of crops will grow there," or "Thinking as social scientists, what conclusions might we draw from this information?" Besides cueing her students to use disciplinary conventions for handling evidence and drawing conclusions, such comments encouraged them to identify with the social science disciplines and to connect what they were learning with their lives outside of school.

Minimize Performance Anxiety

Motivation to learn is likely to develop most fully when students are goal oriented but relaxed enough to be able to concentrate on the task at hand without worrying about whether they can meet performance expectations. You can encourage this by making clear distinctions between instructional activities designed to promote learning and tests designed to evaluate performance. Most classroom activities should be structured as learning experiences rather than as performance assessments.

To the extent that learning activities include testlike events (recitation questions, practice exercises), portray these as opportunities for your students to work with and apply what they are learning rather than as opportunities for you to test their mastery. If you want your students to engage in academic activities with motivation to learn (which implies a willingness to take intellectual risks and make mistakes), you will need to protect them from anxiety or premature concern about performance adequacy.

Eventually you will have to evaluate their performance and assign grades using tests or other assessment devices. Until that point, however, emphasize teaching and learning rather than performance evaluation, and encourage students to respond to evaluations in terms of "Let's assess our progress and learn from our mistakes," rather than "Let's see who knows it and who doesn't." If necessary, add statements such as "We're here to learn, and you can't do that without making mistakes," or caution students against laughing at the mistakes made by classmates.

Shaping Students' Expectations about the Learning

Students are more likely to respond positively to your attempts to induce motivation to learn if they expect the learning to be interesting or important. You can foster and maintain this expectation by being enthusiastic when introducing and implementing learning activities and by shifting into an intense communication style when explaining things that are especially important.

Be Enthusiastic (Regularly)

Students take cues from their teachers about how to respond to school activities. If you present a topic or assignment with enthusiasm, suggesting that it is interesting, important, or worthwhile, your students are likely to adopt this same attitude.

Projecting enthusiasm does not mean pep talks or phony theatrics. Instead, it means identifying good reasons for viewing a topic as interesting, meaningful, or important and then communicating these reasons to your students when teaching about the topic. You can use dramatics or forceful salesmanship if you are comfortable with these techniques, but if not, low-key but sincere statements of the value that you place on a topic or activity will be just as effective. Even a brief comment showing that a topic is food for thought or illustrating how it is interesting, unique, or different from previously studied topics may be sufficient. The primary objective of projecting enthusiasm is to induce students to value the topic or activity, not to amuse, entertain, or excite them.

A history teacher generated a great deal of interest (and also pulled together a great many concepts) by enthusiastically explaining to his students that during the Middle Ages, the Mediterranean Sea was the center of the world. Mediterranean seaports were major trade centers and places like England were outposts of civilization, but this changed drastically with discovery of the New World and the emergence of new centers of trade and culture. His presentation included references to maps, reminders about the primary modes of transportation at the time, and characterizations of the attitudes of the people and their knowledge about other countries and trade possibilities.

Another teacher brought ancient Israel alive by enthusiastically telling his students about David as the slayer of Goliath and ancestor of Jesus, Abraham leading his people to the Promised Land, Solomon as a wise man and builder of the temple, and Moses as the man who presented the Ten Commandments and led the people out of the wilderness. This lesson included locating Jerusalem, Israel, and the Sinai peninsula on a map and speculating about whether the temple might be rebuilt in modern Jerusalem (noting that a major Moslem temple is located next to the spot occupied by Solomon's temple). In each of these examples, the teacher was able to parlay personal interest and detailed knowledge about a topic into an effective presentation that sparked interest and elicited many questions and comments.

The potential power of teacher enthusiasm is captured in the following quotation explaining why certain teachers find a permanent place in their students' memories:

What intrigues students most about these teachers is their enthusiasm for subjects that seemed boring and purposeless in other teachers' classes. Memorable teachers challenge students to expect more than just recognition or a paycheck from the work they choose. Why is Mr. Phillips so fired up about differential equations? How could Ms. Patrelli get so excited about the Crusades? Sometimes it is an encounter with just such a teacher that inspires students to reconsider the intrinsic rewards of exploring a domain of knowledge.

Be Intense (Selectively)

Learn to use timing, nonverbal expressions and gestures, and cueing and other verbal techniques to project a level of intensity that tells students that material is especially important and deserves close attention. Often, an intense presentation will begin with a direct statement of the importance of the message ("I'm going to show you how to invert fractions—now pay close attention and make sure that you understand what this involves, when and why you do it, and how you do it"). Then, present the message itself using verbal and nonverbal public speaking techniques that convey intensity and cue attention: a slow-paced, step-by-step presentation during which you emphasize key words, use unusual voice modulations or exaggerated gestures that focus attention on key terms or procedural steps, and scan the group following each step to look for signs of understanding or confusion (and to allow anyone with a question to ask it immediately). In addition to your words, everything about your tone and manner should communicate to students that what is being said is important and that they should give it full attention and ask questions about anything they do not understand.

"Pick your spots" for using such an intense communication style. You cannot be so intense all the time, and even if you could, your students would adjust to it so that it would lose much of its effectiveness. Therefore, reserve intensity for times in which you want to communicate "This is especially important; pay close attention." Likely occasions include introduction of important new terms or definitions, especially those that might be confusing to students; demonstration of procedures (preparing paint in an art class, serving a volleyball, or handling scientific equipment); modeling of problem-solving techniques, especially when giving instructions for assignments; and any instruction that is intended to eliminate misconceptions (and thus requires making students aware that although they think they already understand the point at issue, their "knowledge" may be incorrect). Exaggerated intensity is less appropriate for more routine instructional situations, although it is wise to slow the pace and be alert for signs of confusion or student desire to ask a question whenever you are covering new or complex material.

Strategies for Inducing Motivation to Learn

Regardless of extrinsic incentives, intrinsic interest, or whatever other motivational influences may be operating, you will need to motivate your students to learn what your lessons and activities are designed to teach. This requires introducing and carrying out lessons and activities in ways that keep both you and the students goal oriented—developing key knowledge and skills in ways that support understanding, appreciation, and life applications.

Awareness of curricular goals should guide both your teaching and your students' learning. You will need to stay aware of the primary learning outcomes that a lesson or activity is designed to develop and how these fit within the curriculum as a whole. This will enable you to make good decisions about what content to emphasize, how to frame it so that students can appreciate its value, and how to develop it so they will not only learn it but be able to apply it in and out of school.

Similarly, clarity about learning goals will help your students to focus on key ideas and applications and thus to learn with a sense of purpose. To the extent that students are aware that the point of their efforts is not just to please you or prepare for a test, they will be more likely to monitor their progress, seek help if they need it, and persist until they have learned what they are supposed to learn.

All of this assumes that your lessons and activities are focused on major instructional goals, phrased in terms of desired student outcomes. Within the context created by this approach to teaching school subjects for understanding, appreciation, and life application, you can use the following strategies to induce motivation to learn in particular situations.

Induce Dissonance or Cognitive Conflict

If a topic is familiar, students may think that they already know all about it and thus may listen to presentations or read texts with little attention or thought. You can counter this tendency by pointing out unexpected, incongruous, or paradoxical aspects of the content; by calling attention to unusual or exotic elements; by noting exceptions to general rules; or by challenging students to solve the "mystery" that underlies a paradox. One teacher implemented several of these principles when he introduced a unit on the Middle Ages by telling students that they would learn about "our ancestors" who chose to remain illiterate and ignorant and who persecuted people who did not share their religion. Later he contrasted the Moslem advances in mathematics, science, and the construction of libraries with the illiteracy of most Christian kings and lords during the Middle Ages. This stimulated his mostly Christian students to develop empathy with and appreciation for the culture of the Moslems of the Middle Ages, instead of viewing them only as faceless enemies of Christian crusaders.

Another teacher used dissonance to stimulate curiosity about the Persian empire by noting that Darius was popular with the people he conquered and asking students to anticipate reasons why this might be so. Another teacher introduced a selection on the Trojan War by telling students that they would read about "how just one horse enabled the Greeks to win a major battle against the Trojans." Another introduced a video on the fall of the Roman Empire by saying, "Some say that the factors that led to the decay of the Roman Empire are currently at work in the United States—as you watch the video, see if you notice parallels."

United States history is full of opportunities to create dissonance, especially in students whose prior exposures have been confined to overly sanitized and patriotic versions of the subject. Exposure to topics such as the Trail of Tears, the Japanese Internment during World War II, or CIA involvement in undermining foreign governments can be startling eye openers for students, especially if approached not just as past history but as grist for discussions about whether such things might still happen today or what their implications might be for current and future government policy.

The school curriculum includes a great many "strange but true" phenomena, especially in mathematics and science. By calling attention to these phenomena, you can get your students to begin asking themselves "How can that be?" Otherwise, students may treat the material as just more information to be absorbed without giving it much thought or even noticing that it seems to contradict their previous learning.

Conceptual Change Teaching. Sometimes students' prior learning includes misconceptions about important concepts. For example, science units on plants typically emphasize their roles as food producers via the photosynthesis process. Students enter these courses knowing little about photosynthesis but a great deal about food, especially food for people. They know that food is something that you consume or eat, that it is taken in from the outside environment, and that there are many different kinds of food. This knowledge produces distorted understandings in students who assume that food for plants is similar to food for people, because unlike people or animals, plants make their own food. Plants' only source of food is that which they manufacture themselves by transforming light energy from the sun into chemical potential energy stored in food by combining the light energy with carbon dioxide, water, and minerals. Neither soil nor fertilizers (even if called "plant food") are taken in as food or consumed for energy.

Science educators have found that, in order to understand the food production function of plants, students must restructure their thinking about the nature of food, focusing on its scientific definition as potential energy for metabolism rather than on reasoning by analogy from their prior experiences with food for humans. Posner and his colleagues suggested that four conditions must be satisfied if students are to be induced to change their understandings of key concepts: (a) dissatisfaction with existing concepts must be induced and the new concepts must (b) be intelligible to the students, (c) be initially plausible, and (d) appear fruitful. These ideas underlie what has become known as conceptual change teaching.

Anderson and Roth developed a version of conceptual change teaching to help middle-school students understand plants' food production function. They began by asking students to define food—and food for plants—and to respond to a problem. This provided information about the students' initial conceptions and made the students more aware of them. Next, students were given explanations about different ways of defining food, including its scientific definition. Then they were asked to address questions that allowed them to appreciate how this new definition of food could explain everyday phenomena (Is water food? Juice? Vitamin pills? Can people live on vitamin pills alone? Why or why not?). Students also were asked to write their ideas about how plants get food, to write about what kind of food plants use, and to draw pictures on a diagram to show how they think food moves inside a plant.

As the unit progressed and students were exposed to scientific information about plants and food production, the instruction frequently referred back to these early exercises, drawing direct contrasts between scientific explanations and the explanations offered based on students' prior knowledge. In addition, students engaged in experimental observations of plants, discussion of similarities and differences between plants and animals, comparisons of materials taken into plants with materials made by plants during photosynthesis, and comparisons between energy-containing and non-energy-containing materials that people consume. These activities encouraged students to make connections between their own ideas and scientific concepts, as well as to use their newly structured conceptions to make predictions and develop more satisfying explanations of familiar everyday phenomena.

Kathleen Roth extended the conceptual change teaching model to history teaching, and noted that it can be used with any subject. In her version, the key steps include

- Establish a question or problem in a way that engages students' interest and then elicit students' ideas about it (students will see that their peers have many different ideas from their own).
- Engage students in exploring phenomena related to the question or problem (preferably through direct, hands-on experiences that will challenge their preconceptions), allowing them opportunities to think through their ideas, gather new evidence, and consider whether their initial ideas still make sense.
- Once students realize the need for new ideas, present scientific explanations and encourage students to compare these with their previous ideas and determine whether they make sense in light of the evidence.
- Provide students with opportunities to apply the scientific concepts to explain real-world situations, scaffolding by providing a lot of initial modeling and coaching but then fading this assistance as students become more comfortable working with the ideas.
- Engage students in reflecting on how their ideas have changed and exploring connections between the newly learned scientific ideas and other ideas.

Alexander, Fives, Buehl, and Mulhern incorporated aspects of conceptual change teaching into a "teaching as persuasion" model developed for science teaching in middle school. Casting teaching as persuasion implies that the lesson will address issues about which there is some dispute and that the teaching will appeal not only to reason but to the emotions. The instruction involved relatively conventional content concerning Galileo's study of planetary movements leading to the conclusion that the earth revolves around the sun instead of vice versa. However, the lesson was framed as an investigation to address a motivating question ("Should scientific evidence be kept from the public if it will cause confusion or unrest?"), and content was developed with an emphasis on Galileo as an individual struggling to hold onto his beliefs and promote his scientific discoveries even in the face of ridicule and banishment. Also included was a role-play activity in which students were asked to assume the position of a designated character in the dispute. The students also wrote reactions to several readings on the topic, and as a culminating activity, re-evaluated their original responses to the motivating question in the light of what they had learned. Analyses indicated that the persuasion classes showed both deeper comprehension and greater interest than comparison classes taught more conventionally.

Make Abstract Content More Concrete

Definitions, principles, and other abstract information may have little meaning for students unless made more concrete. One way to accomplish this is to relate experiences or anecdotes illustrating how the content applies to the lives of individuals that your students are interested in or likely to identify with.

For example, a junior high teacher read aloud a brief selection about Spartacus in order to personalize his instruction about slavery in ancient times. When covering the crusades, this same teacher gave particular emphasis to the Children's Crusade, noting that the children involved were "your age and younger" and that most of them died before the crusade ultimately ended in failure. He also made poignant connections to contemporary Iran, where religion-based zeal led preadolescents to volunteer to go to war. Another teacher brought the medieval guilds alive for her students by describing them in detail and soliciting the students' reactions to the fact that if they had lived during the Middle Ages and wanted to become a journeyman, they would have had to leave their homes as children and spend 7 years apprenticed to a master craftsman.

You can make abstractions concrete by conducting demonstrations or by showing objects, pictures, or videos. In studying another country, for example, teach about its people and culture in addition to its physical features and products. Show students what the country looks like and help them to imagine what it would be like to live there. Perhaps include children's literature sources that offer stories set in the country or follow members of a representative family through a typical day or week in their lives. You also can help your students to relate new or strange content to their existing knowledge by using examples or analogies that refer to familiar concepts, objects, or events.

Sometimes the problem is not that content would be too abstract or unfamiliar for students to understand if it were explained sufficiently, but that the text simply does not provide enough explanation. This is one reason why it is wise to view your texts as outlines to be elaborated on, not as the entire curriculum. For example, one text that we studied explained Russia's exit from World War I by saying only that "the revolution came and a new government was established." This brief statement does not supply enough details to enable students to understand and visualize the events surrounding the Russian revolution. To make these events more understandable, you would need to elaborate on the text by explaining why and how the communists and others organized political and eventual military resistance to the Czar's regime, killed or expelled the Czar's family and key officials, and established a new government. Such elaboration on the text transforms the relatively meaningless statement that "the revolution came and a new government was established" into a meaningful story that students can explain in their own words because they can relate it to their prior knowledge and visualize the events to which it refers. Thus, they can actively process the content instead of just trying to memorize it.

The preceding example also illustrates another technique for making content more concrete and personal for students: Dramatize by telling stories or at least representing the content within narrative formats. In contrast to analytic or impersonal explanatory formats, narrative formats contain the key features of stories: a focus on central figures pursuing some goal, a plot that involves conflict or some barriers to accomplishment of the goal, and a resolution that includes reference to success or failure and the implications of this for subsequent events. Egan has written extensively about the power of narratives for capturing students' imaginations. He has suggested that 8-

to 15-year-olds in particular are highly responsive to the narrative format, and especially to dramatic stories featuring inspiring hero figures struggling to accomplish great feats or to right the wrongs of the world. This narrative approach can be applied not only in language arts and history, but in mathematics and science as well (in stories about how individuals or small groups struggled to solve mathematical problems, unlock scientific mysteries, or develop important inventions).

You may need to adapt your curriculum to make sure that it features gender equity and suitable connections to the ethnic and cultural backgrounds of your students. Even when content is selected and taught effectively in other respects, certain students may feel excluded and lose interest if they come to believe that a school subject is about "them" rather than "us". Consequently, your treatment of history should include sufficient attention to social history, women's roles, and the lives of everyday people along with political and military events, and should include multiple perspectives on their meanings and implica-tions. Similarly, your material on literature, biography, and contributions to the arts and sciences or to society and culture should include sufficient attention to contributions by women and members of minority groups, especially groups represented in your class.

Research assignments connected with this content should include opportunities for students to choose biographical subjects, literature selections, or historical events on which to focus. In this way, those who wish to do so can pursue their interests in content with which they identify in part because of its relevance to gender or cultural identity issues that are important to them.

Induce Task Interest or Appreciation

You can induce appreciation for a topic or activity by verbalizing reasons why students should value it. If it has connections with something that your students already recognize as interesting or important, note these connections. If the knowledge or skills to be taught have applications to everyday living, point out these applications, especially any that will allow students to solve problems or accomplish goals that are important to them. Also, mention any new or challenging aspects of activities that students can anticipate.

Sometimes, instead of just telling students why the content they are about to learn is valuable, you can arrange for them to discover this for themselves by engaging them with a question or problem that requires the content for its solution. This approach is most applicable with mathematical or scientific principles and procedures. Most of these principles were developed in the first place as a by-product of attempts to understand some important phenomenon or solve some practical problem, and since then, other important applications have accumulated. You can make use of these applications in introducing and developing the content.

Arts and humanities knowledge usually lacks such direct linkages to practical applications, but it has value as grist for developing insights into the human condition and advances in personal identity and self-actualization. Stories, for example, whether fictional or historical, usually can be framed with reference to enduring dilemmas or common problems with which your students can identify. When properly framed and developed, stories have value not just as entertainment or cultural literacy knowledge but as case studies and food for thought about the trade-offs involved in alternative ways of responding to situations that provoke fear, rage, jealousy, conflicting loyalties, moral dilemmas, or other powerful emotions. In exposing your students to such stories, encourage them to put themselves in the place of the hero or another key character and think about how they might have handled the situations depicted as the story develops. In considering works of art, help your students not only to appreciate the artist's interpretation of the theme but also to develop their own interpretation and think about how they might express it artistically.

Information about people in the past or in other cultures can be rendered more meaningful and potentially significant to students by helping them to appreciate how these people's experiences contrast in insight-producing ways with their own geographical and cultural experiences. For example, a junior high teacher motivated students to read about the ancient Greek legal system by noting that it was similar to our own system in many ways but it called for 501 jurors. This teacher also motivated his students to study the map of Greece with interest and appreciation by explaining that even though no place in Greece is more than 40 miles from the sea, its jagged contours give it far more coastline than most larger countries.

Sivan and Roehler studied teachers' introductions to activities conducted during small-group reading instruction. They found that when the teachers introduced activities with emphasis on the value of the activities themselves or of the knowledge or skills that the activities would develop, students engaged in the activities with an enhanced sense of their usefulness and with greater metacognitive awareness of their learning strategies and progress. Sansone, Weir, Harpster, and Morgan and Reeve, Jang, Hardre, and Omura reported similar benefits to informing students about the value of text content.

Keller recommended six strategies for enhancing students' perceptions of the relevance or value of curricular content. These included connecting the content with students' existing past experiences, skills, and interests; emphasizing the present worth of the content (how students can use it in their lives right now); emphasizing the future usefulness of the content; need-matching by linking the content to specific student needs; allowing students autonomy and choice in determining how to accomplish curricular goals; and using modeling by personally demonstrating the value of the content or recruiting former students to testify to its value.

Frymier and Shulman identified 12 strategies that teachers might use to help students appreciate the relevance or value of their learning. They asked students to rate how frequently their teachers performed each of the following behaviors:

- uses examples to make the content relevant to me;
- provides explanations that make the content relevant to me;
- uses exercises or explanations that demonstrate the importance of the content;
- explicitly states how the material relates to my career goals or my life in general;
- links content to other areas of content;
- asks me to apply content to my own interests;
- gives assignments that involve the application of the content to my career interests;
- helps me to understand the importance of the content;
- uses own experiences to introduce or demonstrate a concept;
- uses student experiences to demonstrate or introduce a concept;
- uses discussion to help me understand the relevance of the topic;
- uses current events to apply a topic.

Several studies indicated that students reported greater motivation to study for classes in which their teachers used more of these strategies.

Newton noted that helping students appreciate content often involves embedding the content within a wider context, restoring some of the threads that were removed from a larger web when the content was isolated for study. This might be done by asking questions that relate to its relevance, eliciting prior knowledge about it, or setting the scene in ways that highlight the human needs that the content can satisfy. For example, a unit on genetics might be introduced through discussion of beliefs about inheritance before Mendel, how Mendel's discoveries changed our understanding of genetic mechanisms, and how this knowledge eventually led to plant hybridization, cloning, the human genome project, and other contemporary applications of genetic knowledge.

Induce Students to Generate their own Motivation to Learn

You can induce your students to generate their own motivation to learn by asking them to think about topics or activities in relation to their own interests or preconceptions. For example, you can ask them to identify questions about a topic they would like to get answered or to note things they find to be surprising as they read. These techniques help students to understand that motivation to learn must come from within themselves—that it is a property of the learner rather than the activity.

Ortiz developed techniques for inducing this insight with respect to reading assignments. She emphasized to students that their motivational responses to a text—whether interest or boredom—are generated by them and not inherent in the text itself. These exercises helped students to realize that they need to generate interest themselves and to acquire a repertoire of strategies for doing so.

One popular way to induce students to generate their own motivation to learn is to use the K-W-L technique. Developed originally as a way to facilitate reading comprehension, K-W-L promotes learning by helping students to retrieve relevant background knowledge and learn with awareness of purpose and accomplishment. The technique unfolds through several steps. First, as they are about to begin study of a topic, students write down what they already Know (or think they know) about the topic and what they Want to learn about it. Alternatively, this step can be done as a teacher-led group activity, in which students' responses are listed on the board, the chartstand, or the overhead projection screen.

The next steps occur during study of the topic. Here, you address any misconceptions that emerged in your students' "K" responses and provide answers (or arrange for the students themselves to get answers) to the questions they raised in their "W" responses.

Finally, as a culmination of their study of the topic, students write what they Learned about it. At this time, they also revisit their earlier "K" and "W" responses. They may see a need to change some of these earlier statements, if part of what they thought they knew was incorrect. The K-W-L technique is useful not only for its originally intended purpose of helping students to read content selections with greater interest and understanding, but also for developing productive learning sets when introducing new topics in science, social studies, and other content areas.

Spires and Donley noted that giving students permission to bring their personal knowledge into the school context encourages them to establish the relevance of academic content to their own interests and purposes. Consequently, they recommended teaching students not only to activate prior knowledge when they read texts, but also to take note of their personal reactions, things that the content reminds them of, or connections to other knowledge or experience. They reported that students taught to use this strategy showed both better comprehension of and improved attitudes toward text materials that they studied.

Conti, Amabile, and Pollak described a method of inducing an active cognitive learning set that incorporates fantasy elements and creativity. They were to write the three most interesting and unusual questions that came to mind about this dream or about dreams in general. Other students were asked to use the dream paragraph to complete a word substitution exercise that did not engage them in thinking creatively about the dream or about the topic of dreaming. The researchers found that students who completed the creative pretask showed more intrinsic interest in the topic and greater long-term retention for the content of the longer instructional passage.

You can use variations of this technique with a broad range of content. The key elements are: placing students within a fantasy context that calls for them to address some problem or take advantage of some opportunity and asking them to act out this role in a way that involves thinking creatively about the topic to be studied.

Scaffolding Students' Learning Efforts

Scaffolding strategies are needed to complement motivational strategies because, as Blumenfeld et al. noted, motivating students to learn requires not only bringing them to the lesson but bringing the lesson to them. You are off to a good start if you present students with worthwhile learning activities and introduce the activities in ways that help students to appreciate their value. You need to follow this up, however, by asking questions or assigning tasks that will require students to think critically and creatively about the content; apply it in activities calling for inquiry, problem solving, or decision making; and get feedback. In the process, you can supplement and scaffold your students' efforts to respond to these challenges by providing them with learning objectives and advance organizers, modeling task-related thinking and problem solving, and helping them to learn with metacognitive awareness and control of their own learning strategies.

State Learning Goals and Provide Advance Organizers

Instructional theorists have shown that learners retain more information when their learning is goal directed and structured around key concepts. They commonly advise teachers to introduce activities by stating learning goals and by providing advance organizers that characterize what will be learned in general terms. These techniques help students to know what to expect and to prepare to learn efficiently.

Learning goals and advance organizers also serve motivational purposes. These techniques call students' attention to the benefits that they should receive from engaging in an activity and help them to establish a learning set to use in guiding their responses to it. As used here, the term learning goal is meant to have a broader mean-ing than behavioral objective, instructional objective, or other terms that suggest a performance standard that students are expected to reach when their mastery is assessed. The kinds of learning goals likely to contribute to students' motivation to learn are broader and phrased in terms of the added capacities (knowledge, insights, coping strategies) that students will acquire, preferably with reference to their potential application to life outside of school.

Learning goals and advance organizers ordinarily are communicated in the process of introducing a lesson or activity to students. It seems natural to use these occasions to make sure that students understand what they will be doing and why they will be doing it. However, classroom research suggests that few teachers systematically take advantage of these opportunities.

For example, Newby observed 30 first-year elementary teachers over a 4-month period, developing thick-description records of the classroom discourse and activities that occurred during the observation times. These data were later analyzed for the presence of motivational strategies, categorized into four types: focusing attention, emphasizing relevance, building confidence, or imposing rewards and punishments. Data from 168 hours of observation yielded 1,748 instances of teacher behavior coded as one of these motivational strategies, or about 10.4 strategies per hour by each teacher. However, 58% of these were reward or punishment strategies, and most of the rest (27%) were attention-focusing strategies. Only 7.1% of the strategies involved building students' confidence in their abilities to handle the work, and only 7.5% were relevance strategies that involved explaining the value of the learning or why it was being taught. Thus, these teachers mentioned the purpose or value of learning less than once per hour.

Anderson and her colleagues found that first-grade teachers' presentations of assignments to their students typically included procedural directions or special hints (e.g., pay attention to the underlined words), but seldom called attention to the purposes and meanings of the work. Only 5% of the teachers' presentations explicitly described the purpose of the assignment in terms of the content being taught, and only 1.5% included explicit descriptions of the cognitive strategies to use. In these classrooms, the work was mostly low level and repetitive, the directions seldom included statements about what would be learned or how it related to other learning, and the teachers' monitoring focused on the students' work completion progress rather than on their levels of understanding.

What can result from this was summarized in what one student was heard to say to himself as he finished a worksheet: "I don't know what it means, but I did it." The data from this study indicated that many students (especially low achievers) did not understand how to do their assignments.

Rather than ask their teachers or get help in other ways, they often were content to respond randomly or rely on response sets (such as alternating or using geometrical patterns for circling multiple-choice answers or picking one from a list of new words to fill the blank in a sentence without reading the sentence itself). Low achievers tended to be more concerned about finishing their assignments than about understanding the content they were supposed to be learning. High achievers completed most assignments successfully and showed less concern about finishing on time, but even they showed little evidence of understanding the content-related purposes of the assignments. No student consistently explained assignments in terms of their curricular content. Instead, most responses were vague generalities ("It's just our work" or "We learn to read").

These findings are not unique. Rohrkemper and Bershon interviewed elementary students about what was on their minds when they worked on assignments. They found that of 49 students who gave codable responses, 2 were concerned only about getting finished, 45 were concerned about getting the answers correct, but only 2 mentioned trying to understand what was being taught.

If we want students to be aware of the learning goals of classroom activities and to appreciate the potential of these activities for promoting personal growth and enhancing quality of life, we will need to draw the students' attention to these goals and potentials. Teachers do not do this nearly as much as they should. For example, Green interviewed two teachers about their motivational strategies and observed them in their classrooms. Each teacher mentioned both expectancy aspects (e.g., help students become comfortable and confident as learners) and value aspects (e.g., elicit their interest and help them understand the importance of learning activities) in describing her ideas about motivation. Yet, each made reference to usefulness or importance only three times during approximately 15 hours of teaching. Their motivational attempts were focused much more on the expectancy aspects than the value aspects of motivation. Most were made during comments to individual students after activities had begun, rather than in comments to the whole class when introducing the activities.

Plan Questions and Activities to Help Students

Once you have clarified the purposes and goals of an activity and provided any needed introduction to its content base, ask questions and engage students in activities designed to help them develop their understanding of the content by processing and applying it. In developing your plans, emphasize questions and activities that will stimulate students to reflect on what they are learning and engage in thoughtful discussion of its meanings and implications. You may occasionally need to use drill activities to reinforce learning that must be memorized, as well as recitation activities to check and correct understanding of basic knowledge that must be in place to anchor subsequent learning activities. However, most of your questions should be asked not just to monitor comprehension but to stimulate students to think about the content, connect it to their prior knowledge, articulate their understandings of it, and begin to explore its applications.

Types of Questions

Questioning ordinarily should not take the form of rapidly paced drills or attempts to elicit "right answers" to miscellaneous factual questions. Instead, use questions as means for engaging students with the content they are learning. Stimulate them to process that content actively and "make it their own" by rephrasing it into their own words and considering its meanings and implications. Focus your questions on the most important elements of the content and guide students' thinking in ways that move them systematically toward key understandings. The idea is to build an integrated network of knowledge structured around powerful ideas, not to stimulate rote memorizing of miscellaneous information

Questioning Technique

Certain aspects of questioning technique can enhance the power of your questions to stimulate student thinking. First, address most of your questions to the entire class rather than to a single designated student. This will encourage all students, and not just the designated individual, to think about the question. Second, before calling on anyone to respond, allow sufficient wait time to enable students to process and formulate responses to the question. You may need to emphasize to students that you are more interested in thoughtfulness and quality than in speed of response, as well as to discourage overly eager students from blurting out answers. Finally, distribute response opportunities widely rather than allow a few students to answer most of your questions. Students learn more if they are actively involved in discussions than if they sit passively without participating, and distributing response opportunities helps keep all students attentive and accountable.

Thoughtful Discourse

Classroom discourse patterns that are desirable from both an instructional and a motivational perspective develop in students a set of dispositions that together constitute what Newmann called thoughtfulness: a persistent desire that claims be supported by reasons (and that the reasons themselves be scrutinized), a tendency to be reflective by taking time to think through problems rather than acting impulsively or automatically accepting the views of others, a curiosity to explore new questions, and a flexibility to entertain alternative and original solutions to problems.

Model Task-related Thinking and Problem Solving

The information processing and problem solving strategies needed for thinking about particular content or responding to particular tasks may be unknown to many of your students unless you make them overt and observable by modeling them. Such modeling should include the thinking that goes into selecting the general approach to use, deciding on what options to take at choice points that arise during the process, checking on progress as one goes along, and making certain that one is on the right track. It also should include recovery from false starts and from use of inappropriate strategies, so that students can see how to develop a successful strategy even after getting off to a bad start. This kind of cognitive modeling is powerful not just as an instructional device but as a way to show students what it means to approach a task with motivation to learn. That is, it allows you to model the attitudes, beliefs, and strategies that are associated with such motivation (patience, confidence, persistence in seeking solutions through information processing and ratio nal decision making, benefiting from the information supplied by mistakes rather than giving up in frustration, concentrating on the task and how to respond to it rather than focusing on the self and worrying about one's limitations).

Induce Metacognitive Awareness

When motivated to learn, students do not merely let information "wash over them" and hope that some of it will stick. Instead, they process the information actively by concentrating their attention, making sure that they understand, integrating new information with existing knowledge, and encoding and storing this information in a form that will allow them to remember it and use it later. Students are most likely to do these things effectively if they do them with metacognitive awareness—conscious selection of appropriate strategies, monitoring of their effectiveness, noting and correcting their mistakes, and shifting to new strategies if necessary. You can help your students remain aware of their goals and strategy decisions by structuring and scaffolding their engagement in learning activities. To the extent needed, such structuring and scaffolding might include preactivity instructions that emphasize the purposes and goals of the activity, questions or cues offered during the activity to help keep students aware of the processes they are using in responding to it, and postactivity debriefing that focuses on analyzing and appreciating what has been accomplished

A complete activity might include the following stages:

1. *Introduction* (communicate the goals of the activity and cue relevant prior knowledge and response strategies)
2. *Initial scaffolding* (explain and demonstrate procedures if necessary, then ask questions to develop key ideas and make sure that students understand what to do before releasing them to work on their own)
3. *Independent work* (release students to work individually or in collaboration with peers, but monitor their progress and intervene when necessary)
4. *Debriefing/reflection/assessment* (revisit the activity's primary goals with the students and assess the degree to which they have been accomplished)

This sequence operationalizes the point that effective activities require not just physical actions or time on task but cognitive engagement with important ideas. Inductive or discovery learning activities will unfold through different stages, but even these activities require an optimal type and amount of structuring and scaffolding to maximize their impact

Self-regulated Learning

Rohrkemper and Corno suggested that the highest form of cognitive engagement that students can use to learn in classrooms is self-regulated learning—active learning in which students assume responsibility for motivating themselves to learn with understanding. Self-regulated learning should be the ultimate goal of your motivational efforts. You can set the stage for development of selfregulated learning by using teaching strategies that foster intrinsic motivation and motivation to learn. Within this context, you then can promote self-regulated learning more directly by

(1) clarifying goals, modeling strategies, and otherwise working to ensure that students' learning is meaningful and strategic and

(2) withdrawing these learning supports when they are no longer needed and providing opportunities for students to work with increasing autonomy on tasks that challenge them to integrate and apply what they are learning.

Teaching learning skills and strategies empowers students by helping them to truly understand what they are learning (which should improve their attitudes toward it) and to generalize and apply it to tasks of their own choosing. Students' need for instruction in strategy use recedes as their expertise develops. At first they may need interventions designed to increase their awareness and deliberate use of learning strategies, but this kind of assistance can be faded as they begin to acquire the skills of expert learners (e.g., abilities to diagnose the reasons for learning problems and to focus immediately on the most likely solutions rather than working systematically through a larger repertoire, to develop short cuts through longer processes, and to use certain strategies automatically without having to make conscious decisions to do so). Along with the findings of Blumenfeld, Puro, and Mergendoller concerning classroom factors that foster stu dent motivation to learn, the ideas put forth by Rohrkemper and Corno concerning classrooms that foster selfregulated learning again remind us that there are intimate connections between teachers' motivational strategies and their approaches to curriculum and instruction.

References

Ford, M. (1992). *Motivating humans: Goals, emotions, and personal agency beliefs.* Newbury Park, CA: Sage.

Jones, B., & Idol, L. (Eds.). (1990). D*imensions of thinking and cognitive instruction.* Hillsdale, NJ: Lawrence Erlbaum Associates.

Newton, D. (2000). *Teaching for understanding: What it is and how to do it.* London: Routledge/ Falmer.

Tharp, R., & Gallimore, R. (1988). *Rousing minds to life: Teaching, learning, and school in social context.* Cambridge: Cambridge University Press.

Weinstein, C., & Mayer, R. (1986). *The teaching of learning strategies. In M. Wittrock (Ed.), Hand-book of research on teaching* (3rd ed., pp. 315–327). New York: Macmillan.

Wong, E., Pugh, K., & The Dewey Ideas Group at Michigan State University. (2001). Learning sc-ence: A Deweyan perspective. *Journal of Research in Science Teaching,* 38, 317–336.

9

Motivating Apathetic Students

Teaching apathetic students is a great challenge. In some cases, teaching them is equivalent to wiping away a blood stain with nothing but water. But, that is the idea, indeed. Most people would not try to remove a blood stain with water. They might try a more stringent solution, such as alcohol or the appropriate base for the malady. Using the right solution to remove a blood stain from a fine piece of fabric takes a similar approach to teach apathetic students. You simply have to have the right tools. What are the right tools to teach students? There are many. The most effective tool, however, is being proactive and getting to know students before they get to know you. This idea means learning who the little darlings, and in some cases, little monsters, are before they step into your classroom.

Apathy, not discouragement, is the ultimate motivational problem facing teachers. Students who display learned helplessness, failure syndrome, or related performance concerns frequently lose their focus on learning and require special motivational treatment beyond what is needed for the class as a whole. However, these students usually value learning and would like to be able to complete learning activities successfully.

In contrast, apathetic students are uninterested in or even alienated from school learning: They don't find it meaningful or worthwhile, don't want to engage in it, don't value it even when they know that they can achieve success with reasonable effort, and may even resist it if they fear that it will lead to unwanted responsibilities or make them into something that they do not want to become. You will need to make sustained efforts to resocialize such students' attitudes and beliefs. More specifically, you will need to show them what it means to engage in academic activities with motivation to learn, nurture their desire to do so, and follow up with appropriate structuring and scaffolding of their learning efforts.

Students who have not developed motivation-to-learn schemas tend to view school activities as imposed demands rather than as learning opportunities, and thus to engage in them (if at all) only to the extent needed to garner acceptable grades and stay out of trouble. They give little consideration to learning goals, let alone to appreciating the value of the learning or taking pride in their accomplishments.

There is a dearth of theory-based research on strategies for dealing with uninterested or alienated students. However, it is possible to suggest several sets of principles based on what is known about the development and socialization of value-based motivation in homes, schools, and work settings.

Contracting and Incentive Systems

In many respects, students who find no value in school activities are ideal candidates for the use of contracting or other approaches that involve offering incentives in exchange for specified accomplishments. Incentive systems are especially useful with students who know what they are supposed to do and are capable of doing it if they put their minds to it, but currently are not conscientious or motivated enough to do so consistently (i.e., apathetic or alienated students whose motivational problems primarily involve value issues rather than expectancy issues).

Contracting provides built-in opportunities for teacher–student collaboration in negotiating expectations and rewards. If perfect performance is currently an unreasonable expectation, negotiations might yield specifications calling for rewarding a level of improvement that the student views as reasonable and the teacher is willing to accept (at least for now). Contracting also provides opportunities to offer students choices of rewards, thus ensuring that the intended reward is experienced as such.

In contingency contracting, you confer with the student about possible alternatives and then jointly draw up a contract that specifies what the student will be expected to do in order to earn contingent rewards. The contract can be purely oral, although it helps to formalize it by having the student write down the details of the agreement. Solicit the student's input about the extent and nature of the required accomplishments (challenging but doable with reasonable effort) and about desired rewards. If appropriate, the contract might specify several levels of potential accomplishment linked to differential levels of reward, to make it possible for the student to earn a lesser reward even if he does not succeed in qualifying for his most preferred reward.

Contracting can be subsumed within an "earned points" version of a token economy system, in which students earn point credits by fulfilling contracts. These credits can then be "spent" on rewards selected from a menu offering a variety of incentives. The "prices" of the rewards vary according to their attractiveness: The most popular ones cost the most points and thus require the most sustained levels of effort and accomplishment.

Most motivation theorists urge caution in using such incentive systems because they can undermine students' intrinsic motivation to engage in the rewarded activities. Where such intrinsic motivation is lacking, however, there is nothing to undermine. Thus, at least in areas where apathetic students clearly have no intrinsic motivation, you have nothing to lose by using extrinsic incentives.

However, the qualifications and guidelines on how to use extrinsic incentives still apply, especially if you want to move apathetic students away from dependence on these incentives and toward self-regulated motivation to learn. Therefore, avoid offering incentives in ways that reinforce these students' tendencies to view lessons and assignments as unwelcome impositions that must be endured for extrinsic reasons. Instead, use contracting approaches that include collaborative goal setting, and take advantage of the opportunities provided by the goal-setting negotiations to help the students begin to appreciate the value of what they are learning.

Emphasize authentic activities, phrase goal statements in terms of learning accomplishments rather than tasks completed, and use qualitative criteria for assessing progress. Revisit these goals and assessment criteria during post-activity debriefings, and as much as possible, elicit summaries and critiques of accomplishments from the students themselves. If the activity has yielded some noteworthy product, offer to display it in the classroom or suggest that the student share it with classmates or family members.

The point here is not merely to deflect attention from extrinsic rewards and their role in motivating these students' efforts, but to provide the students with concepts and language that they can use to appreciate and take pride in their accomplishments. Students can't appreciate what they don't see or understand. They need concepts and language to help them articulate learning goals, assess progress, and think about end products in terms of understandings, skills, or accomplishments (not merely task completion or compliance with minimal requirements).

Richly descriptive language is especially important for practice activities in subjects such as grammar, computation, or penmanship. To begin with, students should be aware that such practice is important because the ultimate goals—writing and problem solving in life situations—cannot be accomplished efficiently until key subskills are mastered to levels of smooth, accurate performance, such that they can be integrated and applied "effortlessly" when needed. Analogies to the importance of skill practice in preparing for integrated athletic or musical performance might be useful here.

In addition, though, students will need concepts and language to describe the immediate outcomes of their learning efforts. It is more meaningful and motivating to think about a reading assignment in terms of "understanding why slavery flourished in the south but not in the north" rather than "studying history," to "learn to divide when there is both a decimal point and a remainder" rather than to "do your math problems," or to "learn to adjust your writing position so that you stay on the line and maintain the same slant as you move across the page" rather than to "practice your penmanship." Use richly descriptive goal characterizations like these when introducing such activities. As students begin to work on them, phrase your feedback with reference to these goals. In assessing their completed work, refer to specific, qualitative aspects of their performance instead of confining yourself to grades or general evaluative comments.

It may be helpful to explain to apathetic students why learning can be empowering and self-actualizing. However, it almost certainly will be helpful to arrange conditions that allow them to experience these outcomes directly. Therefore, whether or not you use performance contracts or other incentive systems, be sure to negotiate goals and provide feedback to these students in language that they can use to plan and assess their learning. By engaging them in the processes of setting goals and reflecting on their work, you lead them through first-hand experiences in what it means to engage in academic activities with motivation to learn.

As these processes become more familiar, the students can begin to engage in them more naturally without feeling pressed to respond to unfamiliar demands. This will leave more of their cognitive resources free to think about the purposes, meanings, and potential applications of what they are learning. Eventually they should begin to do this spontaneously and thus start to generate and build on their own motivation to learn.

Building Close Relationships with Students

These students are already moving in undesirable directions, so they need to be turned around. This will require exerting counterpressures against, and ultimately prevailing over, whatever forces have led them to become apathetic or resistant learners. If failure syndrome problems are also present, you will have to work on these too, using the techniques described. Sometimes students dismiss a content area or type of learning activity as boring or useless because they fear failure and want to establish an excuse for not trying hard.

Whether or not they are compounded by failure syndrome problems, well-established apathy or resistance problems will not be cleared up quickly with a brief talk or a single key experience. You will need to work for and accept gradual progress, and to stay patient and supportive even if you encounter skepticism or resistance. Be prepared for such reactions, at least from students whose apathy has "hardened" into a well-articulated belief system. After all, why should these students take seriously your attempts to portray school learning as worthwhile if their own prior experiences, and perhaps the messages they get from their peers or even their parents, tell them otherwise?

To establish a potential for succeeding with apathetic students, show them that you care about them personally as individuals and are trying to "get through" to them primarily because you are concerned about their present and future best interests, not just because you want to get them to comply with your demands, and help them to see that their prior experiences have been limited or distorted—that despite the grading system and other performance incentives, the basic reason for engaging in learning activities is to acquire the empowerment and self-actualization potential that these activities are designed to develop. A great deal of modeling, socialization, and reflective discussion of learning experiences will be required to accomplish this agenda. For these efforts to have much effect, your relationships with these students will have to be such that they value your opinions and want to please you.

In getting to know apathetic students, take note of the situations in which they do or do not accomplish learning goals, and adjust accordingly. Also, get them talking about their school experiences in ways that help you to capitalize on their existing motivation. In particular, ask them about situational features (content areas, types of activities, types of learning formats) that they find conducive to learning, and about ways that other learning experiences might be made more worthwhile or helpful. Simply providing such students with opportunities for input is likely to improve your relationships with them and their attitudes toward learning, and their responses may include specific suggestions that you are willing to accept and that actually lead to improved performance.

Discover and Build on Existing Interests

Another reason for developing good relationships with apathetic students as individuals is to learn about their values and interests. Students who are not motivated to learn are pursuing other goal-oriented agendas. Some of these agendas will be incompatible with your own but others might provide motivational bases to use as starting points in working with these students while you nurture their motivation to learn. Almost any substantive interest, for example, can become the basis for developing language arts skills. Students might read books or magazines about sports and entertainment personalities, automobile customizing, computer games, or other topics popular in the youth culture, then write reports summarizing and reflecting on what they read. This may be less desirable than having them read and write about science or social studies topics, but at least it provides opportunities for applying language arts skills and perhaps for developing some important dispositions (reading for key ideas, reflecting on and communicating about them). In fact, you might consider suggesting that these students subscribe to favorite magazines, or even give them such subscriptions as gifts or as rewards for fulfilling achievement contracts. Other possibilities include arranging for students to follow up on significant recent experiences by reading about topics featured in field trips or popular movies or television shows, as well as encouraging students to discuss things they have read and recommend books to one another.

As another example, certain apathetic students might possess social motivation that you could use to substitute in part for their lack of motivation to learn. Such students might learn little or nothing if left to work individually but accomplish some important learning goals if paired with classmates who are more oriented toward learning. You might make frequent use of partner learning formats with these students in the short run, while working toward the long-term goal of developing their capacities as self-regulated learners. You might also arrange for these students to spend time with older students or alumni who value learning and could share life experiences that would help your apathetic or alienated students come to see that they should, too.

John Dewey believed that interest, if construed properly, is basic to good curriculum and instruction. He saw no value in attempting to dress up or sugar coat something that has no fundamental relevance to students, because this will create only momentary or fleeting interest. However, he saw great value in creating genuine interest by helping students to see connections between the school curriculum and their own spontaneously developed interests, goals, and abilities. He believed that curriculum content and learning activities should be selected in relation to students' current experience, abilities, and needs, and should be represented in ways that enable the students to appreciate their relevance and value in relation to what already has significance for them.

Genuine interest implies absorption in the process of learning, not just interest in its final products. It also implies recognition of long-term goals, monitoring of progress toward these goals, and willingness to strive to reach them. The interest-related payoff to the learner is some form of development or self-actualization.

Help to Develop Positive Attitudes

Dewey's ideas about interest connect to what was said in about intrinsic motivation residing in persons rather than objects or events. To develop stable individual interests in apathetic students and use these as bases for motivating their learning, you need to go beyond inducing curiosity or situational interest. In addition or instead, induce these students to identify with the whole idea of learning the content or skills you are teach-ing—to view acquisition of the content or skills as worth the effort for reasons that they can understand. In other words, help these students to see that it is in their own best interests to learn what you are trying to teach them.

Mordecai Nisan made a similar point in stating that schooling does not aim to provide satisfaction of what is desired by students but instead to cultivate in them what the culture construes as desirable. Ultimately, schooling is based on values rooted in images of a state of human perfection that is worth aspiring to attain. Apathetic students need help in understanding that school attendance and the demands of the educational system are part of a set of cultural expectations that are legitimate and desirable because they are designed to help students develop toward the culture's image of the ideal human being. Therefore, students owe it to themselves, as well as to the culture, to take advantage of the opportunities that schooling offers to develop well-differentiated and self-actualized personal identities, as well as the knowledge, skills, values, and dispositions that they will need to function effectively in society.

When phrased in such language, the sense of the desirable sounds like a very abstract value that would be difficult to convey to K–12 students, let alone to cultivate in apathetic students who see no value in schooling. However, Nisan's research with first-, fourth-, and seventh-graders showed that these students already possessed intuitive versions of this value. The students were asked to express opinions about several scenarios, one of which involved a child who did not attend school. Large majorities of students at all three grade levels viewed failure to attend school as undesirable, even when the child was depicted as living in a country in which school attendance was not required and not common. Most of them believed that there should be laws requiring school attendance, and they justified this opinion on the basis of concern about children's long-term well-being. They viewed schooling as necessary for proper development.

These findings imply that, at some level, most if not all students understand that it is in their own best interests not only to attend school but to strive to accomplish learning goals. Apathetic students have suppressed this realization, so you will have to help them rediscover it and confront its implications through sympathetic yet persistent comments and questions. Both your and their efforts should emphasize securing their long-run best interests by promoting their progress in all aspects of the curriculum, not just pursuing their current interests in particular topics or activities.

Just as intrinsic motivation resides in persons, not activities, the same is true of negative reactions to school learning experiences. Emphasize this when working with students who view learning activities as aversive.

Assuming that the activities are well suited to the students' current learning abilities and needs, their aversive experiences are caused by their own negative attitudes and expectations, not by anything inherent to the activities themselves. Other students find these activities meaningful, worthwhile, and even enjoyable; they will too if they learn to engage in them with a more positive mindset.

Csikzentmihalyi noted that people can learn to experience flow even in routine activities if they seek out challenges and relish stretching their limits. For example, they might "complexify" an otherwise boring activity by trying to do it artistically, seeking to increase their efficiency, or setting goals that convert the activity into something more challenging and interesting. In school, students can develop strategies for managing their affective responses to learning activities. They then can use these strategies to maintain task focus and avoid becoming distracted by boredom, anger, frustration, or other negative emotions. You can assist such development by making your students more aware and able to make efficient use of the coping strategies they have developed on their own, as well as by teaching them new ones.

Oldfather interviewed fifth- and sixth-graders about the strategies they had developed for getting started and staying focused on tasks that they found boring or unrewarding. Several emphasized accepting the teacher's assurances that the task was worth doing (or more generally, the idea that there was a significant purpose behind everything that they were asked to do in school). For example, Suki found her science project boring but believed that "I have to think of it as important, because if you thought it wasn't important, you wouldn't do anything about it." Phil identified two factors that helped him overcome resistance to a task: observing peers enjoying the task and gaining a sense of competence (recognizing that he could "figure it out" if he applied himself to the activity, and thus expand his repertoire of knowledge and skills).

McCaslin and Good spoke of scaffolding students' motivation by asking them questions such as the following:

> Do you like the unit we have been studying? How come? (Why not?)
>
> What about-----interests (bores) you?
>
> Do you think that when you like something or find it interesting it is eas-ier to learn? Is it easier to remember?

Are there ways that you can try to make work more interesting or fun for you?

What are some of the things you do? Does that seem to help you learn?

Why do you suppose that is?

Have you ever tried ?

Besides calling students' attention to useful strategies, such scaffolding encourages honest communication because it "legitimizes" the students' view that engagement in learning activities is sometimes boring or aversive. It doesn't endorse this view, but it acknowledges that the students believe it and makes it OK to talk about it.

Making Work More Enjoyable or Satisfying

Many suggestions have been made to adults who would like to derive more satisfaction from their jobs. You can adapt these suggestions as ways to help apathetic students learn to take more satisfaction from their school work.

Waitley and Witt emphasized that the nature of work resides at least as much in the worker's attitude as in the work itself. To illustrate this, they told of three construction workers who were asked to talk about their jobs. The first worker mostly complained about negative aspects of the job (demanding boss, frustrations caused by bad weather or poor materials). The second worker talked more descriptively, but emphasized the steps involved in carrying out discrete tasks (mixing mortar, positioning a brick properly, troweling mortar around the brick and then scraping off the excess). The third worker, who derived the most satisfaction from the job, explained that he was building a cathedral!

Waitley and Witt identified several techniques used by workers to make their jobs more rewarding and enjoyable:

- Adopt positive attitudes and expectations by focusing more on what you expect to accomplish than on the difficulties you expect to encounter
- Develop plans and goal sequences to guide your work but also get feedback and be prepared to revise plans when necessary
- Emphasize perseverance and flexibility over attempts to be perfect from the beginning

- Make routine work more interesting by treating it as a game, trying to surpass self-imposed quotas, trying to do individual portions perfectly, or discovering how you can add personal creativity to it
- Learn to enjoy the challenge of solving problems and to take satisfaction in a job well done
- Congregate with people who share similar attitudes and expectations, while avoiding people who lack goals or who are more into complaining than coping.

Cameron and Elusorr also offered suggestions for making work more interesting. Most are based on psychological principles but some are based on Zen philosophy, especially the notion of present focus.

— *Present focus.* If you stay absorbed in what you are doing, you won't be watching the clock. Therefore, when you show up for a task, really show up: Be there, pay close attention to what you are doing, focus on it, and do it fully. If you catch your mind wandering, notice where it went and why. Make a note of any business that needs to be attended to later so that you can put your concerns on hold and refocus on the task at hand.

— *Ritual.* Starter rituals help you to get into present focus. For example, a "clearing ritual" in which you set up your equipment or clear your desk and arrange your papers might be a useful transition from other activities into getting ready to study or work.

— *Ride the waves.* Don't let situations that are imperfect or do not work out well gnaw at you. Care about what you do, do your best, analyze and try to deal with problems, but don't give up or do less than your best merely because you know that things are not going to be perfect.

— *A personalized approach.* Bring creativity to the job. If you must deal with certain recurring difficulties, stop looking at them as built-in handicaps and begin to view them as opportunities or challenges. If things are going so smoothly that you get bored, get off of automatic pilot and return to present focus by finding ways to make the job less routine or more demanding (by striving to meet personally set goals or varying your routines).

— *Make a game of it.* Turn work into play by creating a game that you can play while doing the job. A medical technician might occasionally take time out to view slides as if she were an art critic, a bartender might become a connoisseur of cliches that he hears from boring customers, a grocery bagger might try to pack items so that they come out level at the fill line, and a waitress might learn the ordering habits of regulars and make bets with herself on their behavior.

— *See your work as an art form.* Any action can be performed with a sense of aesthetics—seek ways to do your work gracefully or to produce an end product that is visually or otherwise pleasing in addition to functional.

— *See your work as a teacher.* Analyze the work to discover what there is to learn about it. If you get bored, figure out at what point you became bored, why you did the same task yesterday without getting bored, or whether something else is irritating you. Analyze differences between when you are bored and when you are not bored for ideas about how to minimize boredom. Also, learn more about the work itself (possibilities for using any equipment involved, ways to do the job more efficiently, shortcuts to use and cues for recognizing when they are relevant).

— *Find a rhythm to your work.* Finding natural rhythms or cycles in work can help make it more enjoyable and reduce the sense that it "never lets up." If possible, take time away from some continuous task so as to vary it with another task and give yourself a chance to relax from that particular form of effort. Pay attention to natural rhythms in work cycles to help keep you aware of the variation that is built into tasks and the progress you are making toward goals.

— *Unwind.* When pressure gets to you, let your mind slip into something more comfortable (but not into doubts, worries, or irritations). Alternate periods of intense concentration and activity with brief periods of relaxation. If you can't walk around or take a break, sit back, close your eyes, and meditate briefly. Sharing jokes and finding humor on the job helps too.

— *Seek excellence.* Learn to seek excellence in doing your work and taking satisfaction from doing so. In the process of seeking excellence, use the following techniques: (a) *just the details* (Pay attention to each detail of the job and do it fully and carefully. This combines present focus with the notion of taking pride in each separate small piece of the job as part of what is involved in completing the job as a whole successfully) and (b) *your life depends on it* (Do the work as if your life depended on doing it well. Think of it as something that you are going to dedicate to people you care about or are going to sign with your name when you finish).

Students develop some of these techniques on their own, although often only the less adaptive ones. You might teach them some of the more adaptive techniques, which should help them to derive satisfactions in the process of carrying out assignments and to sustain the self-regulation needed to see the work through to completion. Techniques for making work more enjoyable should go a long way toward reducing apathy and resistance. However, they apply more to routine tasks calling for expert performance than to tasks designed as learning experiences for novices. As Marshall emphasized, classrooms are better described as learning settings than as work settings.

Socialize Apathetic Students' Motivation to Learn

Values and attitudes ordinarily are acquired primarily through exposure to respected models who exhibit them, rather than through more typical instruction. However, they also can be socialized through persuasive communication (if students accept the message) and developed through participation in powerful learning experiences that foster them. You can socialize motivation to learn indirectly through modeling, persuasion, and scaffolding of students' learning experiences, but you cannot transmit it directly through instruction because it includes elements of emotional involvement and personal commitment that can come only from the students themselves.

The task of socializing motivation to learn is difficult with apathetic students who have not had much exposure to experiences that help them understand what it means to engage in learning activities with the intention of gaining the benefits they were designed to develop. The task is even more challenging with alienated students who have come to view schooling as aversive, because it requires changing existing attitudes and values in addition to building new ones.

You cannot force students to change their attitudes and values, not even with sanctions such as punishments or failing grades. You may be able to force them to do at least a minimum amount of work by requiring them to complete assignments during recess periods, after school, or in in-school detention programs. However, getting work out of students is not the same as motivating them to learn. Therefore, it is better to minimize your reliance on coercive methods and instead build and work within more productive teacher–student relationships.

Apathetic students need the same curiosity-, interest-, and reflection-stimulating experiences that other students do, but they need to encounter them more frequently and carry them out in more personal, intense, and sustained ways. They especially need to be stimulated to reflect on and communicate about their learning. Therefore, keep focusing them on the self-actualizing potential of learning experiences by asking them questions about the content or by making assignments that require them to think about and appreciate new insights, to form and explain opinions, to develop explanations, or to make connections or applications. Scaffold their engagement in learning activities and their post-activity reflections to make sure that they experience empowering or self-actualizing outcomes. Your goal is to induce them to identify with these experiences—to connect learning experiences with their self-concepts and to begin to develop images of their ideal selves that cast them as open-minded, active learners.

To the extent that apathetic students are open to considering it and capable of understanding it, consider trying a "hard sell" approach to socializing their motivation to learn. Perhaps begin by informing them that they have missed the boat on some important opportunities for self-actualization, and that you want to give them a second chance or a chance to catch up.

Ask them questions to initiate discussions about why schools and libraries exist, why people go to museums or watch educational programs, why they read newspapers and magazines, and why they travel and seek other opportunities to broaden their lives. Also, model and provide examples of ways that people with active minds can bring the world to themselves by using their own resources, without depending on other people or media to bring things to them. Draw on examples from your own life to illustrate motivation to learn and the self-talk that accompanies it, while articulating values such as the following:

— *Get worthwhile payoffs from your investments of time and effort.* Whenever you invest in some activity (and especially when your engagement in the activity is required), do so in ways that produce useful outcomes and do not leave you feeling that you have wasted time and effort. If you are going to study, learn. Get the most out of the experience by using generative learning strategies that focus on the meanings and potential applications of key ideas.

— *Take satisfaction in gaining understanding.* Learn to take pleasure in acquiring information and to experience satisfaction in coming to understand how things work. Take time to appreciate the minor epiphanies represented by "aha" reactions, "so that's how it works" insights, or "I never knew that—I'll bet that's why connections.

— *Enjoy the stimulation of novel or surprising input.* New input stimulates the cognitive juices, especially when it extends knowledge of things that we are already interested in or when it violates our expectations, contrasts with what we are familiar with, or in some other way surprises or makes aware that our knowledge is incomplete. It is fascinating to learn about lifestyles or actions that we have never considered or thought possible.

— *Enjoy vicarious experiences.* Especially in reading fiction, but also in keeping up with current events or reading in the social sciences, there are opportunities to identify with focal characters or project ourselves into the situations being depicted. This allows to vicariously experience what happens to the characters or people in these situations, and to think about how we would respond in their place.

— *Appreciate expansion of self-knowledge.* Whenever we learn about particular people or about the human condition in general, we learn more about ourselves. This includes similarities and contrasts with other people as well as information about the motives and intentions that underlie behavior, about different ways of handling life situations, and so on.

— *Take pride in becoming a well-informed person and citizen.* Expanding our knowledge and using our cognitive abilities is unique to the human condition and an important part of what it means to be a fully functioning person. Engagement in these activities provides bases for to take satisfaction in feeling that we are aware of what is going on in the world, that we can follow news and current events knowledgeably, that we are informed voters, and that we have developed well-articulated opinions on policy issues or matters that come up in social discussion.

Along with providing such modeling and expectations yourself, expose your apathetic students to peers or people with whom they identify who model active minds at work. For example, in an intervention study designed to encourage 7 to 11 year-old students to become more intrinsically motivated learners, Hennessey, Amabile, and Martinage had the students watch videotapes that included the following dialogue:

Adult: Tommy, of all the things your teacher gives you to do in school, think about the one thing you like to do best and tell me about it.

Tommy: Well, I like social studies the best. I like learning about how other people live in different parts of the world. It's also fun because you get to do lots of projects and reports. I like doing projects because you can learn a lot about something on your own. I work hard on my projects and when I come up with good ideas, I feel good. When you are working on something that you thought of, and that's interesting to you, it's more fun to do.

Adult: So, one of the reasons you like social studies so much is because you get to learn about things on your own. And it makes you feel good when you do things for yourself; it makes it more interesting. That's great!

As part of your attempt to socialize motivation to learn in apathetic students, you might expose these students to selected videotapes from television talk shows (or at least make reference to certain common types of participants on these shows) in order to draw contrasts between active and passive or closed minds. In the process, draw distinctions between the content and style of communication displayed by interesting, well-informed, and obviously reflective guests and the guests who defeat their own best interests by impulsively blurting out ill-considered ideas, loudly repeating counterproductive arguments, undermining their own credibility, and causing other guests and onlookers to respond to them with derision or irritation. Point out that these people did not have to become the way they are— most of them are not stupid but are passive, unreflective, willfully ignorant, or defensively aggressive rather than open to new information or ideas. They never learned to ask what things mean, why they are important, or what their implications might be for personal or social decision making.

Where it may be productive to do so, you might go on to point out that despite the diversity and richness of the self-actualization opportunities that the modern world presents, some people maintain very restricted mental lives. They think only about work, daily needs, and popular culture. They are not desirable as spouses, parents, friends, or coworkers because they have nothing to say, prattle on about trivia, or aggressively spout uninformed opinions rather than engage in mutually satisfying conversations. They got this way by passing through school without taking advantage of the opportunities it offers, rationalizing by finding everything to be "boring" or "stupid."

The point of all this to emphasize with apathetic students is that schooling is not intended just to teach them basic skills and prepare them for jobs; in addition, it is intended to help them realize their human potential more fully in all aspects of their lives. To put it bluntly, schooling is intended to help them become the kinds of people that others admire rather than the kinds that are mostly ignored because they just pass their time like cows chewing cud or are mostly looked down upon because they act like the people who embarrass themselves on scandal-oriented talk shows.

Teach Skills for Self-regulated Learning

Many students, but especially apathetic or alienated students, will need instruction in cognitive and metacognitive skills for learning and studying effectively. You can teach them to become more aware of their goals during task engagement, to monitor their selection of strategies to use in pursuing those goals, to note the effects of these strategies and adjust them if necessary, and to control their affective responses to these unfolding events. For example, Pressley and Beard El-Dinary reviewed evidence supporting the value of teaching students how to manage six aspects of self regulated learning:

— *Actively preparing to learn.* Teach students to prepare to learn actively by mobilizing their resources and approaching tasks in thoughtful ways: getting ready to concentrate, previewing tasks by noting their nature and objectives, and in the case of complex tasks, developing plans before trying to respond to them.

— *Committing material to memory.* If material must be memorized, teach students techniques for doing so efficiently. Such techniques include active rehearsal; repeating, copying, or underlining key words; making notes; or using imagery or other mnemonic strategies.

— *Encoding or elaborating on the information presented.* Ordinarily you will not want students to memorize information but instead to retain its gist and be able to apply it later. Teach them strategies for identifying and retaining main ideas: paraphrasing and summarizing information to put it into their own words, relating it to what they already know, and assessing their understanding by asking themselves questions.

— *Organizing and structuring the content.* Students also need to learn to structure extensive content by dividing it into sequences or clusters. Teach them to note the main ideas of paragraphs, outline the material, and notice and use the structuring devices built into it. Also, teach them strategies for effective note-taking.

— *Monitoring comprehension.* In giving instructions for assignments, remind students to remain aware of the learning goals, the strategies they use to pursue those goals, and the corrective efforts they undertake if the strategies have not been effective. Also, teach them strategies for coping with confusion or mistakes: backing up and rereading, looking up definitions, identifying places in the text where the confusing point is discussed, searching the recent progression of topics for information that has been missed or misunderstood, retracing steps to see whether the strategy has been applied correctly, and generating possible alternative strategies.

— *Maintaining appropriate affect.* Finally, model and instruct your students in ways of approaching academic activities with desirable affect (relaxed but alert and prepared to concentrate, ready to enjoy or at least take satisfaction in engaging in the task). Also, teach them ways to avoid undesirable affect (anger, anxiety, etc.). Such instruction should include taking satisfaction in accomplishments and using coping skills to respond to frustration or failure.

A literacy program developed by a team of university researchers and elementary school teachers illustrates application of many of the strategies suggested here for scaffolding students' learning efforts. Butler similarly reported positive findings from a program for teaching strategies in the context of writing instruction. Generally, strategy teaching that is embedded in the regular curriculum (and thus is learned in the context of application) is more likely to be effective than more generic strategy instruction, including instruction that occurs in pull-out programs for struggling students.

TEACH VOLITIONAL CONTROL STRATEGIES

In many learning situations, some students begin with goal clarity and motivation to learn and possess the strategies needed to do so, but fail to follow through because they become distracted, fatigued, or preoccupied with competing goals. In recognition of this, some motivational theorists distinguish between motivation and volition.

These theorists use the term motivation to refer to the adoption of goals and the development of goal-related plans, then use the term volition to refer to actions taken to follow through on those plans and make sure that they are implemented. Such actions include concentrating on the task at hand, buckling down to get to work, resisting distractions, and persisting in the face of difficulties.

You may need to teach at least some of your students volitional control strategies such as the following:

- *metacognitive control* (thinking of initial steps to take in order to get started right away; going back over work to check it and making revisions before turning it in);
- *motivation control* (reminding oneself to concentrate and focus on task goals; generating ways to carry out the task that will make it more enjoyable, challenging, or reassuring; imagining completing the task success fully and enjoying the satisfaction of doing so);
- *emotion control* (reassuring oneself when bothered by fear of failure or doubts about one's ability; activating strategies that one has learned for coping when confused or frustrated);
- *controlling the task situation* (developing and revising a step-by-step plan for getting complex tasks accomplished; moving away from noise and distractions; gathering all needed materials before beginning the work);
- *controlling others in the task setting* (asking for help from teacher or class mates; asking others to stop bothering or interrupting).

With highly distractible students, you may need to provide study carrels or other distraction-reduced work environments in addition to teaching them strategies for maintaining their engagement in learning activities.

When working with apathetic or alienated students, it often is especially important to supplement work on motivational issues (eliciting goal commitment) with work on volitional issues (eliciting or working with the student to establish specific plans for when, where, and how the commitment will be carried out). Ostensible goal commitments (stated intentions to accomplish particular agendas) are much more likely to be carried through to fruition if accompanied by specific implementation intentions.

Students with low self-efficacy perceptions or other expectancy-related problems will need attention to aspects of volition that involve managing frustration and negative emotions and maintaining productive task engagement. In contrast, apathetic and alienated students are likely to need work on aspects of volition that involve formulating clear and firm implementation intentions. Help these students learn to follow through on goal commitments by planning such considerations as: when and where they will do the work (estimating and budgeting for the necessary time); how they will protect this time from other interests and commitments; when and how they will obtain and assemble any needed materials; and if necessary, how they will divide the work into a series of subtasks (with associated time schedules).

Students who have particular trouble getting started and following through on assignments can learn to benefit from the "strategic automaticity" or "proceduralization" of implementation intentions. Encourage them to establish standard routines for working in particular places at particular times: develop a "start-up ritual" (e.g., clearing the workspace of all but needed materials, arranged in ready-for-use alignments); turn off the television, the phone, or other potential distractions; do assignments for different subjects in the same order each time; and so forth. Just as the automatized procedures have developed for entering, starting, and beginning to drive a car enable to perform these familiar activities with great efficiency and without much conscious thought, proced-uralizing certain aspects of our implementation of learning commitments can make it easier for to follow through on these commitments efficiently. Standardized procedures and work habits reduce students' needs to make specific implementation plans and help them to begin work more quickly and stick with it more consistently.

References

Csikzentmihalyi, M. (1993). *The evolving self: A psychology for the third millennium*. New York: HarperCollins.

Damon, W. (1995). *Greater expectations: Overcoming the culture of indulgence in America's homes and schools.* New York: The Free Press.

Hartman, H. (Ed.). (2001). *Metacognition in learning and instruction: Theory, research and practice.* Boston: Kluwer.

Kuhl, J., & Beckmann, J. (Eds.). (1985). *Action control: From cognition to behavior.* New York: Springer-Verlag.

Waitley, D., & Witt, R. (1985). *The joy of working.* New York: Dodd, Mead.

Williams, W. (1996). *The reluctant reader: How to get and keep kids reading.* New York: Warner Books.

Zimmerman, B., & Schunk, D. (Eds.). (2001). *Self-regulated learning and academic achievement: Theoretical perspectives* (2nd ed.). Mahwah, NJ: Lawrence Erlbaum Associates.

10

Individual Differences in Student Motivation

Learners are individuals and must be treated as such if expect to optimize their motivation and learning. Over time, a great many claims have been made that teachers need to accommodate this or that dimension of difference among students, but few of these claims have been backed by a significant research base establishing that

(a) differences on the dimension are important enough to justify the effort it would take for teachers to assess students and provide differentiated curriculum and instruction to different subgroups;

(b) the suggestions made to teachers about differentiating instruction are feasible for implementation under normal classroom conditions; and

(c) if provided, such differentiated treatment would serve the long-run best interests of all of the students involved.

For the most part, the motivational strategies suggested here are based on psychological principles believed to apply to people in general, regardless of age, gender, social class, race, cultural background, or personal characteristics. Many motivational theorists would expect these strategies to affect all students similarly rather than to produce contrasting reactions in different subgroups. Certain principles might be more relevant to certain situations, but the principles would apply to all students. Other motivational theorists would maintain that efforts to implement motivational principles need to be tailored not only to situations but to students. They might agree that you can use the same basic set of motivational strategies with all students but argue the need to use some strategies more frequently or intensively with students who belong to certain subgroups or have developed certain personal characteristics.Still other motivational theorists would argue that you face a more complex situation—that different students need different motivational strategies because application of any given strategy is likely to increase motivation in some students but decrease it in others. Some students prefer material rewards, others prefer symbolic rewards, and still others prefer special privilege or teacher rewards.

Eden developed a model that incorporated this idea. His model assumes that, for a given person in a given situation, certain motives are relevant but others are not. Therefore, the effect of tying task engagement to a motive will depend on the relevance of that motive to the person at the time. If task engagement produces a relevant motivational consequence, there is likely to be a (probably substantial) increase in motivation to perform the task. However, if task engagement produces some irrelevant motivational outcome, there is likely to be a (probably small but real) decrease in motivation to perform the task. Eden presented some evidence in support of this model (although not evidence based on students' behavior in classrooms)

Intrinsic motivational theorists might interpret Eden's work as further evidence of the need to provide students with choices of what assignments to do and when and how to do them. Extrinsic motivational theorists might interpret it as further evidence that teachers should not rely on a few incentives but instead offer students a variety of rewards from which to choose, so that all of them will be able to work toward incentives that they find appealing.

Accommodating Students' Preferences

Accommodating students' existing motivational systems does nothing to move them in directions that you would like to see them move. In addition, there are two other reasons for proceeding cautiously when adapting motivational strategies to student differences. First, accommodating students' preferences is not the same as meeting their needs. Allowing students to choose their own learning methods or arranging to teach them as they prefer to be taught may produce less achievement than teaching them in some other way, even if it improves their attitudes toward learning.

Second, accommodating students' existing personal characteristics is likely to reinforce those characteristics, including ones that you would prefer to change if possible. For example, it is tempting to respond reciprocally to passive or alienated students by minimizing your interactions with them—never calling on them during lessons unless they raise their hands and avoiding them during independent work times unless they indicate a need for help. This might maximize both your comfort and that of the students involved, but it would not be in their best interests.

Even where it may be desirable to treat different students differently, your opportunities to do so will be limited unless you teach in a special education resource room or some other setting with a very low student–teacher ratio. If you teach a typical class of 20 or more students, you will have to focus most of your curriculum and instruction on the class as a whole and work at the margins to adapt to individual differences.

With respect to students' motivation, the most important individual differences lie in the degree to which they value what schooling has to offer (and the reasons why they do so), the degree to which they believe that they can meet the demands of schooling if they invest reasonable effort, and the degree to which they emphasize learning goals versus less desirable goals.

As you read this and any other advice about differentiating your motivational strategies, however, keep in mind that your primary responsibility is to induce your students to move in desirable directions, not just to cater to their current preferences and interests.

Differences in Psychological Differentiation

Cognitive style refers to the ways that people process information and use strategies to respond to tasks. People differ, for example, in their tendencies to attend to global features versus fine details of stimuli, to classify stimuli into a few large categories versus many smaller ones, or to make quick, impulsive decisions versus employing a slower, more painstaking approach to problem solving. Cognitive styles are called styles rather than abilities because they refer to how people process information and solve problems, not how well.

A cognitive-style dimension that has implications for motivation is psychological differentiation, also known as field dependence versus field independence or as global versus analytic perceptual style. People who are low in psychological differentiation (field dependent) have difficulty differentiating stimuli from the contexts in which they are embedded, so their perceptions are easily affected by manipulations of the surrounding context. In contrast, people who are high in psychological differentiation (field independent) perceive more analytically. They can separate stimuli from context, so their perceptions are less affected when changes in context are introduced.

These differences apply to social perceptions as well as to perceptions of the physical world. Consequently, field-dependent people's perceptions and opinions are strongly affected by those of other people, whereas field-independent people are more likely to resist social pressures and make up their minds on the basis of their own perceptions. In ambiguous social situations, field-dependent people are more attentive to and make more use of prevailing social frames of reference, monitor the faces of others for cues as to what they are thinking, attend more to verbal messages with social content, and get physically closer to and interact more with others. As a result, they tend to be liked by other people and perceived as warm, tactful, considerate, socially outgoing, and affectionate. In contrast, field-independent people have a more abstract, theoretical, analytical, and impersonal orientation. This makes them more able to resist external pressures toward conformity, but also more likely to be perceived as cold, distant, or insensitive.

In classrooms, field-dependent students tend to prefer to learn in groups and to interact frequently with teachers, whereas field-independent students prefer more independent and individualized learning opportunities. They also tend to prefer and do better in mathematics and science, whereas field-dependent students tend to prefer and do better in the humanities and social sciences.

Most students do not consistently reflect these extremes of psychological differentiation, but they may tend more toward one set of attributes than the other. To the extent that they do, they are likely to be happier in school if they spend most of their time focusing on content and learning within formats matched to their preferences. However, it is not clear that such differentiated treatment would serve their long-term best interests. Extremely field-independent students have social adjustment problems, and extremely field-dependent students are conforming to the point that they seem to lack minds of their own. These students might be better off in the long run if they could learn to appreciate and function more frequently in their nonpreferred orientation.

Therefore, learn to recognize and respect both orientations and to build on students' strengths but also work on their areas of weakness. You might structure field-dependent students' learning experiences enough to enable them to cope effectively, provide frequent encouragement and praise, be supportive when noting their mistakes, and allow them to learn in collaboration with peers most of the time. Field-independent students do not need as much personal support and encouragement, although they will require explicit feedback. With these students, it may be more important for you to respect their needs for privacy and distance, to avoid penalizing them unreasonably for low social participation, and to allow them frequent opportunities to operate autonomously.

Learning Style Differences

Much attention has been focused on the notion of learning styles, especially by people who offer workshops or sell materials purported to help teachers assess their students' learning styles and follow up with differentiated curriculum and instruction. Learning style inventories address questions such as the following: Are the students "verbal learners" who prefer to listen to information or "visual learners" who prefer to read it or see it displayed graphically? Do they prefer to learn alone or with others? Do they prefer to study for frequent short periods or fewer longer periods? Do they like to study in silence, with soothing musical or "white noise" backgrounds, or in potentially distracting environments (amid people who are conversing or next to a playing radio or television)?

For example, McCarthy identified four learning style types by locating students on two dimensions: perceiving (concrete sensing/feeling versus more abstract thinking) and processing. Combinations of high and low scores on these dimensions produce the following four learning styles:

1. Imaginative learners perceive information concretely and process it reflectively. They listen, share, and seek to integrate school experience with self experience.
2. Analytic learners perceive information abstractly and process it reflectively. They appreciate both details and ideas, tend to think sequentially, and value ideas more than people.
3. Commonsense learners perceive information abstractly and process it actively. They tend to be pragmatic learners who value concrete

problem solving and like to "tinker" and experiment to learn by discovery.

4. Dynamic learners perceive information concretely and process it actively. They tend to integrate experience and application, are enthusiastic about new learning, ready to engage in trial-and-error learning, and adept at risk taking.

McCarthy designed the 4MAT system of instruction as a way to accommodate these differences in students' preferences and strengths and thus to improve their motivation and achievement.

The 4MAT system is a model for designing units of study that accommodate the four learning styles as well as the supposed hemispheric (left- versus right-brain) preferences of students. Intended to be applicable to any content area or grade level, it calls for an eight-step cycle of instruction and learning activities relating to the unit topic. Each of the four learning styles is represented by two steps in the cycle, one designed to facilitate right-brain learning and the other to facilitate left-brain learning. According to McCarthy, if the teacher follows the full cycle, each individual student's learning style will be addressed during at least one fourth of the instructional time. During other parts of the cycle the learner will be "stretched," learning other ways to solve problems and thus developing a broader repertoire of problem-solving skills. She reported positive results from an intervention done with elementary students.

Wilkerson and White tested the 4MAT system against a more conventional treatment of a science unit on machines taught to third graders. The 4MAT version was constructed by taking the lessons and activities from the teacher's edition of the textbook and reworking them into the eight-step 4MAT cycle as follows:

Step 1: Students visualize machines they have experienced in everyday life, then draw pictures of these mental images (right mode lesson for innovative learners)

Step 2: Students work in small groups to discuss how the machines they have drawn make their work easier (left mode lesson for innovative learners)

Step 3: Students view a filmstrip depicting six simple machines used in everyday life, then draw pictures of the machines. Also, teacher holds up various objects (e.g., fishing reel, scissors) and students point to pictures of the same types of machines as the objects being shown (right mode lesson for analytic learners)

Step 4: Using the overhead projector, the teacher explains characteristics of each of the six simple machines. Then, students use a flannel board to match new words from the unit with their definitions (left mode lesson for analytic learners)

Step 5: Teacher reads students a book about machines. Then the students complete three worksheets reviewing concepts taught in Steps 4 and 5 (left mode lesson for commonsense learners)

Step 6: Wooden models of simple machines, examples of compound machines, and task cards are placed at work stations. Working in groups of three or four, students examine the machines and discuss potential responses to questions written on the task cards (right mode lesson for commonsense learners)

Step 7: Each student is given a plastic bag containing 11 word cards. The teacher asks questions about machines and the students answer by holding up one of their word cards. Then, each student is given a piece of transparency film and asked to draw a compound machine that would make work easier (left mode lesson for dynamic learners)

Step 8: The pieces of transparency film are used to make a film strip that is shown to the class. As their drawings come up, individual students explain to the class how the machines they drew would work (right mode lesson for dynamic learners).

While the 4MAT group was working through this cycle, students in the conventional group read from the textbook, provided oral and written responses to questions based on this material, and engaged in activities that included making a lever, conducting an experiment on inclined planes, completing a crossword puzzle that reviewed the six simple machines, making a bar graph showing the numbers of machines found in their homes, and watching a commercial filmstrip about machines. Assessment data indicated that the 4MAT approach produced modest but favorable effects on students' attitudes and achievement.

McCarthy and the 4MAT system are unusual within the learning styles literature, for at least three reasons. First, intervention studies based on the system were done with elementary students and encompassed a significant portion of the curriculum and instruction that they experienced. In contrast, most learning style studies have been done at the high school and (especially) the college level and many interventions have been restricted to variations in study or test environments.

Second, McCarthy noted the need for teachers to help students "stretch" to function in learning modes that they use infrequently. Unfortunately, the advice offered by most learning style advocates only emphasizes catering to students' existing preferences, without recognizing that this might not be in their long-run best interests.

Finally, reports of research on the 4MAT system have been published in respected research journals. Unfortunately, most of the sources cited by advocates of learning styles are either position pieces unsupported by classroom research or dissertations and other unpublished studies.

Lack of Research Support for Claimed Effects

Critics have noted that the credibility of learning styles enthusiasts is questionable because:

(a) they tend to make outlandish claims for the effectiveness of the measurement inventories and instructional models they sell;

(b) most of the studies purporting to support learning style approaches are too flawed to survive the peer review standards of research journals; and

(c) most of these studies have been conducted by people with vested interests in positive results who gave instructions to the participants in learning style treatment groups designed to maximize their enthusiasm and positive expectations.

Stellwagen underscored several of these themes in what he described as a challenge to learning style advocates. He was intrigued by the contrast he noted between enthusiasm for learning styles among many school administrators and teachers compared to the skepticism or rejection typically expressed by researchers. Looking into the matter, he found that professional journals typically waxed enthusiastic about learning styles and related fads such as so-called brain-based learning, but research-oriented journals consistently published reports questioning the value of both the instruments purporting to measure learning styles and the educational programs ostensibly based on them. He noted that even the 4MAT approach showed only mixed results in 18 dissertation studies.Stellwagen contrasted the claims of Rita Dunn about her learning style inventory with the conclusions drawn by independent investigators who assessed its validity and reliability. He also expressed concern that learning style categories were being misapplied in ways that led to stereotyping and potentially prejudicial treatment of students.

Similarly, Stahl critiqued Marie Carbo's claims for her so-called reading style inventory and noted that most of the "research" claims of Carbo and the Dunns are citations to dissertations by their own students. He went on to suggest that learning styles have enduring popularity despite a paucity of supporting evidence for the same reason that fortune telling does: They produce statements that are specific enough to sound predictive but ambiguous enough to apply to many different situations.

Brain-Based Education and Multiple Intelligences

Similar comments apply to schemes for differentiating instruction according to student profiles developed using supposed measures of cognitive styles, brain hemisphere preferences, or multiple intelligences. Scientifically based examinations of claims about supposedly brain-based education routinely conclude that knowledge about brain functioning has not yet progressed to a level that would support recommendations about curriculum and instruction, so that educational programs claiming to be based on brain research simply have no validity.

Similarly, although Howard Gardner has updated his multiple intelligences model and also published a book about educational assessments and interventions based on it, scientifically oriented reviewers routinely conclude that there are conceptual problems with his theory (particularly, misapplication of the term intelligences), psychometric problems with his measuring instruments (validity not yet demonstrated), a lack of clarity and specificity about what multiple intelligences theory does and does not imply about educational practice, and a lack of systematic research on (let alone clear support for) educational programs supposedly based on this theory.

Krechevsky and Seidel offered a useful introduction to the theory of multiple intelligences and its potential application to education. They suggested that the theory implies the need to individualize students' education as much as possible, teach subjects in more than one way, use project-based learning, and infuse the arts throughout the curriculum.

However, they cautioned that the theory should not be taken as a mandate to teach every topic in seven or eight ways. For example, asking students to sing songs about operations learned in a unit on fractions or playing classical music in the background during the lessons are not meaningful uses of music to support mathematics learning. They also cautioned against labeling or stereotyping students and against overemphasizing celebration of students' strengths without paying sufficient attention to their weaknesses.

Individual difference concepts such as cognitive styles, multiple intelligences, or learning styles can be useful to teachers if adopted only loosely and used primarily as reminders of the value of including a variety of learning activities and formats in the curriculum. However, scientific validity and practical feasibility problems arise if such concepts are emphasized to the extent of seeking to develop individual curricular prescriptions for each student.

It is worthwhile to learn about your students' preferences and accommodate them by providing opportunities for autonomy and choice whenever doing so will support progress toward learning goals. Sometimes such accommodation is not feasible or advisable, however. For example, in order to attain certain learning goals students must engage in processes that they might prefer to avoid. Or, you might have to limit certain students' opportunities to pursue favorite topics or learn in their preferred mode, because if the students spent too much time indulging these preferences they would fail to develop knowledge or skills needed in school or in life generally. You can accommodate such preferences much of the time, however, and doing so will increase your students' opportunities to experience intrinsic motivation in your classr.

Age and Motivational Patterns

Different grade levels present somewhat different motivational challenges to teachers because of age-related changes in students' motivational patterns. Most students begin schooling enthusiastically, but then show progressive deterioration on measures of school-related attitudes, curiosity, and intrinsic motivation.In addition, most students in the early grades show positive (actually, unreal-istically high) self-concepts and success expectations. These inflated self-perceptions of ability persist until about age seven, when they begin to show more consistent relationships with test scores and other more objective measures. As students become better at understanding and interpreting the feedback they receive, and as they begin to compare themselves with peers, their self-assessments become more accurate or realistic. To the extent that they begin to experience failure and understand its implications, they become susceptible to learned helplessness and other failure syndrome problems. However, even students who doubt their abilities usually do not begin to give up consistently when they encounter difficulties until they are about 10 years old.

Young children's unrealistically positive self-perceptions reflect more than mere childish egocentricity. Developments in their processing of performance feedback and related attributional thinking lead to shifts from intrinsic motivation to a focus on grades, from carefree optimism to social comparison and realism in judging achievement, and (for many students) from an emphasis on effort and an incremental view of ability to an emphasis on ability viewed as a stable entity. Younger students attend primarily to their own accomplishments rather than to those of classmates, so they tend to feel competent and successful if they complete a task or show improvement in their work. They tend to attribute success more to effort than ability, and to believe that they can increase their levels of ability by investing the effort needed to do so. As they develop, however, they begin to see effort and ability as inversely related. By the time they reach seventh grade, most are well aware that the need to expend considerable effort on a task implies limitations in domain-related abilities.

Young children's inflated perceptions of their own competence and lack of sophistication in making social comparisons and interpreting feedback provide certain advantages to primary-grade teachers. For one thing, their students are less susceptible to learned helplessness problems because failure does not faze them the way it fazes older students who are more aware of its potential implications. Also, younger students are less likely to feel embarrassed or to infer that their teacher believes they lack ability if they are encouraged or praised for effort.

These findings imply that primary-grade teachers can afford to be more spontaneous in scaffolding their students' learning, giving them feedback, and praising both their efforts and their accomplishments. Even so, teachers in these grades should follow the praising guidelines given. They also should provide primarily informative rather than evaluative feedback and focus their students' attention on appreciating their accomplishments to date and building on them in the future, not on comparisons with classmates. If feedback emphasizes social comparisons or normative evaluations, even kindergarten students will experience failure and begin to lower their self-evaluations of ability.

Transitional Grades

Within the general trend of steady decreases in intrinsic motivation and self-perceptions of ability, there is a tendency for noteworthy drops to occur when students shift from elementary to middle or junior high schools, or from middle or junior high schools to high schools. Negative effects on motivation are especially likely following the first shift, because it entails movement from a more supportive to a less supportive learning environment. Compared to elementary classrooms, middle school and junior high classrooms confront students with greater emphasis on teacher control and discipline; fewer opportunities to engage in decision making, choice, or self-management; less personal and positive teacher–student relationships; more frequent use of practices such as whole-class teaching, ability grouping, and public evaluation of work; and more stringent standards for grading. The enhanced salience of performance feedback and social comparison, within the context of a new reference group, causes many students to reevaluate their academic abilities.

Adjustments to new levels of schooling need not be so stressful or destructive to students' motivation. When middle and junior high schools provide more personalized and supportive environments suited to their students' psychological needs, the students do not demonstrate the same declines in motivation or increases in rates of misconduct seen in more traditional schools.

School-level changes such as creating "schools within schools" and smaller learning environments, block scheduling and flexible use of time, and assigning an adult advisor to each student can help ease transitions to higher levels of schooling. In particular, teachers at higher school levels who work with transitional students just entering from lower levels should go out of their way to welcome these students, make them feel comfortable in their new surroundings, and scaffold their learning efforts in ways that help them to feel confident that they will be able to meet the challenges that face them. They also should provide their students with frequent autonomy and choice opportunities, because they value these opportunities more than younger students do and because they are better equipped to handle them.

Developments in Children's Interests

Educators have studied children's interests because connecting with those interests is one way to stimulate intrinsic motivation and perhaps motivation to learn. Jersild and Tasch conducted a massive survey of the in-terests of students in Grades 1 to 12, and numerous smaller studies have also been conducted. These studies indicated that interests become differentiated with age, so that younger students have more interests in common than older students. At all ages, however, students tend to be more interested in stories and other content dealing with people than in content dealing with impersonal topics, and to prefer learning experiences that involve active doing over those that are confined to watching and listening.

Students' responses to questions about their interests are heavily influenced by their prior experiences. Consequently, these responses say more about the students' past exposure to interest-generating experiences than about their probable responses to potential future experiences. Even so, certain documented trends are worth noting.

Primary-grade students' interests center on themselves and their personal and family experiences. In school, they tend to prefer language arts, mathematics, and art over science, social studies, and local or world news. For reading, they tend to enjoy stories about other children and familiar experiences; tales of fantasy, fun, and humor; and narratives featuring acts of kindness or bravery.

Students in the intermediate grades tend to be more interested in realistic stories—tales of adventure, sportsmanship, or the work of inventors. They also develop interests in nature study and natural science, and more generally, in science and social studies topics. They tend to become interested in subjects in which they are successful, but to develop negative attitudes toward subjects that are difficult for them. Whereas younger students talk mostly about their own play and recreation or their family and home activities, students in the middle grades talk more about family vacations and other trips away from the local setting, books they have been reading, and television, movies, and other entertainment and youth culture activities.

These trends continue as students progress through secondary schools but their interests broaden to include topics from history and the social sciences and current events in the news, including events occurring in other parts of the world. High school students also develop interests in self-improvement, self-understanding, and vocations. The emergence of these interests reflects progression from a primary focus on competence to a primary focus on identity.

The curriculum scope and sequence followed in most school districts is reasonably well matched to students' developing knowledge and interests. Even so, you can generate additional opportunities to connect with their interests by administering and following up on interest inventories and by allowing for choices of topics for reading assignments and learning projects.

Authors of children's literature tend to be well attuned to the interests and imaginations of the age groups that they write for, as do many authors of educational software. Consequently, it is worth your while to familiarize yourself with literature selections and computerized learning programs that are especially appealing to students at your grade level.

Gender Differences

As children develop in our society, they are exposed to gender role socialization suggesting that certain family and social roles, occupations, personal attributes, and ways of dressing and behaving are primarily feminine, while others are primarily masculine. Gender role socialization pervades most children's experiences. It is modeled by the individuals they encounter in their personal lives and in the media, expressed directly in the messages they receive from their parents and peers (and sometimes their teachers), and reinforced through communication of expectations concerning such things as the toys and games they will want to play with, the books they will enjoy reading, or the things that they will want to do in school or in their free time.

In response to the Women's Movement and other social forces, there has been a loosening of the more restrictive aspects of traditional gender roles in the United States over the last century. Even so, many activities are still associated primarily with one gender or the other. To the extent that an ac-tivity is gender typed, teachers' and students' attitudes and expectations are likely to be affected. They may anticipate gender differences in interest and enjoyment in the activity, and perhaps also in success expectancies and performance attributions (if the gender typing is based on notions of gender differences in ability). Such gender typing has been noted in several aspects of schooling.

One of these involves subject-matter preferences and related motivational responses. Most studies find that boys value and enjoy mathematics and science more than language arts, but girls show the opposite pattern. These differences extend to preferences within subject areas, as well. In reading, for example, boys are more oriented to nonfiction texts, while girls tend to prefer fiction. Within fiction, boys tend to prefer action, adventure, and sports themes, whereas girls tend to prefer plots focusing on romance or personal relationships. Some researchers view these differences merely as carryovers from traditional socialization designed to prepare boys primarily to be breadwinners but girls primarily to be wives and mothers. They point to evidence of reductions in gender differences in recent years and suggest that further reductions can be expected to occur naturally in response to continued reductions in gender role specialization in the home and workplace.

Others urge teachers to try to reduce gender differences in response to school subjects, especially if the differences encompass not only preferences or value perceptions but also beliefs about ability and related attributional inferences. Concern is greatest with respect to science and especially mathematics, where several investigators have found that girls believe themselves to possess less domain-specific ability than boys, or that girls are more likely than boys to attribute their successes to luck or other external factors but to attribute their failures to lack of ability.

This pattern of subject-matter differences in gender-related attitudes and beliefs develops over time, so it is more noticeable in junior high and high school students than in elementary students. Occasionally, somewhat different patterns appear. For example, Chouinard, Vezeau, Bouffard, and Jenkins reported a precipitous decline across the adolescent years in boys' beliefs and attitudes about mathematics, to the point that they showed a less positive pattern than girls did by senior year of high school.

Unusual findings also were reported by Licht, Stader, and Swenson, who found that fifth-grade girls rated themselves as less smart than boys in social studies and science, but not in mathematics or reading. They attributed this finding to the fact that at fifth grade, the performance feedback that students receive for social studies and science is less frequent and more ambiguous than the feedback they receive for mathematics and reading, so the students' self-ratings of ability are more dependent on their general assumptions or beliefs than on specific data.

This interpretation is supported by other studies showing that, especially in the early grades, boys are more likely to have higher (although not necessarily more accurate) ability perceptions and future success expectations than girls. Boys also are more likely to credit their successes to high ability but attribute their failures to bad luck, lack of interest, low effort, or other causes that do not imply a lack of ability. These differences make girls more vulnerable to learned helplessness and other failure syndrome problems than boys, especially in subjects like mathematics or science where the girls might suspect limitations in their domain-specific abilities.

In any case, it is clear that starting around fifth grade and continuing thereafter, girls' ability beliefs and expectancies for future success in mathematics and science tend to drop below those of boys, even though their grades in these subjects are as good or better than boys' grades. Girls also are more likely to opt out of mathematics and science classes when they begin to get the opportunity to do so, thus cutting themselves off from future career opportunities that require academic preparation in these subjects. These patterns develop at least as much among brighter girls as among other girls.

Boys generally place less value on engaging in academic activities than girls do, so that the quality of their engagement is more variable. They are more likely than girls to adopt work-avoidant goals or display task resistance. When they adopt learning or performance goals, however, they are likely to focus on achieving mastery or competitive success. In contrast, girls are more likely to focus on consistently putting forth their best efforts and pleasing their teachers (Berndt & Miller, 1990; Blatchford, 1992; Boggiano, Main, & Katz, 1991; Bouffard, Boisvert, Vezeau, & Larouche, 1995; Harter, 1975; Meece & Holt, 1993; Pomerantz, Altermatt, & Saxon, 2002; Van Hecke & Tracy, 1983). Again, these differences do not always appear. However, they show up often enough to be cause for concern because they further contribute to girls' vulnerability to learned helplessness (because girls more consistently put forth their best efforts and therefore tend to attribute failures to lack of ability, whereas boys more consistently credit their successes to high ability but explain away their failures).

Interactions with Teachers

Other research has focused on gender differences in student behavior and teacher–student interaction patterns in classrooms. These studies indicate that boys are more active and salient in the classroom than girls. They have more of almost every kind of interaction that occurs between students and teachers, although the differences are greatest for interactions that boys initiate themselves by calling out answers or by misbehaving and drawing some form of teacher intervention. However, teachers also initiate interactions more frequently with boys, especially to give them procedural instructions, check their progress on assignments, or generally monitor and control their activities.

Along with differences in the quantity of teacher–student interaction, researchers have identified qualitative differences in the ways in which teachers interact with boys versus girls. In particular, words of encouragement or feedback directed to boys tend to focus exclusively on their achievement striving and accomplishments, but some of what is said to girls in parallel situations focuses instead on neatness, following directions, speaking clearly, or showing good manners. Teachers sometimes pay more attention to, ask more thought-provoking questions of, or provide more extensive feedback to boys in mathematics or science classes but to girls in language arts classes. When groups of students work on computers or carry out scientific experiments, boys are more likely to take active roles but girls are more likely to act as recorders or just observers.

These trends are observed in varying degrees in almost all classrooms, regardless of whether the teachers are male or female. Thus, they are rooted in the gender role expectations that most people acquire through socialization into our culture. Sadker and Sadker suggested that many of these differences reflect gender differences in styles of participation in social conversation that are pervasive in our society and thus carry over into classrooms: Men speak more often and frequently interrupt women; listeners pay more attention to male speakers, even when female speakers use similar styles and make similar points; women participate less actively in conversations but do more gazing and passive listening; and women often transform declarative statements into more tentative statements that reduce their ability to influence others.

Recommendations

Clear-cut teacher favoritism of one gender over the other is rare. Gender differences in teacher–student interaction patterns tend to be relatively small in quantity and subtle in quality. Furthermore, most of them reflect gender differences in student behavior that impact on teachers, rather than consistent teacher tendencies to treat boys and girls differently in parallel situations. Even so, it is wise to remain conscious of gender issues and to monitor your interactions with boys versus girls. This will help you not only to avoid inappropriate gender discrimination but also to take advantage of opportunities to free your students from some of the counterproductive restrictions built into traditional gender role concepts.

With regard to subject matter, help your boys to take full advantage of reading and writing opportunities, and in particular, to appreciate poetry and other forms of literature that they might view as feminine. Information about books popular with boys can be found at www.guysread.com. Similarly, help your girls to value and develop their full potential in mathematics and science. In developing content, use examples and problem contexts that will interest girls as well as boys. Stimulate their interest in and willingness to take courses in these subjects and help them to realize that they have the abilities to enable them to be successful in these subjects if they apply reasonable effort.

Also, where necessary, encourage girls to become more active in the classroom. Make systematic efforts to observe and get to know each girl as an individual (especially girls who achieve satisfactorily and appear to be well adjusted but rarely initiate contact with you or assert themselves in the classroom). Encourage these girls to speak their minds, call on them to participate if they do not volunteer, assign them to leadership roles for group projects, and take other actions to encourage them to become more assertive. Broaden their perspectives by helping them to realize that the full spectrum of career opportunities is open to them and by using learning experiences such as stories involving females in leadership positions or discussions or assignments focusing on the work of female scientists.

Most teachers have been doing these things in recent years, and along with changes in curriculum materials and pervasive messages about gender equality in the culture generally, they have had a significant effect. Gender gaps in mathematics and science achievement are disappearing rapidly. In fact, gender-related concerns about student motivation and achievement have begun to shift to boys, because recent trends indicate that fewer boys are earning good grades in school, graduating from high school, or attending college.

Differences in Sociocultural Backgrounds

Students from lower social class backgrounds or from racial or ethnic minority groups may experience difficulties at school to the extent that the values, language, behavioral expectations, and other aspects of the school culture contrast with what these students have been exposed to in their families and local subcultures. However, these difficulties can be minimized by teachers who are knowledgeable about and respectful of their students' home cultures and who work with the assets that the students bring to school with them rather than focus on deficiencies or problems.

Theory and research on these issues have developed in ways that reflect these distinctions. Early studies focused on group comparisons and yielded conclusions suggesting, for example, that lower class students preferred material rewards whereas middle-class students preferred intrinsic rewards, that Hispanic students were oriented toward cooperative learning, that Native American students responded negatively to public praise, and that African-American students had lower success expectations and less favorable attribution patterns than other students.

Subsequent research indicated that these and other sweeping statements about group differences were either incorrect or exaggerated, and that in any case, general sociological categories such as social class, race, ethnicity, or minority group membership were not nearly as useful as knowledge about individual students' family backgrounds and home cultures for understanding and suggesting ways to improve their adjustment to schooling. When researchers focused on specific families, and especially on the frequency and nature of the interactions that children had with their parents, they discovered many dimensions of family life and home culture that affect the degree to which children are comfortable at school, prepared to meet its challenges successfully, and confident in their ability to do so.

Task Structure

The task structure includes all activities conducted at home that may be related to school learning (household chores, play and hobby activities, school assignments done as homework, learning opportunities designed by the parents). Some families do much more than others to prepare their children for school and support their schooling experiences. They interact with their children frequently in cognitively stimulating ways, provide them with instruction and learning opportunities suited to their developmental levels, expose them to educational games and media at home, take them to museums and zoos, and encourage their talents and interests. Interaction around these activities builds important knowledge and skills and also has positive effects on children's developing curiosity, interest, attitudes toward school, acceptance of challenge, and tendency to engage in activities with learning goals rather than less desirable goals.

Authority Structure

The authority structure concerns the types and frequencies of children's responsibilities, self-directed activities, and opportunities to participate in family decision making. Families support their children's development of desirable motivational patterns by using authoritative child-rearing methods that include age-appropriate sharing of authority, negotiation of rules and expectations, and opportunities for children to make their own decisions. These home experiences develop desirable motivational patterns on variables such as locus of control, personal responsibility, efficacy perceptions, tendency to seek success and not fear failure, and orientation toward self-regulated learning. Families that rely on authoritarian or laissez-faire childrearing methods develop less desirable motivational patterns in their children.

Reward Structure

The reward structure refers to the degree to which parents pay attention to and reward their children's efforts and accomplishments. Parents support their children's school motivation by emphasizing encouragement and reward over threat and punishment, and by focusing their encouragement and rewards on school-related accomplishments. It also helps if parents recognize improvement as well as excellence, cooperative as well as competitive behavior, and intrinsic satisfactions as well as extrinsic rewards.

Grouping Structure

Students' readiness to get along and collaborate with peers is affected by the degree to which their families encourage them to display nurturing behavior (in caring for younger siblings or elderly family members), monitor their interactions with peers and teach them to negotiate plans and resolve disagreements productively, model tolerance and appreciation of diversity, and help them to balance responsibilities to peers with responsibilities to parents, teachers, and others in their lives.

Evaluation Structure

The evaluation structure concerns the standards set for learning and behavior, the procedures used for monitoring and evaluating attainment of those standards, and the methods used to provide feedback about accomplishments and needed improvements. Supportive parental activities within this structure include emphasizing private and in- formative feedback over public and evaluative judgments, being flexible in adjusting standards to accommodate developments in children's abilities, and discussing the reasons for and implications of these developments in ways that help children to appreciate their accomplishments and set appropriate goals in the future.

Time Structure

The time structure concerns the schedules that families set for their children's activities and assignments. Especially when children have busy schedules it is important for them to learn to develop realistic plans and manage their time effectively. Parents need to see that their children have sufficient time to do all of the things that they are expected to do, but also to see that these things are in fact accomplished and that a high priority is placed on school-related tasks if time is tight.When parents fail to do these things that help prepare children for school and support their progress as students, it is usually because they do not realize their importance or know how to do them. Most parents care about their children's success at school and will respond positively to information sharing and requests from teachers. Furthermore, one of the distinctive features of the teachers and schools that are most effective with students at risk for school failure is that they reach out to these students' families, get to know them, keep them informed of what is going on at school, and involve them in decision making.

Stereotype Threat

Claude Steele has shown that members of stereotyped groups may perform below their capacities on tasks that their group is expected to do poorly on, especially if they are reminded of their group membership before or during the task. For example, African-American students usually are aware that African-Americans tend to score lower than European-Americans on tests of intelligence or academic achievement, leading to stereotyped expectations that African-American students will perform poorly on such tests. Even subtle reminders of this expectation can cause African-American students to become concerned about confirming this stereotype when they take tests, and this concern can distract the students from the tests and reduce their coping capacities in the same ways that efficacy concerns and fear of failure can. Steele and Aronson demonstrated these dynamics in studies indicating that Black students showed variable levels of performance on a test compared to White students, depending on how the test was presented. Black students did not do as well when the test was described as diagnostic of intellectual ability, and even when the test was not so described, the Black stu- dents did not do as well when the students were asked to identify their race immediately before taking it.

Stereotype threat phenomena can occur with respect to members of any group who might be expected to perform poorly in a particular domain, especially if they are reminded of the existence of this stereotype and their membership in the group when they are about to perform. So far, this has been demonstrated for Latino students, for women relative to men on tests of mathematics ability, for men relative to women on an affective processing task, for European-American students relative to Asian-American students on a mathematics test, for White athletes relative to black athletes on an ostensible test of natural athletic ability, and for students from lower socioeconomic status backgrounds relative to students from higher socioeconomic status backgrounds.

Wise teachers will create optimistic relationships with their students, focusing not on academic problems and failures but on encouraging these students to feel a sense of belonging in the classroom and helping them to reach realistic achievement goals. In interacting with these students, and especially when giving feedback on their work, teachers should combine articulation of high standards with expression of confidence that the students can meet these standards if they apply themselves.

Motivating Minority and At-Risk Students

It is important to establish collaborative relationships with all of your students' parents, but especially with the parents of students who are struggling, apathetic, or resistant to you or your curriculum. The parents may have had similar problems in school themselves, may feel guilty about their child's problems, or may be inhibited or suspicious at first in dealing with you. However, they are likely to be grateful and become more responsive if they see that you care about their child and want to work with them to pursue the child's best interests, not merely to give them bad news and then expect them to "do something."

The same is true of their child. Minority students and others whose family backgrounds place them at risk for school failure do especially well with teachers who share warm, personal interactions with them but also hold high expectations for their academic progress, require them to perform up to their capabilities, and see that they progress as far and as fast as they are able. These teachers break through social-class differences, cultural differences, language differences, and other potential barriers to communication in order to form close relationships with at-risk students, but they use these relationships to maximize the students' academic progress, not merely to provide friendship or sympathy to them.

At-risk students also do especially well in classrooms that offer warm, inviting social environments. Therefore, help your students to value diversity, learn from one another, and appreciate different languages and traditions. Treat the cultures that they bring to school as assets that provide students with foundations of background knowledge to support their learning efforts and provide you with opportunities to enrich the curriculum for everyone. Think in terms of helping minority students to become fully bicultural rather than in terms of replacing one culture with another. If you are unfamiliar with a culture that is represented in your classroom, educate yourself by reading about it, talking with community leaders, visiting homes, and most importantly, talking with students to learn about their past history and future aspirations.

Moll and Gonzalez noted that teachers could usefully integrate these funds of knowledge into classrooms through such activities as having students do research on community issues, understanding the architectural principles used in building community houses, or developing awareness of how the community functioned socially. They also emphasized the value of integrating parents intellectually into the life of the school. Similarly, Leacock noted that opportunities for connecting the curriculum to the students' home backgrounds are often missed because instruction stays too close to what is in the textbooks. As an example, she noted "community helpers" lessons in elementary social studies classes. Usually at least some students in a class, and frequently a great many students, have parents who are police officers, fire fighters, postal workers, and other service workers studied in these units, but few teachers think to invite these parents to come to the classroom and speak with the students about their jobs.

If necessary, modify your curricula to infuse a multicultural perspective and feature the cultures represented by your students. Modifications might include a somewhat different selection of content (especially in history and literature) as well as treatment of many more topics as issues open to multiple perspectives rather than as bodies of factual information that admit to only a single interpretation. In covering cultures and customs, emphasize instructional materials that focus on universal human experiences and parallels between comparable cultural practices over materials that encourage chauvinism by focusing on exotic practices. Expose students to literature or multimedia content sources that not only feature models who come from minority groups represented in your classroom but also portray these models in ways that encourage all students to identify with them. In addition, expose your students to actual, living models by arranging for classroom speakers, field trips, or current events discussions that will raise minority students' consciousness of roles and accomplishments to which they might aspire.

Knapp analyzed ways in which teachers working in ethnically heterogeneous classrooms responded to the cultural diversity of their students. Some teachers did not respond constructively because they held negative stereotypes of certain ethnic or socioeconomic groups. These stereotypes led them to treat students from these groups in ways that limited their learning opportunities and communicated low expectations. In contrast, constructive teachers held more positive expectations of their students and possessed a basic knowledge of their cultures. The most effective ones explicitly accommodated the students' cultural heritages by communicating to them that their cultural backgrounds were not problems to be overcome but rather strengths to be acknowledged and drawn upon in schooling.

Counteracting Peer Pressures

A positive approach that honors diversity and focuses on helping all students to achieve their potentials should carry you a long way in motivating your students to learn, regardless of their social class, racial, or ethnic backgrounds. However, you may encounter consistent resistance to adoption of learning goals by alienated students who have come to view putting forth consistent effort in school as "selling out," "sucking up to teachers," or "acting white" (as well as sporadic resistance by other students who are being pressured by alienated peers). You will need to take actions designed to turn around the alienated students, and in the meantime, to minimize their negative influences on classmates.

The most effective way to turn around resistant students is to put them in contact with respected models with whom they identify and ask the models to help these students see that their attitudes undermine their own best interests. Ideal models might be teenagers and young adults who formerly attended your school and could tell your students true stories about local people that illustrate how life paths begin to diverge when students their age decide either to take advantage of or to reject what schooling has to offer them.

In addition, try to resocialize resistant students' attitudes, whatever your (and their) social class and ethnic backgrounds may be. Toward this end, we recommend three strategies. First, do not scoff at the students' ideas (about "acting white," etc.) or dismiss them out of hand. Accept them as genuinely held beliefs, although beliefs that you do not share. If you try to undermine these beliefs using persuasion methods, make sure that everything about your tone and manner and all of the arguments that you present to the students communicate your concern about their best interests. If they view your behavior as an attempt to manipulate them for your own purposes, your persuasion attempts will backfire. In the case of minority group students, even if they concede your good intentions, they may not accept your arguments if they believe that you essentially are pressuring them to give up their cultural heritage in exchange for economic opportunities in the larger society.

Second, draw these students out by using "active listening," reflection, and related counseling techniques. In private conversations, ask them to elaborate on their views and listen carefully as they do so. Occasionally, paraphrase or reflect to show that you have heard and understood what the student is saying ("So, your friends taunt you when you contribute good ideas to class discussion or get good grades on tests. How does that make you feel?"). If you continue in this vein, the student may begin to see for himself that he doesn't really believe what peers are telling him, that the peers are pursuing their own questionable agendas rather than acting as true friends concerned about his best interests, that they are pressuring him to subvert his own values, and that he needs to find ways to resist this peer pressure without significant cost to his social relationships (or perhaps to cultivate friendships with more compatible peers).

Third, with students who begin to develop such insights, you might use the "inoculation" techniques that have been developed for helping people to cope with stressful situations. For example, techniques for helping timid children to become more assertive include role playing or discussing vignettes in which someone ignores or mistreats them, then analyzing how the situation might be handled effectively or how the role-played response might have been improved. Similar techniques can be used to help socially pressured students plan ahead for and practice possible responses to situations in which peers taunt them for displaying motivation to learn at school.

Along with your own efforts, improvements in the school's culture and in school–community relations will be needed to turn around the most hostile and resistant students, especially if they belong to a local subculture that detests or distrusts schooling as an institution. You cannot simply wait for these improvements to occur, however, because you must work with your students each day, dealing with them and the school milieu as they are at the moment. You may not be able to eliminate resistant students' negative attitudes toward the school as a whole, but at least you can get them to view you as an exception and begin to "go along with the program" in your classroom.

References

Dunn, R., & Dunn, K. (1992). *Teaching elementary students through their individual learning styles.* Boston: Allyn & Bacon.

Gardner, H. (1993). *Multiple intelligences: The theory in practice.* New York: Basic Books.

Head, J. (1999). *Understanding the boys: Issues of behaviour and achievement.* London: Falmer.

Jersild, A., & Tasch, R. (1949). *Children's interests and what they suggest for education.* New York: Bureau of Publications, Teachers College, Columbia University.

McCarthy, B. (1980). *The 4MAT system.* Oakbrook, IL: Excel.

Morgan, H. (1997). *Cognitive styles and classroom learning.* Westport, CT: Praeger.

Stevenson, H., & Stigler, J. (1992). *The learning gap.* New York: Summit.

Bibliography

Abbott, J. (1978). *Classroom strategies to aid the disabled learner*. Cambridge, MA: Educators Publishing Service.

Aronson, E., Blaney, N., Stephan, C., Sikes, J., & Snapp, M. (1978). *The Jigsaw classroom*. Beverly Hills, CA: Sage.

Atkinson, J. (1964). *An introduction to motivation*. Princeton, NJ: VanNostrand.

Berndt, T., & Miller, K. (1990). Expectancies, values, and achievement in junior high school. *Journal of Educational Psychology*, 82, 319–326.

Blanco, R., & Bogacki, D. (1988). *Prescriptions for children with learning and adjustment problems: A consultant's desk reference* (3rd ed.). Springfield, IL: Charles C. Thomas

Boekaerts, M. (2001). Motivation, learning, and instruction. In N. Smelser & P. Baltes (Eds.), *Inter-national encyclopedia of the social and behavioral sciences* (pp. 10112–10117). New York: Elsevier Science.

Brophy, J. (Ed.). (1998). *Advances in research on teaching. Vol. 7: Expectations in the classroom*. Greenwich, CT: JAI Press.

Covington, M. (2000). Goal theory, motivation, and school achievement: An integrative review. *Annual Review of Psychology*, 51, 171–200.

Csikszentmihalyi, M. (1993). *The evolving self: A psychology for the third millennium*. New York: HarperCollins

Csikzentmihalyi, M. (1993). *The evolving self: A psychology for the third millennium*. New York: HarperCollins.

Damon, W. (1995). *Greater expectations: Overcoming the culture of indulgence in America's homes and schools*. New York: The Free Press.

deCharms, R. (1976). *Enhancing motivation: Change in the classroom*. New York: Irvington.

Deci, E., & Ryan, R. (1985). *Intrinsic motivation and self-determination in human behavior*. New York: Plenum.

Dunn, R., & Dunn, K. (1992). *Teaching elementary students through their individual learning styles*. Boston: Allyn & Bacon.

Dweck, C. (1999). *Self-theories: Their role in motivation, personality, and development*. Philadelphia: Taylor & Francis.

Eckblad, G. (1981). *Scheme theory: A conceptual framework for cognitive-motivational processes*. New York: Academic Press.

Ford, M. (1992). *Motivating humans: Goals, emotions, and personal agency beliefs*. Newbury Park, CA: Sage.

Freitas, A., & Higgins, E. T. (2002). Enjoying goal-directed action: The role of regulatory fit. *Psychological Science,* 13,1–6.

Gardner, H. (1993). *Multiple intelligences: The theory in practice.* New York: Basic Books.

Good, T., & Brophy, J. (2003). *Looking in classrooms* (9th ed.). Boston: Allyn & Bacon.

Hartman, H. (Ed.). (2001). *Metacognition in learning and instruction: Theory, research and practice.* Boston: Kluwer.

Head, J. (1999). *Understanding the boys: Issues of behaviour and achievement.* London: Falmer.

Heckhausen, H. (1991). *Motivation and action* (2nd ed.). New York: Springer-Verlag.

Jersild, A., & Tasch, R. (1949). *Children's interests and what they suggest for education.* New York: Bureau of Publications, Teachers College, Columbia University.

Johnson, D., & Johnson, R. (1999). *Learning together and alone: Cooperative, competitive, and indi-vidualistic learning* (5th ed.). Boston: Allyn & Bacon.

Jones, B., & Idol, L. (Eds.). (1990). D*imensions of thinking and cognitive instruction.* Hillsdale, NJ: Lawrence Erlbaum Associates.

Kuhl, J., & Beckmann, J. (Eds.). (1985). *Action control: From cognition to behavior.* New York: Springer-Verlag.

Levine, D. (1985). *Improving student achievement through mastery learning programs.* San Francisco: Jossey-Bass.

Maehr, M., & Meyer, H. (1997). Understanding motivation and schooling: Where we've been, where we are, and where we need to go. *Educational Psychology Review*, 9, 371–409.

McCarthy, B. (1980). *The 4MAT system.* Oakbrook, IL: Excel.

Morgan, H. (1997). *Cognitive styles and classroom learning.* Westport, CT: Praeger.

Newmann, F., & Associates. (1996). *Authentic achievement: Restructuring schools for intellectual quality.* San Francisco: Jossey-Bass.

Newton, D. (2000). *Teaching for understanding: What it is and how to do it.* London: Routledge/ Falmer.

Purkey, W., & Novak, J. (1996). *Inviting school success: A self-concept approach to teaching, learning, and democratic practice* (3rd ed.). Belmont, CA: Wadsworth.

Reeve, J. (1996). *Motivating others: Nurturing inner motivational resources.* Boston: Allyn & Bacon.

Rogoff, B., Turkanis, C., & Bartlett, L. (2001). *Learning together: Children and adults in a school community.* New York: Oxford University Press

Sansone, C., & Harackiewicz, J. (2000). *Intrinsic and extrinsic motivation: The search for optimal motivation and performance.* San Diego: Academic Press.

____, & Morgan, C. (1992). Intrinsic motivation and education: Competence in context. *Motivation and Emotion,* 16, 249–270.

Somuncuoglu, Y., & Yildirim, A. (1999). Relationship between achievement goal orientations and use of learning strategies. *Journal of Educational Research,* 92, 267–277.

Stevenson, H., & Stigler, J. (1992). *The learning gap.* New York: Summit.

Stipek, D. (1996). Motivation and instruction. In D. Berliner & R. Calfee (Eds.), *Handbook of educa-tional psychology* (pp. 85–113). New York: Macmillan.

____. (2002). Motivation to learn: *Integrating theory and practice* (4th ed.). Boston: Allyn & Bacon.

Tharp, R., & Gallimore, R. (1988). *Rousing minds to life: Teaching, learning, and schooling in social context.* Cambridge, England: Cambridge University Press.

Thrash, T., & Elliot, A. (2001). Delimiting and integrating achievement motive and goal constructs. In A. Efklides, J. Kuhl, & R. Sorrentino (Eds.), *Trends and prospects in motivation research* (pp. 3–21). Boston: Kluwer.

Urdan, T. (1997). Achievement goal theory: Past results, future directions. In P. Pintrich & M. Maehr (Eds.), *Advances in motivation and achievement* (Vol. 10, pp. 99–141). Greenwich, CT: JAI.

Valle, A., Cabanach, R., Nunez, J., Gonzalez-Pienda, J., Rodriguez, S., & Pineiro, I. (2003). Multiple goals, motivation and academic learning. *British Journal of Educational Psychology*, 73, 71–87.

Waitley, D., & Witt, R. (1985). *The joy of working.* New York: Dodd, Mead.

Weinstein, C., & Mayer, R. (1986). *The teaching of learning strategies. In M. Wittrock (Ed.), Hand-book of research on teaching* (3rd ed., pp. 315–327). New York: Macmillan.

____, & Mignano, A., Jr. (1993). *Elementary classroom management: Lessons from research and practice.* New York: McGraw-Hill.

Williams, W. (1996). *The reluctant reader: How to get and keep kids reading.* New York: Warner Books.

Wlodkowski, R. (1978). *Motivation and teaching: A practical guide.* Washington, DC: National Education Association.

Wolters, C., Yu, S., & Pintrich, P. (1996). The relation between goal orientation and students' be-liefs and self-regulated learning. *Learning and Individual Differences*, 8, 211–238.

Wong, E., Pugh, K., & The Dewey Ideas Group at Michigan State University. (2001). Learning sc-ence: A Deweyan perspective. *Journal of Research in Science Teaching,* 38, 317–336.

Zimmerman, B., & Schunk, D. (Eds.). (2001). *Self-regulated learning and academic achievement: Theoretical perspectives* (2nd ed.). Mahwah, NJ: Lawrence Erlbaum Associates.